LITERARY SAVANNAH

LITERARY SAVANNAH

edited by

PATRICK ALLEN

HILL STREET PRESS   ATHENS, GEORGIA

Published by

HILL STREET PRESS, LLC

191 East Broad Street

Suite 209

Athens, Georgia 30601-2848

www.hillstreetpress.com

First printing

1   3   5   7   9   10   8   6   4   2

ISBN # 1-892514-01-X

LIBRARY OF CONGRESS CATALOG # 98-87991

Printed in the United States of America by Maple-Vail.

The paper in this book contains a significant amount of
post-consumer recycled fiber.

Text and cover design by Anne Richmond Boston.

Contents

CONTENTS

Preface

Editing an anthology on as rich a topic as the literature of Savannah involves an inevitable tug-of-war between what must go in and what must be left out. My decisions ultimately were made in an effort to give not an encyclopedic history or strict chronology, but a revealing portrait of the city. The resulting portrait is impressionistic—evocative of a mood—rather than cubistic—showing all angles simultaneously. I have included pieces representative of every era of the city's history, from many different literary forms, and with an eye to diversity of race, gender, and class. Native Savannahians, transplants, transients, and visitors give their views. Readers will no doubt be troubled by some of the language and attitudes concerning race contained in this anthology. Knowing that such attitudes are unfortunate historical realities in some sections of Savannah, as they have been throughout the whole of American society, I have made no effort to hide or eliminate them. I rely on the historical understanding and conscience of the reader to put them in proper perspective.

The case of the triumvirate of Savannah's most important writers—Conrad Aiken, Flannery O'Connor, and Julien Green—presented a great challenge to selection and excerption. Aiken, known first as a poet, is represented here by a short story set in Savannah, although the effect of his hometown experience on his work could also have been shown through his long poem "The Coming Forth of Day of Osiris Jones," (1931) or his experimental, autobiographical *Ushant: An Essay* (1952). Although O'Connor is best known in the short story form, the occasional piece I have chosen to include here is an excellent example of her charm: her sly humor and her economical, elegant style. O'Connor's story "Temple of the Holy Ghost," for example, was doubtlessly influenced by her Catholic schooling in Savannah and justifiably could have been included here, as well. Those familiar with Julien Green's prodigious body of work will understand the difficulty of excerpting from his over sixty volumes of novels, essays, and journals. Students of the literature of Savannah would be rewarded by reading his *Les etoiles du Sud: roman* (1989), translated as *The Stars of the South: A Novel* (1996) and *Terre Lointaine* (1966), translated as *Love in America* (1994).

My hope is that *Literary Savannah* not only gives readers insight into the city's history and cultural life, but will also inspire discussion and debate. Some readers may be dubious of particular inclusions and others may decry what they see as obvious omissions, but hopefully both categories of readers will seek to read more of the literature of the city. I could recommend Francis Moore, Jonathan Odell, Samuel Quincy, and John Joachim Zubly as poets and writers of the colonial period worth noting. A generation later, the geographer Jedidiah Morse wrote interestingly of his travels on the Savannah River. Antebellum novelists William Alexander Caruthers and William John Grayson wrote about a city they loved. Frances Anne Kemble's *Journal of a Residence on a Georgian Plantation in 1838–1839* (1863) and Francis Butler Leigh's *Ten Years on a Georgia Plantation since the War* (1883) give insight into Savannah and environs in those turbulent times. Some writers native to Savannah, including Philip Robert Dillon, Willie Snow Ethridge, Anne Green (Julien's sister and frequent translator), and Marie Conway Oemler are most associated with other areas, but are well worth reading. James B. Connolly and Eugene Jolas are likewise fine writers. Would that I could have included more documents ephemeral to Savannah literature, including Margaret Mitchell's 1941 letter to the Alfred Lunts recommending island hotels, an account of Langston Hughes's afternoon with guitar pickers and bluesmen on the Savannah docks, and one of the dozens of Civil War ditties of James Pierpont, the Boston-born Savannah transplant who wrote "The One Horse Open Sleigh" (1857), later renamed "Jingle Bells." Noteworthy also is that Japanese-American photographer and critic Sadakichi Hartmann delivered a lecture on photography in Savannah in 1943. Several diverse literary figures have spent time in the city, but if they committed their experiences to paper it is unknown to me. For example, John Dos Passos paid a long visit to the city, William S. Burroughs Jr. worked as an exterminator there in 1968, and Melissa Faye Green worked as a paralegal in a Savannah firm from 1975 to 1979.

Doubtless many have discovered Hamilton Basso's *View from Pompey's Head* (1954) from its mention in what is known locally as "The Book," and have gone on to enjoy The Lady Chablis's *Hiding My Candy: The Autobiography of the Grand Empress of Savannah* (1996) after its author's notoriety from the John Berendt bestseller. Other authors beloved by Savannahians include Malcolm Bell Jr., Betsy Fancher, Richard Harwell, Mills Lane, and William Robert Mitchell Jr. Richard Kluger's *Members of the Tribe* (1977), a survey of the city's Jewish history, is also locally popular. The Beehive Press; Oglethorpe Press; and Frederic C. Beil, Publishers; all based in Savannah, have produced many fine titles of regional interest. The Savannah Writers' Workshop, through its annual *Savannah Literary Journal*, festivals, and other literary events, encourages and promotes fine writing in the city.

Readers will be interested in the African American writers Albery Allson Whitman and Whittington B. Johnson. Students of black Savannah will want to know that New Jersey-born poet Conrad Rivers Kent went to high school in Savannah for a time. In 1951 he won the Savannah State Poetry Prize for his poem "Poor Peon."

Journalism has figured prominently in Savannah's cultural life. The first newspaper in colonial Georgia, the *Georgia Gazette*, was founded there in 1763. The city was the starting point for Mortimer Thomson's *The Great Auction of Slaves at Savannah, Georgia* (1859)—printed in Northern newspapers and later in book form by the American Anti-Slavery Society—which had a significant impact on the abolition movement. In 1867, Reverend James M. Simms founded the *Southern Radical and Freedmen's Journal*, the first African American publication in Savannah after the Civil War. *Savannah Morning News* editor William Tappan Thompson was an important mentor to many journalists and a well-known humorist in his own right. Albert Scardino founded his controversial weekly *Georgia Gazette* there in 1978 and won a Pulitzer Prize in 1984 for his editorial writing on political corruption and environmental issues. Savannah-born Bruce Feiler has written articles and books on music, circus life, and Japanese travel; and journalist Arthur Gordon has contributed to national magazines.

The vision and experience of the many fine writers represented in *Literary Savannah* is a solid start to a portrait of this fascinating city. One's continued pursuit of literature from and about the city will provide the changes in perspective and fine shading needed to round out the sketch I provide. No better places to continue one's reading of Savannahiana exist than the impressive library and archives of the Georgia Historical Society; the well-stocked shelves of E. Shaver, Bookseller, and other fine bookstores in the city; and the Hargrett Rare Book and Manuscript Library of the University of Georgia in Athens. All provided me with invaluable assistance in researching this collection, for which I am grateful. My thanks also go to Mr. and Mrs. Leopold Adler II for their kind permission to use a lithograph from their collection on the cover of this book, and to acclaimed photographer Van Jones Martin for his assistance in the arrangements.

Patrick Allen
Editor

from *An Account of Carolina and Georgia*

JAMES OGLETHORPE (1696–1785)

Founder of colonial Georgia, politician, philanthropist, and soldier James Oglethorpe was educated at Eton and Corpus Christi College, Oxford. In addition to distinguishing himself on the battlefield and in the House of Commons, Oglethorpe wrote a powerful pamphlet, *The Sailor's Advocate*, which railed against the practice of impressment and called for its abolition. In recognition of this work, he was named to a committee to inquire into the conditions of English prisons. His investigation led to a plan combining impulses of empire and philanthropy in a uniquely eighteenth-century way: settle the "Debatable Land" between the Savannah and Altamaha rivers with the inhabitants of debtors' prisons. The plan was designed to bring resources to England, while allowing settlers to rebuild their finances with honor, and spreading the Anglican faith at the same time. Oglethorpe's adventure in the New World began with his landing at the chosen site for Savannah on February 12, 1733. He negotiated a peace treaty with Yamacraw mico (or chief) Tomochichi—ratified on May 21, 1733—pursuant to which Georgia was settled. Oglethorpe laid out the strict geometry of Savannah's squares himself, a plan that with little modification has dominated the city's civic planning ever since. Oglethorpe returned to England in 1743 and resumed his career in Parliament. Oglethorpe's journal, published as *An Account of Carolina and Georgia*, appeared in 1733.

The province of Georgia is watered by three great rivers, which rise in the mountains, viz. the Alatamaha, the Ogechee, and the Savannah, the last of which is navigable six hundred miles for canoes, and three hundred miles for boats. The British dominions are divided from the Spanish Florida by a noble river called

St. John's. These rivers fall into the Atlantick ocean; but there are besides them, the Flint, the Catooche, and even the Mississippi river, which pass through part of Carolina, or Georgia, and fall into the gulph of Apellachee or Mexico.

All Carolina is divided into three parts: North Carolina, which is divided from South Carolina by Clarendon river, and of late by a line marked out by order of the council; South Carolina; which on the south is divided from Georgia by the river Savannah. Carolina is divided into several counties; but in Georgia there is but one yet erected, viz. the county of Savannah: it is bounded on the one side by the river Savannah, on the other by the sea, on the third by the river Ogechee, on the fourth by the river Ebenezer, and a line drawn from the Ebenezer to the Ogechee. In this country are the rivers of Vernon, Little Ogechee, and of Westbrook. There is the town of Savannah, where there is a seat of judicature, consisting of three bailiffs and a recorder. It is situated upon the banks of the river of the same name. It consists of about two hundred houses, and lies upon a plain of about a mile wide, the bank steep to the river, forty five foot perpendicularly high: the streets are laid out regular. There are near Savannah, in the same country, the villages of Hampstead, Highgate, Skydoway, and Thunderbolt; the latter of which is a translation of a name: their fables say, that a thunderbolt fell, and a spring thereupon arose in that place, which still smells of the thunder. This spring is impregnated with a mixture of sulphur and steel, and from this smell probably the story arose. In the same county is Joseph's Town, and the town of Ebenezer, both upon the river Savannah, and the villages of Abercorn and Westbrook. There are saw-mills erecting on the river Ebenezer, and the fort Argyle lies upon the pass of this county over the Ogechee. In the southern divisions of the province lies the town of Frederica, with its district, where there is a court with three bailiffs and a recorder. It lies on one of the branches of the Alatamaha.

There is also the town of Darien, upon the same river, and several forts, upon the proper passes, some of four bastions, some are only redoubts; besides which there are villages in different parts of Georgia. At Savannah there is a publick store-house built of large square timbers; there is also a handsome court-house, guard-house, and work-house: their church is not yet begun, but materials are collecting, and it is designed to be a handsome edifice. The private houses are generally sawed timber, framed and covered with shingles; many of them are painted, and most have chimneys of brick. At Frederica, some of the houses are built of brick; the rest of the province is mostly wood. They are not got into luxury yet in their furniture, hewing only what is plain and needful; the winters being mild, there are yet but few houses with glass-windows.

The Indians are a manly well-shaped race; the men tall, the women little: they, as the ancient Greeks did, anoint with oil, and expose themselves to the sun, which occasions their skins to be brown of colour. The men paint themselves of various colours, red, blue, yellow and black: the men wear generally a girdle, with a piece of cloth drawn through their legs, and turned over the girdle both before and behind, so as to hide their nakedness. The women wear a kind of petticoat to their knees. Both men and women in the winter wear mantles, something less than two yards square, which they wrap round their bodies, as the Romans did their toga, generally keeping their arms bare: they are sometimes of woollen, bought of the English; sometimes of furs, which they dress themselves. They wear a kind of pumps, which they call morgisons, made of deer skins, which they dress for that purpose. They are a generous good-natured people, very humane to strangers; patient of want and pain; slow to anger, and not easily provoked; but when they are thoroughly incensed, they are implacable; very quick of apprehension, and gay of temper. Their publick conferences shew them to be men of genius, and they have a natural eloquence, they never having had the use of letters. They love eating, and the English have taught many of them to drink strong liquors, which, when they do, they are miserable sights. They have no manufactures but what each family makes for its own use; they seem to despise working for hire, and spend their time chiefly in hunting and war; but plant corn enough for the support of their families, and of the strangers that come to visit them. Their food, instead of bread, is flour of Indian corn boiled, and seasoned like hasty-pudding; and this is called homminy. They also boil venison and make broth: they also roast or rather broil their meat. The flesh they feed on is buffaloe, deer, wild-turkeys, and other game; so that hunting is necessary, to provide flesh, and planting for corn. The land belongs to the women, and the corn that grows upon it; but meat must be got by the men, because it is they only that hunt. This makes marriage necessary, that the women may furnish corn, and the men meat. They have also fruit-trees in their gardens, viz. peaches, nectarines and locusts, melons and watermelons; potatoes, pumpkins, and onions, &c. in plenty, and many wild kinds of fruits; as parsimonies, grapes, chinquepins, and hickary-nuts, of which they make oil. The bees make their combs in the hollow trees, and the Indians find plenty of honey there, which they use instead of sugar. They make what answers salt of wood-ashes, and long-pepper which grows in their gardens; and bay-leaves supply their want of spice. Their exercises are a kind of ball-playing, hunting, and running; and they are very fond of dancing: their musick is a kind of a drum, as also hollow cocoa-nut shells. They have a square in the middle of their towns, in which the warriors sit, converse, and smoke together; but in rainy weather they meet in the King's house.

They are very healthy people, and have hardly any diseases, except those occasioned by the drinking of rum, and the small pox: those who do not drink rum are exceeding long-lived. Old Brim, Emperor of the Creeks, who died but a few years ago, lived to one hundred and thirty years; and he was neither blind nor bed-rid, till some months before his death. They have sometimes pleurisies and fevers, but no chronical distempers. They know of several herbs that have great virtues in physick, particularly for the cure of venomous bites and wounds.

The native animals are, first the urus or zorax, described by Caesar, which the English very ignorantly and improperly call the buffaloe. They have deer of several kinds, and plenty of roe-bucks and rabbits. There are bears and wolves, which are very small and timerous; and a brown wild-cat, without spots, which they very improperly call a tyger; otters, beavers, foxes, and a species of badgers, which they call racoon. There is great abundance of wild fowls, viz. the wild turkey, the partridge, doves of various kinds; wild geese, wild ducks, teal, cranes, herons of many kinds, not known in Europe: there are great variety of eagles and hawks, and great numbers of small birds, particularly the rice bird, which is very like the ortelan. There are also some rattle snakes, but not near so frequent as is generally reported. There are several species of snakes, some of which are not venomous. There are crocodiles, porpoises, sturgeon, mullets, cat-fish, bass, drum, devil-fish, and many species of fresh water fish, that we have not in Europe; oysters upon the sea islands in great abundance. But what is most troublesome here, is flies and gnats, which are very troublesome near the rivers; but as the country is cleared, they disperse and go away. Besides the animals that are natives, there are all the same animals as in Europe, cows, sheep, hogs, &c.

The vegetables are innumerable; for all that grow in Europe grow there; many that cannot stand in our winters thrive there.

"Origin Legend of the Creek People"

CHEKILLI (DATES UNKNOWN)

Chekilli was the principal chief of the Creek confederacy during the settlement of Georgia by the British. Together with Yamacraw chief Tomochichi, he was instrumental in establishing peaceful relations with the British, precipitating the founding of the colony at Savannah in 1733. He may have been one of the group of Native Americans who visited the court of George II with Tomochichi and General James Oglethorpe in 1734. In 1735, Chekilli headed a delegation of over sixty representatives of the Creek Nation in a council with the British at Savannah. On that occasion he recited the origin legend of the Creek people. The presentation took place in Savannah's first square, Johnson Square, site of the presentation of another important document: the Declaration of Independence was read there on August 10, 1776. After his recitation, Chekilli presented the settlers with a buffalo skin giving his text in red and black pictographs. Taken to the London office of the colony, the skin has since been lost. A simultaneous English translation survived in the German diary of Philipp Georg Friederichs von Reck and follows below.

At a certain time, the Earth opened in the West, where its mouth is. The earth opened and the Cussitaws came out of its mouth, and settled near by. But the earth became angry and ate up their children; therefore, they moved further West. A part of them, however, turned back, and came again to the same place where they had been, and settled there. The greater number remained behind, because they thought it best to do so.

Their children, nevertheless, were eaten by the Earth, so that, full of dissatisfaction, they journeyed toward the sunrise.

They came to a thick, muddy, slimy river; came there, camped there, rested there, and stayed overnight there.

The next day, they continued their journey and came, in one day, to a red, bloody river. They lived by this river, and ate of its fishes for two years; but there were low springs there; and it did not please them to remain. They went toward the end of this bloody river, and heard a noise as of thunder. They approached to see whence the noise came. At first, they perceived a red smoke, and then a mountain which thundered; and on the mountain was a sound as of singing. They sent to see what this was; and it was a great fire which blazed upward, and made this singing noise. This mountain they named the King of Mountains. It thunders to this day; and men are very much afraid of it.

They here met a people of three different Nations. They had taken and saved some of the fire from the mountain; and, at this place, they also obtained a knowledge of herbs and of many other things.

From the East, a white fire came to them; which, however, they would not use.

From Wahalle came a fire which was blue; neither did they use it.

From the West, came a fire which was black; nor would they use it.

At last, came a fire from the North, which was red and yellow. This they mingled with the fire they had taken from the mountain; and this is the fire they use today; and this, too, sometimes sings.

On the mountain was a pole which was very restless and made a noise, nor could anyone say how it could be quieted. At length, they took a motherless child, and struck it against the pole; and thus killed the child. They then took the pole, and carry it with them when they go to war. It was like a wooden tomahawk, such as they now use, and of the same wood. There, they also found four herbs or roots, which sang and disclosed their virtues: First, *Pasaw*, the rattlesnake root; Second, *Micoweanockaw*, red-root;

Third, *Sowatchko*, which grows like wild fennel; and Fourth, *Eschalapootchke*, little tobacco.

These herbs, especially the first and third, they use as the best medicine to purify themselves at their Busk.

At this Busk, which is held yearly, they fast, and make offerings of the first-fruits.

Since they learned the virtues of these herbs, their women, at certain times, have a separate fire, and remain apart from the men five, six, and seven days, for the sake of purification. If they neglect this, the power of the herbs would depart; and the women would not be healthy.

About that time a dispute arose, as to which was the oldest and which should rule; and they agreed, as they were four Nations, they would set up four poles, and make them red with clay, which is yellow at first, but becomes red by burning. They would then go to war; and whichever Nation should first cover its pole, from top to bottom, with the scalps of their enemies, should be the oldest.

They all tried, but the Cussitaws covered their pole first, and so thickly that it was hidden from sight. Therefore, they were looked upon, by the whole Nation, as the oldest.

The Chickasaws covered their pole next; then the Atilamas; but the Obikaws did not cover their pole higher than the knee.

At that time, there was a bird of large size, blue in color, with a long tail, and swifter than an eagle, which came every day and killed and ate their people. They made an image, in the shape of a woman, and placed it in the way of this bird. The bird carried it off, and kept it a long time, and then brought it back. They left it alone, hoping it would bring something forth. After a long time, a red rat came forth from it, and they believe the bird was the father of the rat.

They took council with the rat, how to destroy its father. Now the bird had a bow and arrows; and the rat gnawed the bow-string, so that the bird could not defend itself; and the people killed it. They called this bird the King of Birds. They think the eagle is also a great King; and they carry its feathers when they go to War or make Peace: the red mean War, the white, Peace. If an enemy approaches with white feathers and a white mouth, and cries like an eagle, they dare not kill him.

After this, they left that place, and came to a white foot-path. The grass and everything around were white; and they plainly perceived that people had been there. They crossed the path, and slept near there. Afterward, they turned back to see what sort of path that was, and who the people were who had been there, in the belief that it might be better for them to follow that path. They went along it, to a creek, called *Coloosehutche*, that is Coloose-creek, because it was rocky there and smoked.

They crossed it, going toward the sunrise, and came to a people and a town named Coosaw. Here they remained four years. The Coosaws complained that they were preyed upon by a wild beast, which they called man-eater or lion, which lived in a rock.

The Cussitaws said they would try to kill the beast. They digged a pit and stretched over it a net made of hickory bark. They then laid a number of branches, crosswise, so that the lion could not follow them, and going to the place where he lay, they threw a rattle into his den. The lion rushed forth, in great anger, and pursued them through the branches. Then they thought it better that one should die rather than all, so they took a motherless child, and threw it before the lion, as he came near the pit. The lion rushed at it, and fell in the pit, over which they threw the net, and killed him with blazing pinewood. His bones, however, they keep to this day; on one side, they are red, on the other, blue.

The lion used to come every seventh day to kill the people. Therefore, they remained there seven days after they had killed him. In remembrance of him, when they prepare for War, they fast six days and start on the seventh. If they take his bones with them, they have good fortune.

After four years, they left the Coosaws, and came to a River which they called *Nowphawpe*, now *Callasihutche*. There they tarried two years; and as they had no corn, they lived on roots and fishes, and made bows, pointing the arrows with beaver teeth and flint-stones, and for knives they used split canes.

They left this place, and came to a creek, called *Wattoolahawka hutche*, Whooping-creek, so called from the whooping of cranes, a great many being there. They slept there one night.

They next came to a river, in which there was a waterfall; this they named the *Owatuaka*-river.

The next day, they reached another river, which they called the *Aphoosa pheeskaw*.

The following day, they crossed it, and came to a high mountain, where were people who, they believed, were the same who made the white path. They, therefore, made white arrows and shot them, to see if they were good people. But the people took their white arrows, painted them red, and shot them back. When they showed these to their Chief, he said that was not a good sign; if the arrows returned had been white, they could have gone there and brought food for their children, but as they were red they must not go. Nevertheless, some of them went to see what sort of people they were; and found their houses deserted. They also saw a trail which led into the River; and as they could not see the trail on the opposite bank, they believed that the people had gone into the River, and would not again come forth.

At that place, is a mountain, called *Moterell*, which makes a noise like beating on a drum; and they think this people live there. They hear this noise on all sides, when they go to War.

They went along the River, till they came to a waterfall, where they saw great rocks; and on the rocks were bows lying; and they believed the people who made the white path had been there.

They always have, on their journeys, two scouts who go before the main body. These scouts ascended a high mountain and saw a town. They shot white arrows into the town; but the people of the town shot back red arrows.

Then the Cussitaws became angry, and determined to attack the town, and each one have a house when it was captured.

They threw stones into the River, until they could cross it, and took the town (the people had flattened heads), and killed all but two persons. In pursuing these, they found a white dog, which they slew. They followed the two who escaped, until they came again to the white path and saw the smoke of a town, and thought that this must be the people they had so long been seeking. This is the place where now the tribe of Palachucolas live, from whom Tomochichi is descended.

The Cussitaws continued bloody-minded; but the Palachucolas gave them black drink, as a sign of friendship, and said to them: Our hearts are white, and yours must be white, and you must lay down the bloody tomahawk, and show your bodies, as a proof that they shall be white.

Nevertheless, they were for the tomahawk; but the Palachucolas got it by persuasion, and buried it under their beds. The Palachucolas likewise gave them white feathers; and asked to have a Chief in common. Since then they have always lived together.

Some settled on one side of the River, some on the other. Those on one side are called Cussitaws, those on the other, Cowetas; yet they are one people, and the principal towns of the Upper and Lower Creeks. Nevertheless, as the Cussitaws first saw the red smoke and the red fire, and make bloody towns, they cannot yet leave their red hearts, which are, however, white on one side and red on the other.

They now know that the white path was the best for them. For, although Tomochichi was a stranger, they see he has done them good; because he went to see the great King with Esquire Oglethorpe, and hear him talk, and had related it to them, and they had listened to it, and believed it.

from "On Love"

JOHN WESLEY (1703–1791)

John Wesley is recognized as cofounder of Methodism with his younger brother Charles. Disappointed with what he perceived as tepid participation in the apostolate over which he ministered at his Oxford alma mater, Wesley volunteered in 1735 to serve as a missionary to Native Americans in Georgia. When political circumstances rendered this service impossible, he was retained by General James Oglethorpe to serve as minister to the newly arrived English colonists. In a drama reminiscent of his clergyman father's alienation from his own flock (the senior Wesley's rectory may have been set afire by one of his many disgruntled parishioners), John's High Church strictness and formality made him immensely unpopular with his Georgia flock. His public feuds with parishioners and an unhappy love affair precipitated his return to England in 1738. While in the colony, Wesley was impressed by the simplicity and stalwartness of faith of a group of German Pietists, or "Moravians," and the experience had a profound influence on his later ministering. The sermon to the congregants of Christ Church appearing here, "On Love," was the first Wesley preached in Savannah, on March 7, 1736. A bronze tablet marks the spot on the corner of Bull and Bay streets where the sermon was delivered.

Though I bestow all my goods to feed the poor, and though I give my body to be burned, and have not love, it profiteth me nothing.
1 Corinthians 13:3

There is great reason to fear that it will hereafter be said of most of you who are here present, that this scripture, as well as all those you have heard before, profited you nothing. Some, perhaps, are not serious enough to attend to it; some who do attend, will not believe it; some who do believe it, will yet think it a hard saying, and so forget it as soon as they can; and, of those few who receive it gladly for a time, some, having no root of humility, or self-denial, when persecution ariseth because of the word, will, rather than suffer for it, fall away. Nay, even of those who attend to it, who believe, remember, yea, and receive it so deeply into their hearts, that it both takes root there, endures the heat of temptation, and begins to bring forth fruit, yet will not *all* bring forth fruit unto perfection. The cares or pleasures of the world, and the desire of other things, (perhaps not felt till then), will grow up with the word, and choke it.

Nor am I that speak the word of God any more secure from these dangers than you that hear it. I, too, have to bewail "an evil heart of unbelief." . . .

Why then do I speak this word at all? Why? Because a dispensation of the gospel is committed unto me: and, though what I shall do to-morrow I know not, to-day I will preach the gospel. And with regard to you, my commission runs thus: "Son of man, I do send thee to them; and thou shalt say unto them, Thus saith the Lord God;—whether they will hear, or whether they will forbear." . . .

It concerns us all, therefore, in the highest degree, to know,

I. The full sense of these words, "Though I bestow all my goods to feed the poor, and though I give my body to be burned;"

II. The true meaning of the word love; and,

III. In what sense it can be said, "that without love all this profiteth us nothing."

I. As to the first: It must be observed that the word used by St. Paul properly signifies, *To divide into small pieces, and then to distribute what has been so divided*: and, consequently, it implies, not only divesting ourselves at once of all the worldly goods we enjoy, either from a fit of distaste to the world, or a sudden start of devotion, but an act of choice, and that choice coolly and steadily executed. It may imply, too, that this be done not out of vanity, but in part from a right principle; namely from a design to perform the command of God, and a desire to obtain his kingdom. It must be farther observed, that the word *give* signifies actually to deliver a thing according to agreement, and, accordingly, it implies, like the word preceding, not a hasty, inconsiderate action, but one performed with opened eyes and a determined heart, pursuant to a resolution before taken. The full sense of the words, therefore is this, which he that hath ears to hear, let him hear: Though I should give all the substance of my house to feed the poor; though I should do so upon mature choice and deliberation; though I should spend my life in dealing it out to them with my own hands, yea, and that from a principle of obedience; though I should suffer, from the same view, not only reproach and shame, not only bonds and imprisonment, and all this by my own continued act and deed, not accepting deliverance, but moreover, death itself,—yea, death inflicted in a manner the most terrible to nature; yet all this, if I have not love ("the love of God, and the love of all mankind shed abroad in my heart by the Holy Ghost given unto me"), it profiteth me nothing.

II. Let us inquire what this life is: what is the true meaning of the word? We may consider it either as to its properties or effects: And that we may be under no possibility of mistake, we will not at all regard the judgment of men, but go to our Lord himself for an account of the nature of love; and, for the effects of it, to his inspired apostle.

The love which our Lord requires in all his followers is the love of God and man;—of God, for his own, and of man, for God's sake. Now, what is it to love God, but to delight in him, to rejoice in his will, to desire continually to please him, to seek and find our happiness in him, and to thirst day and night for a fuller enjoyment of him? . . .

The effects or properties of this love, the apostle describes in the chapter before us. And all these being infallible marks whereby any man may judge of himself, whether he hath this love or hath it not, they deserve our deepest consideration. . . .

III. It remains to inquire in what sense it can be said, "That though I bestow all my goods to feed the poor, yea, though I give my body to be burned, and have not love, it profiteth me nothing."

The chief sense of the words is, doubtless, this: that whatsoever we do, and whatsoever we suffer, if we are not renewed in the spirit of our mind, by "the love of God shed abroad in our hearts by the Holy Ghost given unto us," we cannot enter into life eternal. None can enter there, unless in virtue of covenant which God hath given unto man in the Son of his love.

But, because general truths are less apt to affect us, let us consider one or two particulars, with regard to which all we can do or suffer, if we have not love, profiteth us nothing. And first, all without this profiteth not, so as to make life happy; nor, secondly, so as to make death comfortable.

And, first; without love nothing can so profit us as to make our lives happy. By happiness I mean, not a slight, trifling pleasure, that perhaps begins and ends in the same hour; but such a state of well being as contents the soul, and gives it a steady, lasting satisfaction. But that nothing without love can profit us, as to our present happiness, will appear from this single consideration: you cannot want it in any one single instance without pain; and the more you depart from it, the pain is the greater. Are you wanting in long-suffering? Then, so far as you fall short of this, you fall short of happiness. The more the opposite tempers—anger, fretfulness, revenge—prevail, the more unhappy you are. You know it; you feel it; nor can the storm be allayed, or peace ever return to your soul, unless meekness, gentleness, patience, or, in one word, love take possession of it. . . .

Secondly: Without love, nothing can make death comfortable.

By comfortable I do not mean stupid, or senseless. I would not say, he died comfortably who died of an apoplexy, or by the shot of a cannon, any more than he who, having his conscience seared, died as unconcerned as the beasts that perish. Neither do I believe you would envy any one the comfort of dying raving mad. But by a comfortable death, I mean, a calm passage out of life, full of even, rational peace and joy. And such a death, all the acting and all the suffering in the world cannot give, without love.

To make this still more evident, I cannot appeal to your own experience; but I may to what we have seen, and to the experience of others. And two I have myself seen going out of this life in what I call a comfortable manner, though not with equal comfort. One had evidently more comfort than the other, because he had more love.

I attended the first during a great part of his last trial, as well as when he yielded up his soul to God. He cried out, "God doth chasten me with strong pain; but I thank him for all; I bless him for all; I love him for all!" When asked, not long before his release, "Are the consolations of God small with you?," he replied aloud, "No, no, no!" Calling all that were near him by their names, he said, "Think of heaven, talk of heaven: all the time is lost when we are not thinking of heaven." Now, this was the voice of love; and, so far as that prevailed, all was comfort, peace, and joy. . . .

It was in this place that I saw the other good soldier of Jesus Christ grappling with his last enemy, death. And it was, indeed, a spectacle worthy to be seen, of God, and angels, and men. Some of his last breath was spent in a psalm of praise to Him who was then giving him the victory; in assurance whereof he began the triumph even in the heat of the battle. When he was asked, "Hast thou the love of God in thy heart?," he lifted up his eyes and hands, and answered, "Yes, yes!" with all the strength he had left. To one who inquired if he was afraid of the devil, whom he had just mentioned as making his last attack upon him, he replied, "No, no: my loving Savior hath conquered every enemy: He is with me. I fear nothing." Soon after, he said, "The way to our loving Saviour is sharp, but it is short." Nor was it long before he fell into a sort of slumber, wherein his soul sweetly returned to God that gave it.

Here, we may observe, was no mixture of any passion or temper contrary to love; therefore, there was no misery: perfect love casting out whatever might have occasioned torment. And whosoever thou art who hast the like measure of love, thy last end shall be like his.

from *The Interesting Narrative of the Life of Olaudah Equiano, or Gustavus Vassa, the African*

OLAUDAH EQUIANO (1745–1797)

Olaudah Equiano was born in the Essaka region of central Nigeria. At eleven, Equiano was kidnaped with his sister by tribal Africans who spoke a language other than his native Ibo and the youngsters were taken west and south across a large river, probably the Niger. Arriving at the coast, Equiano and his sister were sold to a British slaver sailing to the American colonies. In his *Narrative* (1789), excerpted here, Equiano recounts his enslavement, the horrors of the slave ship, his separation from his sister, his education in England, and his experience of slavery in the West Indies, North America, and the British Isles. (Equiano's slave name is that of the sixteenth-century Swedish king.) In his English home after his manumission, Equiano became an ardent abolitionist and lectured against the cruelty of British slave owners in Jamaica. In 1787 he was appointed commissary aboard the *Vernon*, which carried over 500 freed slaves to Freetown, Sierra Leone, to establish a settlement there. Equiano visited Savannah twice. His first trip was a month after he was released from slavery in July 1766. His second visit, recounted here, came a short time after, on his return from the West Indies sailing under Captain William Phillips. After leaving Georgia he was "determined never more to revisit it."

We sailed about four o'clock in the morning with a fair wind, for Georgia; and about eleven o'clock the same morning, a sudden and short gale sprung up and blew away most of our sails; and, as we were still among the keys, in a very few minutes it dashed the sloop against the rocks. Luckily for us the water was deep;

and the sea was not so angry, but that, after having for some time labored hard, and being many in number, we were saved, through God's mercy; and, by using our greatest exertions, we got the vessel off. The next day we returned to Providence, where we soon got her again refitted. Some of the people swore that we had spells set upon us by somebody in Montserrat; and others that we had witches and wizards amongst the poor helpless slaves; and that we never should arrive safe at Georgia. But these things did not deter me; I said, "Let us again face the winds and seas, and swear not, but trust to God, and he will deliver us." We therefore once more set sail; and with hard labor, in seven days time, we arrived safe at Georgia.

After our arrival we went up to the town of Savannah; and the same evening I went to a friend's house to lodge, whose name was Mosa, a black man. We were very happy at meeting each other; and after supper we had a light till it was between nine and ten o'clock at night. About that time the watch or patrol came by; and, discerning a light in the house, they knocked at the door: we opened it; and they came in and sat down and drank some punch with us; they also begged some limes of me, as they understood I had some, which I readily gave them. A little after this they told me I must go to the watch-house with them: this surprised me a good deal, after our kindness to them; and I asked them, Why so? They said that all Negroes who had a light in their houses after nine o'clock were to be taken into custody, and either pay some dollars or be flogged. Some of those people knew that I was a free man; but, as the man of the house was not free, and had his master to protect him, they did not take the same liberty with him they did with me. I told them that I was a free man, and just arrived from Providence; that we were not making any noise, and that I was not a stranger in that place, but was very well known there: "Besides," said I, "what will you do with me?"—"That you shall see," replied they, "but you must go to the watch-house with us." Now, whether they meant to get money from me or not I was at a loss to know; but

I thought immediately of the oranges and limes at Santa Cruz: and seeing that nothing would pacify them I went with them to the watch-house, where I remained during the night. Early the next morning these imposing ruffians flogged a Negro man and woman that they had in the watch-house, and then they told me that I must be flogged too. I asked "why?" and "if there was any law for free men?" and told them if there was I would have it put in force against them. But this only exasperated them the more, and instantly swore they would serve me as Doctor Perkins had done; and were going to lay violent hands on me; when one of them more humane than the rest, said that as I was a free man they could not justify stripping me by law. I then immediately sent for Doctor Brady, who was known to be an honest and worthy man; and on his coming to my assistance they let me go.

This was not the only disagreeable incident I met with while I was in this place; for one day, while I was a little way out of the town of Savannah, I was beset by two white men, who meant to play their usual tricks with me in the way of kidnaping. As soon as these men accosted me, one of them said to the other, "This is the very fellow we are looking for, that you lost:" and the other swore I was the identical person. On this they made up to me, and were about to handle me; but I told them to be still and keep off; for I had seen those kind of tricks played upon other free blacks, and they must not think to serve me so. At this they paused a little, and one said to the other—it will not do; and the other answered that I talked too good English. I replied, I believed I did; and I had also with me a revengeful stick equal to the occasion; and my mind was likewise good. Happily, however, it was not used; and, after we had talked together a little in this manner the rogues left me.

I stayed in Savannah some time, anxiously trying to get to Montserrat once more, to see Mr. King, my old master, and then to take a final farewell of the American quarter of the globe. At last I met with a sloop called the *Speedwell*, Captain John Bunton, which belonged to Grenada, and was bound to Martinico, a French island, with a cargo of rice, and I shipped myself on board of her.

Before I left Georgia, a black woman who had a child lying dead, being very tenacious of the church burial service, and not able to get any white person to perform it, applied to me for that purpose. I told her I was no parson; and besides, that the service over the dead did not affect the soul. This however did not satisfy her; she still urged me very hard: I therefore complied with her earnest entreaties, and at last consented to act the parson for the first time in my life. As she was much respected, there was a great company both of white and black people at the grave. I then accordingly assumed my new vocation, and performed the funeral ceremony to the satisfaction of all present; after which, I bade adieu to Georgia, and sailed for Martinico.

"Letter to Savannah's Hebrew Congregation"

GEORGE WASHINGTON (1732–1799)

> George Washington was unanimously elected the first president
> of the United States in 1789, and was unanimously reelected for
> a second term. The following 1790 letter was in reply to Levi
> Sheftall, president of the Hebrew Congregation of Savannah. It
> is the first official declaration of fealty by American Jews to an
> American president. Savannah's Jewish population, formed by a
> group of immigrant Sephardic Jews in 1733, is one of the oldest
> in the western hemisphere.

*Address from the Hebrew Congregation of the City of Savannah to the
President of the United States.*

Sir,

We have long been anxious of congratulating you on your
appointment by unanimous approbation to the Presidential dignity of this country, and of testifying our unbounded confidence
in your integrity and unblemished virtue: Yet, however exalted
the station you now fill, it is still not equal to the merit of your
heroic services through an arduous and dangerous conflict,
which has embosomed you in the hearts of her citizens.

Our eccentric situation added to a diffidence founded on the
most profound respect has thus long prevented our address, yet
the delay has realized anticipation, given us an opportunity of
presenting our grateful acknowledgments for the benedictions of
Heaven through the energy of federal influence, and the equity
of your administration.

Your unexampled liberality and extensive philanthropy have
dispelled that cloud of bigotry and superstition which has long,
as a veil, shaded religion—unrivetted the fetters of enthusiasm—

enfranchised us with all the privileges and immunities of free citizens, and initiated us into the grand mass of legislative mechanism. By example you have taught us to endure the ravages of war with manly fortitude, and to enjoy the blessings of peace with reverence to the Deity, and benignity and love to our fellow-creatures.

May the great Author of worlds grant you all happiness—an uninterrupted series of health—addition of years to the number of your days, and a continuance of guardianship to that freedom, which, under the auspices of Heaven, your magnanimity and wisdom have given these States.

Levi Sheftall, President
in behalf of the Hebrew Congregation

To The Hebrew Congregation of the City of Savannah

Gentlemen,

I thank you with great sincerity for your congratulations on my appointment to the office, which I have the honor to hold by the unanimous choice of my fellow-citizens: and especially for the expressions which you are pleased to use in testifying the confidence that is reposed in me by your congregation.

As the delay which has naturally intervened between my election and your address has afforded an opportunity for appreciating the merits of the federal-government, and for communicating your sentiments of its administration—I have rather to express my satisfaction than regret at a circumstance, which demonstrates upon experience your attachment to the former as well as approbation of the latter.

I rejoice that a spirit of liberality and philanthropy is much more prevalent than it formerly was among the enlightened nations of the earth; and that your brethren will benefit thereby in proportion as it shall become still more extensive. Happily the people of the United States of America have, in many instances, exhibited examples worthy of imitation—The salutary influence of which will doubtless extend much farther, if gratefully enjoying those blessings of peace which (under favor of Heaven) have been obtained by fortitude in war, they shall conduct themselves with reverence to the Deity, and charity towards their fellow-creatures.

May the same wonder-working Deity, who long since delivering the Hebrews from their Egyptian oppressors planted them in the promised land—Whose providential agency has lately been conspicuous in establishing these United States as an independent nation—still continue to water them with the dews of Heaven and to make the inhabitants of every denomination participate in the temporal and spiritual blessings of that people whose God is Jehovah.

G. Washington

from *Travels through North and South Carolina, Georgia, East and West Florida*

WILLIAM BARTRAM (1739–1823)

William Bartram, son of famed naturalist John Bartram, attended the Academy of Philadelphia, precursor of the University of Pennsylvania. Although his *Travels through North and South Carolina, Georgia, East and West Florida* (1791) is valuable as an empirical field journal, his early grounding in the classics make the book as much a literary as a scientific work. Using Charleston, South Carolina, as his base, Bartram began four years of travels in March 1773 along the Georgia coastline into Florida, up the Savannah River into north Georgia, and later into Alabama and Louisiana. As much as the natural wonders he describes, Bartram himself is one of the most endearing aspects of his book, his mix of learned analysis with awed religiosity make him a fresh, enthusiastic, and utterly sincere guide to the South's landscape. *Travels* is the only book he produced in his long life.

Arriving in Carolina very early in the spring, vegetation was not sufficiently advanced to invite me into the western parts of this state; from which circumstance, I concluded to make an excursion into Georgia; accordingly, I embarked on board a coasting vessel, and in twenty-four hours arrived in Savanna, the capital, where, acquainting the governor, Sir J. Wright, with my business, his excellency received me with great politeness, shewed me every mark of esteem and regard, and furnished me with letters to the principal inhabitants of the state, which were of great service to me. Another circumstance very opportunely occurred on my arrival: the assembly was then sitting in Savanna, and several members lodging in the same house where I took up my quarters, I became acquainted with several worthy characters, who invited me to call at their seats occasionally, as I passed through the country; particularly the Hon. B. Andrews, Esq., a distinguished, patriotic, and liberal character. This gentleman's seat, and well-cultivated plantations, are situated near the south high road, which I often traveled; and I seldom passed his house without calling to see him, for it was the seat of virtue, where hospitality, piety, and philosophy, formed the happy family; where the weary traveler and stranger found a hearty welcome, and from whence it must be his own fault if he departed without being greatly benefitted.

After resting, and a little recreation for a few days in Savanna, and having in the mean time purchased a good horse, and equipped myself for a journey southward, I sat off early in the morning for Sunbury, a seaport town, beautifully situated on the main, between Medway and Newport rivers, about fifteen miles south of great Ogeeche river. The town and harbor are defended from the fury of the seas by the north and south points of St. Helena and South Catherine's islands; between which is the bar and entrance into the sound: the harbor is capacious and safe, and has water enough for ships of great burthen. I arrived here in the evening, in company with a gentleman, one of the inhabitants, who politely introduced me to one of the principal families, where I supped and spent the evening in a circle of genteel and polite ladies and gentlemen. Next day, being desirous of visiting the islands, I forded a narrow shoal, part of the sound, and landed on one of them, which employed me the whole day to explore. The surface and vegetable mould here is generally a loose sand, not very fertile, except some spots bordering on the sound and inlets, where are found heaps or mounds of sea-shell, either formerly brought there by the Indians, who inhabited the island, or which were perhaps thrown up in ridges, by the beating surface of the sea: possibly both these circumstances may have contributed to their formation. These sea-shells, through length of time, and the subtle penetrating effect of the air, which dissolve them to earth, render these ridges very fertile; and, when clear of their trees, and cultivated, they become profusely productive of almost every kind of vegetable. Here are also large plantations of indigo, corn, and potatoes (Convolvulus batata), with many other sorts of esculent plants. I observed, amongst the shells of the conical mounds, fragments of earthen vessels, and of other utensils, the manufacture of the ancients: about the center of one of them, the rim of an earthen pot appeared amongst the shells and earth, which I carefully removed, and drew it out, almost whole: this pot was curiously wrought all over the outside, representing basket work, and was undoubtedly esteemed a very ingenious performance, by the people, at the age of its construction. The natural produce of these testaceous ridges, besides many of less note, are, the great Laurel Tree; (Magnolia grandiflora) Pinus taeda; Laurus Borbonia; Quercus sempervirens, or Live Oak; Prunus Lauro-cerasus; Ilex aquifolium; Corypha palma; Juniperus Americana. The general surface of the island being low, and generally level, produces a very great variety of trees, shrubs and herbaceous plants; particularly the great long-leaved Pitch-Pine, or Broom-Pine; Pinus palustris; Pinus squamosa; Pinus lutea; Gordonia Lisianthus, Liquid ambar (Styraciflua) Acer rubrum; Fraxinus excelcior; Fraxinus aquatica; Quercus aquatica; Quercus phillos; Quercus dentata; Quercus humila varietas; Vaccinium varietas; Andromeda varietas; Prinos varietas; Ilex varietas; Viburnum prunifolium; V. dentatum; Cornus florida; C. alba; C. sanguinea; Carpinus betula; C. Ostrya; Itea Clethra alnifolia; Halesia tetraptera; H. diptera; Iva; Rhamnus frangula; Callicarpa; Morus rubra; Sapindus; Cassine; and of such as grow near water-courses, round about ponds and savannas, Fothergilla gardini, Myrica cerifera, Olea Americana, Cyrilla racemiflora, Magnolia glauca, Magnolia pyramidata, Cercis, Kalmia angustifolia, Kalmia ciliata, Chionanthus, Cephalanthos, Aesculus parva; and the intermediate spaces, surrounding and lying between the ridges and savannas, are intersected with plains of the dwarf prickly fan-leaved Palmetto, and lawns of grass variegated with stately trees of the great Broom-Pine, and the spreading ever-green Water-Oak, either disposed in clumps, or scatteringly planted by nature. The upper surface, or vegetative soil of the island, lies on a foundation, or stratum, of tenacious cinereous-colored clay, which perhaps is the principal support of the vast growth of timber that arises from the surface, which is little more than a mixture of fine white sand and dissolved vegetables, serving as a nursery bed to hatch or bring into existence the infant plant, and to supply it with aliment and food, suitable to its delicacy and tender frame, until the roots, acquiring sufficient extent and solidity to lay hold of the clay, soon attain a magnitude and stability sufficient to maintain its station. Probably if this clay were dug out, and cast upon the surface, after being meliorated by the saline or nitrous qualities of the air, it would kindly incorporate with the loose sand, and become a productive and lasting manure.

The roebuck, or deer, are numerous on this island; the tiger, wolf, and bear, hold yet some possession; as also raccoons, foxes, hares, squirrels, rats, and mice, but I think no moles. There is a large ground rat, more than twice the size of the common Norway rat. In the night time it throws out the earth, forming little mounds, or hillocks. Opossums are here in abundance, as also polecats, wildcats, rattlesnakes, glass-snake, coach-whip-snake, and a variety of other serpents.

Here are also a great variety of birds, throughout the seasons, inhabiting both sea and land. First I shall name the eagle, of which there are three species. The great grey eagle is the largest, of great strength and high flight; he chiefly preys on fawns and other young quadrupeds.

The bald eagle is likewise a large, strong, and very active bird, but an execrable tyrant: he supports his assumed dignity and grandeur by rapine and violence, extorting unreasonable tribute and subsidy from all the feathered nations.

The last of this race I shall mention is the falco-piscatorius, or fishing hawk: this is a large bird, of high and rapid flight; his wings are very long and pointed, and he spreads a vast sail, in proportion to the volume of his body. This princely bird subsists entirely on fish which he takes himself, scorning to live and grow fat on the dear-earned labors of another; he also contributes liberally to the support of the bald eagle.

Water fowl, and the various species of land birds, also abound, most of which are mentioned by Catesby, in his Hist. of Carolina, particularly his painted finch (Emberiza Ceris Linn.) exceeded by none of the feathered tribes, either in variety and splendor of dress, or melody of song.

Catesby's ground doves are also here in abundance: they are remarkably beautiful, about the size of a sparrow, and their soft and plaintive cooing perfectly enchanting.

How chaste the dove! "never known to violate the conjugal contract."
She flees the seats of envy and strife, and seeks the retired paths of peace.

The sight of this delightful and productive island, placed in front of the rising city of Sunbury, quickly induced me to explore it; which I apprehended, from former visits to this coast, would exhibit a comprehensive epitome of the history of all the sea-coast Islands of Carolina and Georgia, as likewise in general of the coast of the main. And though I considered this excursion along the coast of Georgia and northern border of Florida a deviation from the high road of my intended travels, yet I performed it in order to employ to the most advantage the time on my hands, before the treaty of Augusta came on, where I was to attend, about May or June, by desire of the Superintendent J. Stewart, Esq., who, when I was in Charleston, proposed, in order to facilitate my travels in the Indian territories, that, if I would be present at the Congress, he would introduce my business to the chiefs of the Cherokees, Creeks, and other nations, and recommend me to their friendship and protection; which promise he fully performed, and it proved of great service to me.

Obedient to the admonitions of my attendant spirit, curiosity, as well as to gratify the expectations of my worthy patron, I again sat off on my southern excursion, and left Sunbury, in

company with several of its polite inhabitants, who were going
to Medway meeting, a very large and well-constructed place of
worship, in St. John's parish, where I associated with them in
religious exercise, and heard a very excellent sermon, delivered
by their pious and truly venerable pastor, the Rev. —— Osgood.
This respectable congregation is independent, and consists
chiefly of families, and proselytes of a flock, which this pious
man led about forty years ago, from South Carolina, and settled
in this fruitful district. It is about nine miles from Sunbury to
Medway meeting-house, which stands on the high road opposite
the Sunbury road. As soon as the congregation broke up, I re-
assumed my travels, proceeding down the high road towards
Fort Barrington, on the Alatamaha, passing through a level
country, well watered by large streams, branches of Medway
and Newport rivers, coursing from extensive swamps and
marshes, their sources: these swamps are daily clearing and
improving into large fruitful rice plantations, aggrandizing the
well inhabited and rich district of St. John's parish. The road is
straight, spacious, and kept in excellent repair by the industrious
inhabitants; and is generally bordered on each side with a light
grove, consisting of the following trees and shrubs: Myrica,
Cerifera, Calycanthus, Halesia tetraptera, Itea stewartia,
Andromeda nitida, Cyrella racemiflora entwined with bands
and garlands of Bignonia sempervirens, B. crucigera, Lonicera
sempervirens and Glycene frutescens; these were overshadowed
by tall and spreading trees, as the Magnolia grandiflora, Liquid
ambar, Liriodendron, Catalpa, Quercus sempervirens, Quercus
dentata, Q. Phillos; and on the verges of the canals, where the
road was causwayed, stood the Cupressus disticha, Gordonia
Lacianthus, and Magnolia glauca, all planted by nature, and left
standing by the virtuous inhabitants, to shade the road, and perfume the sultry air. The extensive plantations of rice and corn,
now in early verdure, decorated here and there with groves of
floriferous and fragrant trees and shrubs, under the cover and
protection of pyramidal laurel: and plumed palms, which now
and then break through upon the sight from both sides of the

way as we pass along; the eye at intervals stealing a view at the
humble, but elegant and neat habitation, of the happy propri-
etor, amidst harbors and groves, all day, and moonlight nights,
filled with the melody of the cheerful mockbird, warbling non-
pareil, and plaintive turtle-dove, altogether present a view of
magnificence and joy, inexpressibly charming and animating.

In the evening I arrived at the seat of the Hon. B. Andrews,
Esq. who received and entertained me in every respect, as a worthy gentleman could a stranger; that is, with hearty welcome,
plain but plentiful board, free conversation, and liberality of
sentiment. I spent the evening very agreeably, and the day following (for I was not permitted to depart sooner): I viewed with
pleasure this gentleman's exemplary improvements in agriculture; particularly in the growth of rice, and in his machines for
shelling that valuable grain, which stands in the water almost
from the time it is sown, until within a few days before it is
reaped, when they draw off the water by sluices, which ripens it
all at once, and when the heads or panicles are dry ripe, it is
reaped and left standing in the field, in small ricks, until all the
straw is quite dry, when it is hauled, and stacked in the barn
yard. The machines for cleaning the rice are worked by the force
of water. They stand on the great reservoir which contains the
waters that flood the rice-fields below.

Towards the evening we made a little party at fishing. We
chose a shaded retreat, in a beautiful grove of magnolias, myr-
tles, and sweet bay-trees, which were left standing on the bank
of a fine creek, that, from this place, took a slow serpentine
course through the plantation. We presently took some fish, one
kind of which is very beautiful; they call it the red-belly. It is as
large as a man's hand, nearly oval and thin, being compressed on
each side; the tail is beautifully formed; the top of the head and
back of an olive-green, besprinkled with russet specks; the sides
of a sea-green, inclining to azure, insensibly blended with the
olive above, and beneath lightens to a silvery white, or pearl
color, elegantly powdered with specks of the finest green, russet
and gold; the belly is of a bright scarlet-red, or vermillion, dart-

ing up rays or fiery streaks into the pearl on each side; the ultimate angle of the branchiostega extends backwards with a long spatula, ending with a round or oval particolored spot, representing the eye in the long feathers of a peacock's train, verged round with a thin flame-colored membrane, and appears like a brilliant ruby fixed on the side of the fish; the eyes are large, encircled with a fiery iris; they are a voracious fish, and are easily caught with a suitable bait.

The next morning I took leave of this worthy family, and sat off for the settlements on the Alatamaha, still pursuing the high road for Fort Barrington, till towards noon, when I turned off to the left, following the road to Darian, a settlement on the river, twenty miles lower down, and near the coast. The fore part of this day's journey was pleasant, the plantations frequent, and the roads in tolerable good repair; but the country being now less cultivated, the roads became bad. I pursued my journey almost continually through swamps and creeks, waters of Newport and Sapello, till night, when I lost my way: but coming up to a fence, I saw a glimmering light, which conducted me to a house, where I stayed all night, and met with very civil entertainment. Early next morning I sat off again, in company with the overseer of the farm, who piloted me through a large and difficult swamp, when we parted; he in chase of deer, and I towards Darian. I rode several miles through a high forest of pines, thinly growing on a level plain, which admitted an ample view, and a free circulation of air, to another swamp: and crossing a considerable branch of Sapello river, I then came to a small plantation by the side of another swamp: the people were remarkably civil and hospitable. The man's name was M'Intosh, a family of the first colony established in Georgia, under the conduct of general Oglethorpe. Was there ever such a scene of primitive simplicity, as was here exhibited, since the days of the good king Tammany! The venerable grey-headed Caledonian smilingly meets me coming up to his house. "Welcome, stranger; come in, and rest; the air is now very sultry; it is a very hot day." I was there treated with some excellent venison, and here found friendly and secure shelter from a tremendous thunderstorm, which came up from the N. W. and soon after my arrival began to discharge its fury all around. Stepping to the door to observe the progress and direction of the tempest, the fulgour and rapidity of the streams of lightning, passing from cloud to cloud, and from the clouds to the earth, exhibited a very awful scene; when instantly the lightning, as it were, opening a fiery chasm in the black cloud, darted with inconceivable rapidity on the trunk of a large pine-tree, that stood thirty or forty yards from me, and set it in a blaze. The flame instantly ascended upwards of ten or twelve feet, and continued flaming about fifteen minutes, when it was gradually extinguished by the deluges of rain that fell upon it.

I saw here a remarkably large turkey of the native wild breed; his head was above three feet from the ground when he stood erect; he was a stately beautiful bird, of a very dark dusky brown color, the tips of the feathers of his neck, breast, back, and shoulders, edged with a copper color, which in a certain exposure looked like burnished gold, and he seemed not insensible of the splendid appearance he made. He was reared from an egg, found in the forest, and hatched by a hen of the common domestic fowl.

Our turkey of America is a very different species from the meleagris of Asia and Europe; they are nearly thrice their size and weight. I have seen several that have weighed between twenty and thirty pounds, and some have been killed that weighed near forty. They are taller, and have a much longer neck proportionally, and likewise longer legs, and stand more erect; they are also very different in color. Ours are all, male and female, of a dark brown color, not having a black feather on them; but the male exceedingly splendid, with changeable colors. In other particulars they differ not.

The tempest being over, I waited till the floods of rain had run off the ground, then took leave of my friends, and departed. The air was now cool and salubrious, and riding seven or eight miles, through a pine forest, I came to Sapello bridge, to which the salt tide flows. I here stopped, at Mr. Bailey's, to deliver a letter from the governor. This gentleman received me very civilly, inviting me to stay with him; but upon my urging the necessity of my accelerating my journey, he permitted me to proceed to Mr. L. M'Intosh's, near the river, to whose friendship I was recommended by Mr. B. Andrews.

Perhaps, to a grateful mind, there is no intellectual enjoyment, which regards human concerns, of a more excellent nature, than the remembrance of real acts of friendship. The heart expands at the pleasing recollection. When I came up to his door, the friendly man, smiling, and with a grace and dignity peculiar to himself, took me by the hand, and accosted me thus: "Friend Bartram, come under my roof, and I desire you to make my house your home, as long as convenient to yourself; remember, from this moment, that you are a part of my family, and, on my part, I shall endeavor to make it agreeable," which was verified during my continuance in, and about, the southern territories of Georgia and Florida; for I found here sincerity in union with all the virtues, under the influence of religion. I shall yet mention a remarkable instance of Mr. M'Intosh's friendship and respect for me; which was, recommending his eldest son, Mr. John M'Intosh, as a companion in my travels. He was a sensible virtuous youth, and a very agreeable companion through a long and toilsome journey of near a thousand miles.

Having been greatly refreshed, by continuing a few days with this kind and agreeable family, I prepared to prosecute my journey southerly.

"The Lament of the Captive"

RICHARD HENRY WILDE (1789–1847)

Richard Henry Wilde emigrated with his family to America from his native Dublin at the age of eight. After studying law in Augusta, Georgia, he went on to act as attorney general of his district and served multiple terms in the U.S. House of Representatives before returning to the private practice of law. As much as for his original works of poetry, including *Hesperia* (1867), he is remembered for his presumed authorship of the epitaph on his brother James's Savannah gravestone. The young duelist is remembered on his Colonial Cemetery tombstone thusly:

> *This humble stone records the filial piety, fraternal affection and manly virtues of* JAMES WILDE, *Esquire, late District Paymaster in the army of the U.S. He fell in a Duel on the 16th of January, 1815, by the hand of a man who, a short time ago, would have been friendless but for him; and expired instantly in his 22d year: dying, as he had lived: with unshaken courage & unblemished reputation. By his untimely death the prop of a Mother's age is broken: The hope and consolation of Sisters is destroyed, the pride of Brothers humbled in the dust and a whole Family, happy until then, overwhelmed with affliction.*

The poet Wilde's most-loved work, a fragment known as "The Lament of the Captive" (composed between 1813 and 1814), is from a never-finished epic inspired by James's service in the U.S. Army's campaign against the Seminoles of Florida. The "Lament" was first published in 1815 or 1816 from a private copy without Wilde's knowledge or approval. Wilde was accused of plagiarizing the work of Irish poet Patrick O'Kelly, a controversy not laid to rest—in Wilde's favor—until the mid-1830s with the documentation of Savannahian Anthony Barclay.

My life is like the summer rose
That opens to the morning sky,
And, ere the shades of evening close,
Is scattered on the ground to die:
Yet on that rose's humble bed
The softest dews of night are shed;
As if she wept such waste to see—
But none shall drop a tear for me!

My life is like the autumn leaf
That trembles in the moon's pale ray;
Its hold is frail—its date is brief—
Restless, and soon to pass away:
Yet, when that leaf shall fall and fade,
The parent tree will mourn its shade,
The wind bewail the leafless tree,
But none shall breathe a sigh for me!

My life is like the print, which feet
Have left on Tampa's desert strand.
Soon as the rising tide shall beat,
Their track will vanish from the sand:
Yet, as if grieving to efface
All vestige of the human race,
On that lone shore loud moans the sea,
But none shall thus lament for me!

from *Pleasure and Pain*

Reminiscences of Georgia in the 1840s

EMILY PILLSBURY BURKE (1814–1887)

Emily Pillsbury Burke took a teaching post at the Female Orphan Asylum in Savannah in 1840 and spent the next decade teaching and traveling in Georgia. Like many of the teachers at Southern plantation schools, seminaries, and colleges, Burke was a Puritan and Northeasterner. She married the Reverend A. B. Burke in 1848 while employed at the Female Seminary in Alexandria, Georgia. Soon widowed, Burke took a position in 1850 as principal of the Female Department of Oberlin College and published *Pleasure and Pain: Reminiscences of Georgia in the 1840s* the same year. (Accused of kissing a male student, she was dismissed from this position despite the backing of three petitions: one from female students, one from male students, and a third from citizens of Oberlin.) In addition to describing daily life in the South, its plantations, churches, and camp meetings, in *Pleasure and Pain* Burke tried to answer questions commonly put to her by her Northern students about their Southern counterparts. A staunch abolitionist, she wrote that "with all the faults of the South, I love her still."

LETTER III

Savannah received its name, originally, from its general appearance, which was justly called a savanna, a term that signifies an open, marshy plain, without timber, as its first settlers found it. But though it still retains its first name with merely the addition of one letter, it can no longer be literally applied to it. For now it looks like a city built in a forest, so numerous are the shade trees in every part of it. Beneath these trees, the lamps are suspended that give light to the city in the evening. These lights, interspersed with the many long black shadows that fall everywhere around, heighten the romantic effect that the first sight of these streets would naturally produce in the mind of one unaccustomed to Southern scenes.

The city is laid out in squares, each of which is surrounded by a beautiful growth of ornamental trees. The Pride of India is the most common, the preference being given to these trees because they attain their full growth sooner than any others. They become large trees in six or seven years, and, when they arrive at maturity, they are as large as our oldest elms. For a long time in the summer season they are completely covered with blossoms in color like our lilac and growing in clusters like the snowball. Then the blossoms are succeeded by a yellow, dry kind of fruit about as large as our English cherry, which remains on the tree till the blossoms again appear. Many of the squares in Savannah are left open for places of public resort and promenade and planted with beautiful shade trees of various kinds. In the midst of these grounds, wells are dug for the accommodation of the public, there being but few, if any, private wells and reservoirs of water. One of these beautiful sites is ornamented with a splendid monument erected to the memory of General Pulaski, who lost his life near this spot in the defense of our country's liberties. As all these grounds are named from some particular circumstance, this is called the Monument square; another is called the Market square, because the city market stands upon it, and so on.

On the evening of my arrival, seeing none but white people in the streets, the fact that I was in a land where the largest proportion of its inhabitants were slaves did not occur to my mind. Neither was I forcibly reminded of this unpleasant truth till the following morning. For all the slaves in the city are obliged to retire within the precincts of their own dwellings at eight o'clock in the evening, the hour when the bell rings to summon the city patrol to their several posts. After that hour every slave who is found in the streets without a passport is taken up and confined in the guard house till he has had a trial. If then he can prove he had a reasonable excuse for being out at an unreasonable hour, he is liberated. If it is found he is a runaway slave, then he is advertised for a certain number of days and sold at public auction, if the owner of the slave does not make his appearance and prove property before the advertisement is out. A pail carried by a slave in the evening serves for a legal passport. The propriety of this law I do not understand unless it is this: that a slave, running away, would not be likely to encumber himself with so much of a burden, and, besides, the pail would naturally signify an errand.

Soon after I had taken tea, I retired to a chamber already prepared for my reception. Words cannot express how sweet it was to be once more where the creaking of masts and the eternal clattering of the ropes and sails and the dashing of the waves against the sides of the ship could no longer reach my ears. I could not for some time sleep, I so much enjoyed the consciousness of being where I was not constantly tumbled from one side of my bed to the other, and where too I was not expecting to be thrown out of my bed if I did not exert all my strength in clinging to it all night!

In the morning, no sooner had the sky begun to look a little grey than a confused jargon of strange sounds broke upon my ear. I arose and threw aside my curtain to learn the cause that had deprived me of my morning nap, when to my surprise I saw a great many colored persons, with now and then a white man among them, and animals of various kinds, among which mules were the most numerous, all of which were assembled together under a sort of shelter. That, from the appearance of things, I soon judged to be the city market, a description of which, perhaps, will not be uninteresting to those who have not visited the South. It is not a closed building like our markets at the North but merely a roof, supported by pillars. This roof covers quite an extent of ground, laid with bricks for a floor. In the middle stands a pump, where water is obtained that is used in the market. This building is furnished with stalls, owned by individuals in the city who send produce there to sell.

In each of these stalls stands a servant woman to sell her master's property, who is careful to deck out his saleswoman in the most gaudy colors to make her as conspicuous as possible that she may be successful in trade. I once heard a gentleman, whose saleswoman had not been very successful, say, "he must get her a new handkerchief for her head and see if she would not sell more!" Bonnets are not worn by the colored people at the South, not even to church. The fashion of their headdress is a sort of turban, made by folding a cotton handkerchief in that peculiar kind of way known only to themselves. They select for this purpose the most gaudy that can be found. I never saw any of the kind before or since. During my stay in Georgia, I saw many of those red and yellow articles worn by the colored people. These turbans are so arranged, as to entirely conceal their own hair. But those who are particularly desirous to make a good external appearance wear false braids and curls as long as those that grace the face of any white lady.

The market is free for trade from five o'clock in the morning till ten. Then the bell rings and all are obliged to disperse and take with them their unsold articles, for everything that remains on the ground after ten o'clock belongs to the keeper. Trade is not allowed in the market excepting on Saturday evening, when it is more crowded than at any other time. For the people come then to purchase for the Sabbath, and many go just because they want to see a great crowd. It has been estimated that on some pleasant evenings there are no less than four thousand people in the market at one time. Here almost every eatable thing can be found. Vegetables fresh from the garden are sold the year round. All kinds of fish, both shell and finny, may be had there; birds of all kinds, both tame and wild; and the most delicious tropical fruits, as well as those which are brought from cold countries. People travel a great distance for the purpose of buying and selling in the market. I have known women to come one hundred miles to sell the products of their own industry.

LETTER VIII

Notwithstanding the great precaution which is used to prevent the mental improvement of the slaves, many of them steal knowledge enough to enable them to read and write with ease. It is often the case that the white children of a family impart much of that information they have acquired at school to those among the black children who happen to be their favorites. For it must be understood that not only every little boy and girl has each a favorite slave, but also every young man and woman has his favorite servants, to whom he not only often imparts much useful information but confides in them more as companions than merely waiting men and women. And it is not uncommon to see the favorite slave nearly as wise as his master. A lad about eleven years of age in the family where I once visited made it his practice, unknown to the family, to spend an hour or two every day in teaching a black boy to read, an act exposing the father of the noble-hearted boy to a heavy fine if found out. This fact came to my knowledge by a colored woman who had sufficient confidence in me to believe I should not betray the child.

Clerks often instruct the slaves who labor in the back stores, and many by this means acquire a decent education. I have often seen a young man belonging to one of the largest firms in Savannah who could read, write, cipher and transact business so correctly that his masters often committed important trusts to his care. The firm valued him at fifteen hundred dollars. He read with great eagerness every Northern paper that came within his reach and had by this means gained a good knowledge of the political state of our country. At the time I was there, he was deeply interested in the election of President Harrison, as were the slaves generally in the Southern states, for they were all Harrison men. And they were bold enough to assert publicly that "when William Henry Harrison became President of the United States they should have their freedom!"

I do not know that ever I was more deeply impressed with a sense of the cruelty of depriving the slaves of the means of instruction than one evening while on my way to my room I met two little colored children, apparently about eight years old, trying to find out between themselves some of the letters of the alphabet. It appeared that one of them had found an old, crumpled, soiled leaf torn from a toy book, upon which a few of the large letters were still legible, and then they had seated themselves upon the stairs to study them out. One of the children was saying just as I reached them that she heard somebody say that the round letter was O; the other replied that she heard such a little girl say the straight letter was L; so alternately each was teacher and scholar. Oh, if the children at the North, who are almost compelled to go to school, could have witnessed that scene, it would I think have taught them a lesson not soon to be forgotten.

As a general thing the slaves in the city wear good clothing. Many even dress extravagantly and decorate their persons with a great deal of costly jewelry. I have seen colored men with no less than six or eight rings upon one finger. Many in the city have good houses and expensive furniture. I have seen ladies in the streets with such light complexions and dressed so elegantly that when told they were Negroes I could not willingly credit the assertion. I ought here to say that at the South all who have a drop of the African blood in their veins, however white their skins may be, are called Negroes. But those who dress and live in the manner above described, purchase their time, and all they can earn besides paying a certain sum per week or month to their masters they use in any manner they choose. A gentleman informed me he had a slave who accumulated more property than himself after paying nine dollars per month for his time!

It is quite common for a master to give his slave all his time, if he will take care of himself after he has become so old and worn out as to be of no service to him. It often happens that infirm old slaves are by the death or failure of their masters left without any sort of a home or means of subsistence. As a remedy for this evil in Savannah a kind of asylum has been prepared for all such helpless old people among the black population. But from what

I have been able to learn respecting the institution it is next to having no home at all, and those who avail themselves of the comforts it affords only do it when every other resource for the means of subsistence fails them. I have known poor old men almost bent to the ground by hard labor, with locks which age had bleached as white as newly washed wool, rather than to go to this asylum travel from one plantation to another, begging a potato from one slave and a morsel of hominy from another, sleeping at night in some corner of an old outhouse or in the woods, till they were finally compelled by those who thought themselves doing a deed of mercy to take up their residence in a place as much dreaded by these unfortunate creatures as the almshouse is at the North by poor people.

But those among this downtrodden race of people in our country, whom I commiserated as much as any while in Savannah, were the little chimney sweeps. These were the most forlorn, half-starved, emaciated looking beings I ever beheld. Their masters always accompanied them about the city, because they could not trust them to go to their labor alone, for they were invariably obliged to beat them before they would ascend a chimney, the task was so revolting. But notwithstanding this task seemed so dreadful, extreme hunger often compelled them to climb upon the outside of the house in the nighttime and then descend the chimney to steal something to eat.

In the city it is not unusual to hear of colored boys gaining admittance to a house by descending through the chimney. An instance of this kind came under my observation while in Savannah. Two young men who boarded at one of the public houses, lodged in rooms over their office, one of which they had furnished for a parlor. It was their custom to send a servant into this room every evening to prepare a table of refreshments, which having done, he would lock the door and hand the key to his masters. At length they discovered that depredations were committed every evening upon their wines, cigars, etc. And, notwithstanding they took great pains, they were not able to get the least clue to the source of this mischief, till one evening when going into the room as usual, they found the culprit lying upon the floor in a state of intoxication. When he recovered his senses sufficiently to give an account of himself, he confessed he had been in the practice of entering the room by the way of the chimney and taking whatever he wanted. This time he had partaken too freely of champagne to escape detection.

The slaves carry all their burdens upon their heads, and to me it is quite unaccountable how they can sustain such weights as they do in this manner. They will transport from one place to another tubs of water, large, heavy, iron-bound trunks or any other burden they can raise to their heads. I have seen the man who had the care of the city lamps going from one street to another with a ladder in one hand, a large wooden box in the other and a heavy can of oil on his head. Even the white children often learn from their nurses to carry things in this way. It is quite common to see a little group of school girls with all their books on their heads going to or returning from school, and almost the first thing the little child tries to do when it begins to walk is to balance its toys upon its head. I have often heard the old washerwomen complain of pain in their necks after supporting on their heads a large tub of water or basket of wet clothes.

The dog is the Negroe's favorite pet, and almost every man and woman owns one or two of these faithful animals. Consequently they are exceedingly numerous in the city. Efforts are often made to diminish their numbers, but they seldom avail much, as their owners generally succeed in concealing them. In the daytime the dogs usually left the city to seek their food in the woods, but they always returned at night to the city. And they often collected together in such companies that people could not sleep in consequence of their howling and barking. This circumstance made the poor beasts many enemies.

Just hearing the sound of martial music, I am reminded of the appearance and of the manner in which military parades are conducted at the South. In the first place all their musicians are colored men, for the white gentlemen would consider it quite beneath their dignity to perform such a piece of drudgery as to play for a company while doing military duty. These colored musicians are dressed in the full uniform of the company to which they belong, and, on the morning of the day in which the several companies are to be called out, each band in uniform, one at a time, marches through all the streets to summon all the soldiers to the parade ground. This performance also calls out all the servants that can obtain permission to attend the training, and it is not a few of them that not only follow but go before the companies wherever they march. They are excessively fond of such scenes, and crowds of men, women and children never fail of being present on all such occasions, some carrying their masters' young children on their heads and shoulders, while many are seen with large trays on their heads, loaded with fruit, sweetmeats and various kinds of drinks to sell to those who always wish to purchase on such days. In Savannah there are five of that kind of companies that exist in all the states and are called by all names, composed of all such persons as only perform military duty because they are obliged. In Savannah they are called ragamuffins, and I never heard a name more appropriately applied. Scarcely any two were dressed alike or took the same step, and, whenever I saw them approaching, some with a shoe on one foot and a boot on the other, some with their guns wrong end up and others with them on their shoulders, wearing their knapsacks bottom up and wrong side out, I could not help thinking one might suppose they were learning how to catch up their guns and knapsacks and effect the most speedy escape in time of danger instead of facing an enemy. The independent companies are a credit to the militia system. They are well disciplined and wear elegant and expensive uniforms. The Hussars are a noble and splendid company, mounted on fine spirited steeds so well-trained that they understand the word of command nearly as well as their riders.

"Letter to Kate Perry"

WILLIAM MAKEPEACE THACKERAY

(1 8 1 1 – 1 8 6 3)

William Makepeace Thackeray was one of the most critically acclaimed and widely read British novelists of the nineteenth century. Today he is remembered mostly for *Vanity Fair* (1847–1848). Thackeray made two lecture tours of America, visiting what he called "jolly, friendly, little Savannah" on both occasions. The first tour was in 1853 during which he presented some of his six lectures on *The English Humourists of the Eighteenth Century*, and the second was from 1855–1856 during which he spoke on *The Four Georges of England: Sketches of Manners, Morals, Court, and Town Life*. A Judge Norwood heard the latter delivered at St. Andrew's Hall, and, in James Grant Wilson's *Thackeray in the United States*, called it "as delightful literary morsel as the intellectual palate of Savannah ever tasted." The following letter, dating from 1855, was written by Thackeray during the second tour to his friend Kate Perry in England. (In it, he makes mention of the fact that he, like his Savannah host, had two daughters.) The desk on which Thackeray composed the letter may still be seen in the Andrew Low house on Lafayette Square at 329 Abercorn Street, the villa in which Girl Scouts founder Juliette Gordon Low also resided.

SAVANNAH, GEORGIA—
Feast of St. Valentine

This welcome day brought me a nice long letter from K.E.P., and she must know that I write from the most comfortable quarters I have ever had in the United States. In a tranquil old city, wide-streeted, tree-planted, with a few cows and carriages toiling through the sandy road, a few happy Negroes sauntering here and there, a red river with a tranquil little fleet of merchant-men taking in cargo, and tranquil warehouses, barricaded with packs of cotton—no row, no tearing northern bustle, no ceaseless hotel racket, no crowds drinking at the bar—a snug little languid audience of three or four hundred people, far too lazy to laugh or applaud; a famous good dinner, breakfast, etc., and leisure all the morning to think and do and sleep and read as I like. The only place I say in the States where I can get these comforts—all free gratis—is in the house of my friend Andrew Low of the great house of A. Low and Co., Cotton Dealers, brokers, Merchants—what's the word? Last time I was here he was a widower with two daughters in England, about whom—and other two daughters—there was endless talk between us. Now there is a pretty wife added to the establishment, and a little daughter number three crowing in the adjoining nursery. They are tremendous men these cotton merchants. . . .

"Sut Blown Up with Soda"

GEORGE WASHINGTON HARRIS

(1814-1869)

George Washington Harris's early biography remains sketchy. In his adult years, he worked as a silversmith, journalist, steamboat captain, farmer, politician, and railroader. In 1856, Harris met William Tappan Thompson, author of the *Major Jones's Courtship* collections and editor of the *Savannah Morning News*. Two years earlier Harris had begun developing the character of Sut Lovingood, an irascible mountain man with a disdain for pretension and showy piety as great as his libido for woman and drink, in a sketch published in *Spirit of the Times* magazine. As Sut's popularity grew, Harris went on to publish approximately twenty-five humorous sketches, stories, and letters in the voice of the self-described "nat'ral born durn'd fool." Several appeared in Thompson's *Savannah Morning News*. The following story first appeared in that newspaper circa 1857. Several posthumously collected volumes of the Sut tales exist.

Sut's hide is healed—the wounds received in his sudden separation from his new shirt have ceased to pain, and, true to his instincts, or rather "a famerly dispersition," es he calls it, he "pitches in," and gets awfully blown up by a wild mountain girl. Hear him, poor fellow!

"George, did yu ever see Sicily Burns? Her dad lives at the Rattil-snake Spring, clost ontu the Georgia line."

"Yes, a very handsome girl."

"Handsome! that ar word don't kiver the case; hit souns sorter like callin good whiskey strong water, when yu ar ten mile frum a still-hous, hit a rainin, an' yer flask only haf full. She shows amung wimen like a sunflower amung dorg fennil, ur a hollyhawk in a patch ove smartweed. Sich a buzzim! Jis' think ove two snow balls wif a straw-berry stuck but-ainded intu bof on em. She takes adzactly fifteen inches ove garter clar ove the knot, stans sixteen an' a 'haf hans hi, an' weighs one hundred an' twenty-six in her petticoatail afore brekfus'. She cudent crawl thru a whisky barrel wif bof heads stove out, nur sit in a common armeheer, while yu cud lock the top hoop ove a chun, ur a big dorg collar, roun the huggin place."

"The *what*, Sut?"

"The *wais'* yu durn oninishiated gourd, yu! Her har's es black es a crow's wing et midnite, ur a nigger hianlin charcoal when he's hed no brekfus'; hit am es slick es this yere bottil, an' es long es a hoss's tail. I've seed her jump over a split-bottim cheer wifout showin her ankils, ur ketchin her dress ontu the knobs. She cud cry an' larf et the same time, an' either lov'd ur hated yu all over. Ef her hate fell ontu yu, yu'd feel like yu'd been whipp'd wif a pizen vine, ur a broom made outen nettils when yer breeches an' shut wer bof in the wash-tub. She kerried enuf devil about her tu run crazy a big settlment ove Job's children; her skin wer es white es the inside ove a frogstool, an' her cheeks an' lips es rosey es a pearch's gills in dorgwood blossum time—an' sich a smile! Why, when hit struck yu far an' squar hit felt jis like a big ho'n ole onrectified ole Munongahaley, arter yu'd been sober fur a month, a tendin ove a ten hoss prayer-meetin twist a day, an' mos' ove the nites.

"Three ove her smiles when she wer a tryin ove herself, taken keerfully ten minutes apart, wud make the gran' captin ove a temprunce s'iety so durn'd drunk, he wudn't no his britches frum a par ove bellowses, ur a pledge frum a—a—warter-pot. Oh! I be durned ef hits eny use talkin, that ar gal cud make me murder ole Bishop Soul, hissef, ur kill mam, not tu speak ove dad, ef she jis' hinted she wanted sich a thing dun. Sich an 'oman cud du more devilmint nur a loose stud hoss et a muster ground', ef she only know'd what tools she totes, an' I'se sorter beginin tu think she no's the use ove the las' durnd wun, tu a dot. Her ankils wer es roun', an' not much bigger nur the wrist ove a rifle-gun, an' when she wer a-dancin, ur makin up a bed, ur gittin over a fence—Oh durn sich wimen! Why ain't they all made on the hempbreak plan, like mam, ur Betts Carr, ur Suke Miller, so they wudn't bother a feller's thinker et all.

"George, this worl am all 'rong enyhow, more temtashun than preventitive; ef hit wer ekal, I'd stand hit. What kin the ole prechurs an' the ugly wimen 'spect ove us, 'sposed es we ar tu sich invenshuns es she am? Oh, hits jis' no use in thar talkin, an' groanin, an' sweatin tharsefs, about hit; they mus' jis upset nater ontu her head, an' keep her thar, ur shet up. Less taste this yere whisky."

Sut continued, wiping his mouth on his shirt-sleeve:

"I'se hearn in the mountins a fust rate fourth proof smash ove thunder cum onexpected, an' shake the yeath, bringin along a string ove litenin es long es a quarter track, an' es bright es a weldin heat, a-racin down a big pine tree, tarin hit intu broom splits, an' toof pickers, an' raisin a cloud ove dus', an' bark, an' a army ove lim's wif a smell sorter like the devil wer about, an' the long darnin needil leaves fallin roun wif a tif—tif—quiet sorter soun, an' then a quiverin on the yeath es littil snakes die; an' I felt quar in my in'ards, sorter ha'f cumfurt, wif a littil glad an' rite smart ove sorry mix'd wif hit.

"I'se seed the rattil-snake squar hisself tu cum at me, a sayin z-e-e-e-e, wif that nisey tail ove his'n, an' I felt quar agin—mons'rous quar. I've seed the Oconee River jumpin mad frum rock tu rock wif hits clear, cool warter, white foam, an' music"—

"What, Sut?"

"Music; the rushin warter dus make music; so dus the wind, an' the fire in the mountin, an' hit gin me an oneasy queerness agin; but every time I look'd at that gal Sicily Burns, I hed all the feelins mix'd up, ove the litenin, the river, an' the snake, wif a totch ove the quicksilver sensashun a huntin thru all my veins fur my ticklish place.

"Tu gether hit all in a bunch, an' tie hit, she wer gal all over, frum the pint ove her toe-nails tu the aind ove the longes' har on the highis knob on her head—gal all the time, everywhar, an' wun ove the exhitenis kine. Ove corse I lean'd up tu her, es clost es I dar tu, an' in spite ove these yere yaigs, an' my appertite fur whisky, that ar shut-skinin bisness an' dad's actin hoss, she sorter lean'd tu me, jis' a scrimpshun, sorter like a keerful man salt uther pepil's cattil in the mountin, barly enuf tu bring em back tu the lick-bog sum day—that's the way she salted me, an' I 'tended the lick-log es reg'lar es the old bell cow; *an'* I wer jis' beginin tu think I wer ontu the rite trail tu es much cumfurt, an' stayin 'awake a-purpus, es ole Brigham Young wif all his saddil-culler'd wimen, an' the papers tu fetch more, ef he wants em.

"Well, wun day a cussed, palaverin, Inyun-eatin Yankee ped-lar, all jack-nife an' jaw, cum tu ole man Burns wif a carryall full ove appil-parin-mersheens, jewsharps, calliker, ribbons, sody-powder, an' uther durn'd truck.

"Now mine, I'd never hearn tell ove sody-powder in *my* born'd days; I didn't know hit frum Beltashazur's off ox; but I no's now that hit am wus nur gunpowder fur hurtin, an' durn'd ni es smart tu go off.

"That ar Yankee pedlar hes my piusest prayer, an' I jis wish I hed a kaig ove the truck intu his cussed paunch, wif a slow match cumin out at his mouf, an' I hed a chunk ove fire. The feller what foun a mossel ove 'im big enuf tu feed a cockroach, orter be turn'd loose tu pastur amung seventy-five purty wimen, an' foun in whisky fur life, becase ove his good eyes in huntin los' things. George, a Yankee pedlar's soul wud hev more room in a turnip-seed tu fly roun in than a leather-wing bat hes in a meetin-hous; that's jis' so.

"Sicily hed bot a tin box ove the cold bilin truck an' hid hit till I cum tu the lick-log agin, yu know. Well, I jis' happen'd tu pass nex' day, an' ove corse stopp'd tu injoy a look at the temtashun, an' she wer mity luvin tu me. I never felt the lik—put wun arm roun my naik, an' tuther whar the susingil goes roun a hoss, tuck the inturn ontu me wif her lef' foot, an' gin me a kiss. Sez she—

"Sutty, luv, I'se got sumthin fur yu, a new *sensashun*—"

"An' I b'leve in hit strong, fur I begun tu feel hit pow'ful. My toes felt like I wer in a warm krick wif minners a-nibblin at em; a cole streak wer a racin up an' down my back like a lizzard wif a tucky hen arter 'im; my hans tuck the ager, an' my hart felt hot an' on-satisfied like. Then hit wer that I'd a-cut ole Soul's froat wif a hansaw, an' never batted my eye, ef she'd a-hinted the needsesity.

"Then she pour'd 'bout ten blue papers ove the fizilin powder intu a great big tumbler, an' es meny white papers intu anuther, an' put ni ontu a pint ove warter intu bof on em, stir'd em up wif a case-nife, an' gritted a morsel ove nutmaig on top, the 'saitful she torment lookin es solemn es a jasack in a snow storm, when the fodder gin out. She hilt wun, an' tole me tu drink tuther. I swaller'd hit at wun run; tasted sorter salty like, but I tho't hit wer part ove the sensashun. But I wer slitely mistaken'd; hit wer yet tu cum, an' warn't long 'bout hit, hoss, better b'leve. Ternally durn all sensashuns ove every spot an' stripe! I say. Then she gin me tuther, an' I sent hit a chasin the fus' instalmint tu the sag ove my paunch, race-hoss way. Yu see I'd got the idear onder my har that hit wer *luv-powders*, an' I'd swaller'd the devil red hot frum home, a-thinkin that. Luv-powders *frum her*! Jis' think ove hit yerse'f solemnly a minit, an sit still ef yu kin.

"Jis bout the time I wer ketchin my breff, I tho't I'd swaller'd a thrashin-meersheen in full blast, wif a cuppil ove bull-dorgs, an' they hed sot intu fitin; an' I felt sum thin cumin up my swaller, monstrus like a hi pressur steamboat. I cud hear hit a-snortin, and scizzin. *Kotch agin, by the great goly!* tho't I; same famerly 'dispersishun tu make a durn'd fool ove myse'f jis' es ofen es the sun sets, an' fifteen times ofener ef thar's a half a chance. Durn dad evermore, amen! I say.

"I happen'd tu think ove my hoss, an' I broke fur him. I stole a hang-dorg look back, an' thar lay Sicily, flat ove her back in the porch, clapin her hans, screamin wif laughin, her feet up in the air, a-kickin em a-pas' each uther like she wer tryin tu kick her slippers off. I'se pow'ful sorry I wer too bizzy tu look at em. Thar wer a road ove foam frum the hous' tu the hoss two foot wide, an' shoe mouf deep—looked like hit hed been snowin—a poppin, an' a-hissin, an' a-bilin like a tub ove soap-suds wif a red hot mole-board in hit. I gethered a cherry tree lim' es I run, an' I lit a-straddil ove ole Blackey, a-thrashin his hide like the devil beatin tan-bark, an' a-hissin wus nur four thousin mad ganders outen my mouf, eyes, nose, an' years. All this waked the ole hoss, an' he fotch one rar, one kick, an' then he went—he jis' mizzel'd, skar'd. Oh lordy! how the foam rolled, an' the hoss flew! Es we turned the corner ove the gardin lot, I hearn Sicily call, es clar es a bugle:

"Hole hit down, Mister Lovingood! Hole hit down! Hits a cure fur puppy luv; hole hit *down*!"

"Hole hit down! Hu ever hearn sich a onpossibil—Why, *rite then* I wer a-feelin the bottim ove my paunch cumin up arter hit, inside out, jis' like the bottim ove a green champain bottil. I wer spectin tu see hit every blast. That, wif what Sicily sed, wer a-hurtin my thinker pow'ful bad, an' then the ise-warter idear, that hit warn't a luv-powder arter all that hurtin—takin all tugether, I wer sorter wishin hit mout keep on till I wer all biled tu foam, plum tu my heel-strings.

"I wer aimin fur Dr. Goodman's, at the Hiwasee Copper Mine, tu git sumthin tu simmer hit down wif, when I met ole Clapshaw, the suckit-rider, a-travelin to'ards sumbody's hot biskit an' fried chicken. As I cum tarin along, he hilt up his hans like he wanted tu pray fur me; but es I wanted sumthin tu reach furder, an' take a ranker holt nur his prars cud, I jis' rambled ahead. I wer hot arter a ten-hoss dubbil-actin steam paunch-pump, wif wun aind sock'd deep intu my soda lake, an' a strong manbody doctur at tuther; hit wer my *big want* jis' then. *He* tuck a skeer, es I wer cumin strait fur him; his faith gin out, an' he dodged flat hat, hoss, an' saddil-bags, intu the thicket. I seed his hoss's tail fly up over his back, es he disappear'd intu the bushes; thar mus' a-been spurrin gwine on 'bout thar. I liked his moshuns onder a skeer rite well; he made that dodge jis' like a mud-turkil draps ofen a log when a big steamboat cums tarin a-pas'. Es he pass'd ole man Burns's, Sicily hailed 'im tu ax ef he met enybody gwine up the road in a sorter hurry. The poor devil tho't that p'raps he mout; warnt sure, but he hed seed a dreadful forewarnin, ur a ghos', ur ole Belzebub, ur the Tariff. Takin all things together, however, in in the litil time spar'd tu 'im fur 'flection, hit mus' a-been a crazy, long-laiged shakin Quaker, fleein frum the rath tu cum, on a black an' white spotted hoss, a-whipin 'im wif a big brush; an' he hed a white beard what cum frum jis onder his eyes down tu the pumil ove the saddil, an' then forked an' went tu his knees, an' frum thar drapp'd in bunches es big es a crow's nes', tu the groun; an' he hearn a soun like ontu the rushin ove mitey warters, an' he were pow'fully exersized 'bout hit enyhow. Well, I guess her wer, an' so wer his fat hoss, an' so wer ole Blackey, an' more so by a durn'd site wer me mysef. Arter he cumpos'd hissef he rit out his fool noshuns fur Sicily, that hit wer a new steam invenshun tu spread the Catholic doctrin, an' tote the Pope's bulls tu pastur in distunt lans, made outen sheet iron, ingin rubber, tann'd leather, ise cream, an' fat pine, an' that the hoss's tail wer made outen iron wire, red hot at the pint, an' a stream ove sparks es long es the steerin-oar ove a flatboat foller'd thararter; an' takin hit all tugether hit warnt a safe thing tu meet in a lane ove a dark nite; an' he tho't he hed a call over the mountin tu anuth sarkit; that chickens warnt as plenty over thar, but then he were a self-denyin man.

"Now, George, all this beard, an' spotted hoss, an' steam, an' fire, an' snow, an' wire tails, wer durn'd skeer'd suckit rider's humbug, hit all cum outen my paunch, wifout eny vomitin ur coaxin, an' ef hit hedn't, I'd a dun been busted intu more scraps nur thar's aigs in a big catfish.

"'Hole hit down, Mister Lovingood! Hole hit down!' Now warnt that jis' the durndes' onreasonabil reques' ever an o'man made ove man? She mout jis es well ax'd me tu swaller my hoss, an' then skin the cat on a cob-web. She's pow'ful on docterin tho', I'll swear tu that."

"Why, Sut?"

"Kase she cur'd my puppy-luv wif wun dost, durn her! George, am sody *pizen*?"

"No; why?"

"I sorter 'spected hit wer, an' I sot in, an' et yarbs, an' grass, an' roots, till I'se pounch'd out like ontu a ole cow; my hole swaller an' paunch am tann'd hard es sole leather. I axes rot-gut no odds now. Yere's a drink tu the durndes' fool in the worl'—jis' me!"

And the bottom of Sut's flask flashed in the sun light.

from *Fast and Loose in Dixie*

J. MADISON DRAKE (1837–1913)

> J. Madison Drake's Civil War memoir, *Fast and Loose in Dixie*
> (1880) is subtitled "An unprejudiced narrative of personal expe-
> rience as a prisoner of war at Libby, Macon, Savannah, and
> Charleston, with an account of a desperate leap from a moving
> train of cars, a weary tramp of forty-five days through swamps
> and mountains, places and people visited, etc., etc." He was the
> publisher of several New Jersey newspapers and started the
> *Evening News* (1857) and *Wide Awake* (1860), both in New
> Jersey. He served in the Union Army from 1861–1865 and
> unfurled the first Union flag on Virginia soil on May 24, 1861.
> Drake was awarded the Congressional Medal of Honor for dis-
> tinguished gallantry.

The news which we received from Sherman's army grew more
and more encouraging to us, and correspondingly depressing to
the rebels. From what we could overhear, when the sentinels
conversed loud enough for us to distinguish what they said, we
became satisfied that our early removal to another place had
been decided upon. Accordingly, on the 27th of July, six hundred officers were sent off to Charleston, and two days later, six
hundred others were transported to Savannah. Our keepers
could not deceive us, for on every hand we saw evidences of
Sherman's triumphant march into the heart of the Confederacy,
heretofore exempt from the horrors of war. Hundreds of freight
cars along the railroad contained "poor white trash," refugees
from the upper part of Georgia. These people had been driven
from their hitherto peaceful homes, and now they began to suffer some of the horrors which they had provoked. How they
would be able to subsist was a mystery.

The ride to Savannah occupied some twelve hours. The country was a wilderness, or nearly so. Only here and there did we

see a house, or a farm which looked as if it could be made productive. On leaving the train at the depot in Savannah, we were surrounded by a company called the Blues, headed by a black band, and were escorted to our new prison-home, which we found to be the old Marine Hospital grounds, property of the United States, luxuriously shaded by beautiful live-oak trees. The streets through which we marched were crowded with people anxious to get a "look at the Yankees." Many females displayed the flag of the stars and bars, and took great pride in attracting our attention thereto. Some even indulged in singing a ridiculous song called "The Bonnie Blue Flag," which, to say the least, did not show very good taste on their part.

I was fearful of leaving Macon that we might be taken to a worse place, if such could be found, but on entering the hospital grounds, my mind was happily set at rest on that score. Indeed, I congratulated myself on the change when I found ample shade, green grass on which to sleep, and a well of good water, of a sulphurous taste—yet said to contain medicinal properties of a high order. I found the place, which was surrounded on all sides by a high brick wall, to be delightful, and I never slept more tranquilly.

From the fact that no preparation had been made for our reception, we decided that the rebels must have been greatly alarmed when they sent us from Macon. The morning after our arrival at Savannah a number of carpenters entered the yard and erected a "dead line," a necessary appendage to a camp for prisoners. This afforded us a chance to secure pieces of boards, which we used in constructing bunks on which to sleep. During the day, one hundred clean tents were issued to us, also an abundance of cooking utensils, etc., and we were further surprised a few days after by receiving boards sufficient to stockade every tent in the yard. With all these things, together with plenty of cornmeal, rice, beans, salt, fresh beef, etc., we made ourselves quite comfortable. The commandant of the camp, Colonel Wayne, of the First Georgia Regulars, and his gentlemanly officers, did all in their power to ameliorate our condition, and none who were there will ever forget the many favors so generously shown. This camp was Elysium itself. I attributed the generosity of our new keepers to the fact that they had been to the front, knew what war was, and treated us accordingly. Had they been home-guards, our condition would have been made as unpleasant as possible, for home-guards must always do something to show their importance.

The tents answered a double purpose, several of them serving to screen tunneling operations, a work which some of us at once engaged in. Two tunnels were commenced at the same time—one from the large privy vault, the other from Captain Grant's tent. I worked actively on the latter. The soil being of a light, sandy nature, we were enabled to make astonishing progress, succeeding beyond our sanguine expectations. It was while disposing of dirt from the tunnel, one dark night, that I detected a comrade, Captain John Parker, First New Jersey Volunteers, engaged in a similar occupation. We seated ourselves under a huge live-oak tree and made an arrangement by which both parties should work in unison, and in the event of one tunnel being completed in advance of the other, the one thus finished should be used by all in common. As luck would have it, Parker's tunnel was first completed, and we were notified to get ready for flight. I lost no time in cooking what meal, etc., I had, and at about ten o'clock at night stood waiting in the vault, expecting momentarily to receive the signal to descend the shaft and enter the tunnel, the narrow yet certain path, I fondly hoped, to freedom. Parker, Donovan, and several others had crawled in. What could the matter be? Why so much delay? Our anxiety was finally set at rest by the sudden appearance of those who had but a few minutes before gone into the mouth of the tunnel with such high hopes. Covered with perspiration—for it must be borne in mind that a tunnel of that nature is a close corporation—Parker gave the following explanation. Reaching the farthest end of the tunnel, he probed the opening, and was about to emerge therefrom when his attention was attracted to a sentinel who stood leaning against the prison wall a few yards away. Satisfied that our designs were suspected and that egress was impossible, the gallant captain "kicked back," and the party retreated, feet fore-most, to the starting-point, and a more crest-fallen crowd I never saw. We had no means of covering our tracks, it being impossi-ble to refill the hole in the sidewalk outside the prison yard, and as we knew the gap would be discovered when daylight came, we slunk away to our quarters, and slept soundly till the sun rose the next morning. When daylight came, the tunnel was dis-covered in a singular manner. A cow, in passing along, had fallen into the pit, from which she was unable to extricate herself. A vigilant sentinel, seeing her predicament, raised an alarm, which was speedily responded to by the officer of the day, who hastened to the spot, accompanied by two reliefs.

The prison commandant subsequently entered the yards: he expressed his surprise at our conduct, especially as he had shown much forbearance, and had been uniformly kind and obliging. He forbade further tunneling. Should the attempt be made, however, discovery was certain, and would lead to unpleasant results. We congratulated ourselves upon the non-discovery of the tunnel in Grant's tent, and this we determined to push forward to an early completion, although we felt that it would be necessary to extend it into a grove on the opposite side of the street. But during the afternoon the commandant again appeared, this time with a party of officers, each of whom car-ried an iron ramrod. With these they probed the ground in each tent. They were about to cease their examination, when one of the officers accidentally dropped his rammer, which on being picked up, by some unaccountable means, became attached to the strap of one of the bags sunk in the shaft, and exclaiming, "Hallo, what's this?" stooped down, and after exerting consid-erable strength, hauled out a bag filled with dirt. Although the occupants of that tent expressed surprise at the discovery, noth-ing which they could say in explanation would satisfy the Confederates, who ordered the removal of the tent to another spot. The tunnel was destroyed during the afternoon, and again were we doomed to bitter disappointment.

A day or two after this we commenced two other tunnels, and

had made considerable headway with them, when one night we were discovered in the act of dragging the bags therefrom. Captains Grant and Benson, acknowledging that they were the responsible parties (although none of us saw any crime in the transaction), were marched to the city prison, where they were kept in close confinement for a week. They were on the point of escaping therefrom, when they were escorted back to the yard. They reported to us that there were many Unionists in the city, and that if any of us could get away, the prospect of meeting with friendly assistance was extremely good.

There was one amusing, if not ridiculous feature of prison-life which may be worth mentioning: that was the all-absorbing question of "exchange." This word was in everyone's mouth, and but little else was thought of or talked about. Every day, through the dreary months of our captivity, we heard rumors of a contemplated exchange. It, being a question of vital importance, was debated *pro* and *con* by all. We credited almost everything that we heard in relation to this matter, especially if the report corresponded with our wishes and our hopes. The subject finally became a farce, and when two officers or more were seen conversing together, cries of "Louder on Exchange" were sure to greet them. No term was used as much as "Louder on Exchange," and the phrase prompted the following, written by Lieutenant J. B. Vance, Company K, 95th Ohio Volunteers:

"LOUDER ON EXCHANGE"

AIR—PUTTING ON AIRS

Of slang words there are many,
    Which this war about did bring,
And among the rest, now there is one,
    About which I shall sing.
You need not think I mean you ill,
    Nor take it very strange,
When I tell you that the words I mean,
Are "Louder on Exchange."

CHORUS—Every day, and every day,
    To me it is not strange,
    To hear the prisoners calling out,
    "Louder on Exchange."

A group of friends together meet,
    With all the arrangements made,
Just to while away a pleasant hour,
    Some place in the shade.
They are talking o'er the various plans
    Our government could arrange,
When someone suddenly bellows out,
    "Louder on Exchange."

        CHORUS—Every day, etc.

Then you chance to get a paper,
    That contains a little news—
Not enough to raise your spirits up,
    Or drive away the blues.
A crowd gathers round you, and
    The first thing they exclaim,
What's the news from our army,
    Next—"Louder on Exchange!"

        CHORUS—Every day, etc.

Then you hear of General Foster,
    And the rebel General Jones,
How they swapped off fifty men,
    And sent them to their homes.
You think the news is good enough,
    And nothing now remains;
You cannot help from calling out,
    "Louder on Exchange!"

        CHORUS—Every day, etc.

Our authorities at Washington,
    That very well we know,

Will release us all in course of time,
    But it seems so very slow.
And when we do get out of this,
    And have our freedom gained,
There will be no more this calling out,
    "Louder on Exchange."

CHORUS—Every day, etc.

This song became very popular, and was sung by all the prisoners with a vim peculiar to themselves and their condition.

One morning, noticing that the Johnnies were more quiet than usual, we suspected that something had gone wrong with them, and we became decidedly anxious to learn the news. Towards noon the sergeant of the guard gave us a copy of the *Republican*, which explained the cause of grief on the part of our keepers. We read with pleasure of the capture of the "Gate City" (Atlanta), by Sherman. Seeing the officer of the day passing through camp shortly after, we inquired whether there was any news from Atlanta. "No-o, gentlemen! I—oh! I haven't seen a paper in a week," and he walked hurriedly away, as if he had an important engagement elsewhere. We felt sorry for him.

While we had many comforts in Savannah that had been denied us elsewhere, we never could account for the caution which the Confederates took to prevent us from ascertaining the news. We petitioned General McClaws for permission to purchase the papers, but he disapproved our request.

During the cool of mornings and evenings we took such exercise as was available, and felt all the better therefor. Take it all in all, our sojourn in Savannah was pleasant, far better than we expected, and my recollections of the place are of an agreeable character. Many a time afterward I regretted leaving it.

Nothing in particular occurred to disturb the monotony of our existence at Savannah. After we found tunneling unproductive, we settled down to the natural order of things, becoming quite philosophic the more we reflected upon the hopelessness of making our escape.

from *Treasure Island*

ROBERT LOUIS STEVENSON (1850–1894)

Robert Louis Stevenson was born a sickly child in Edinburgh, Scotland. Despite lifelong frailty and ill health, Stevenson's body of essays, poetry, travel books, and fiction is as prodigious as his globetrotting travel. Savannah lore holds that the basis for the Admiral Benbow Inn appearing in his *Treasure Island* (1883) was the Pirate's House, a 1734 building at the Trustee's Garden Site at 20 East Broad Street.

THE OLD SEA-DOG AT THE "ADMIRAL BENBOW"

Squire Trelawney, Dr. Livesey, and the rest of these gentlemen having asked me to write down the whole particulars about Treasure Island, from the beginning to the end, keeping nothing back but the bearings of the island, and that only because there is still treasure not yet lifted, I take up my pen in the year of grace 17—, and go back to the time when my father kept the "Admiral Benbow" inn, and the brown old seaman, with the sabre cut, first took up his lodging under our roof.

I remember him as if it were yesterday, as he came plodding to the inn door, his sea-chest following behind him in a handbarrow; a tall, strong, heavy, nut-brown man; his tarry pigtail falling over the shoulders of his soiled blue coat; his hands ragged and scarred, with black, broken nails; and the sabre cut across one cheek, a dirty, livid white. I remember him looking round the cove and whistling to himself as he did so, and then breaking out in that old sea-song that he sang so often afterwards:

> "Fifteen men on the dead man's chest—
> Yo-ho-ho, and a bottle of rum!"

in the high, old tottering voice that seemed to have been tuned and broken at the capstan bars. Then he rapped on the door with a bit of stick like a handspike that he carried, and when my father appeared, called roughly for a glass of rum. This, when it was brought to him, he drank slowly, like a connoisseur, lingering on the taste, and still looking about him at the cliffs and up at our signboard.

"This is a handy cove," says he, at length; "and a pleasant sittyated grog-shop. Much company, mate?"

My father told him no, very little company, the more was the pity.

"Well then," said he, "this is the berth for me. Here you, matey," he cried to the man who trundled the barrow; "bring up alongside and help up my chest. I'll stay here a bit," he continued. "I'm a plain man; rum and bacon and eggs is what I want, and that head up there for to watch ships off. What you naught call me? You mought call me captain. Oh, I see what you're at—there"; and he threw down three or four gold pieces on the threshold. "You can tell me when I've worked through that," says he, looking as fierce as a commander.

And, indeed, bad as his clothes were, and coarsely as he spoke, he had none of the appearance of a man who sailed before the mast; but seemed like a mate or skipper, accustomed to be obeyed or to strike. The man who came with the barrow told us the mail had set him down the morning before at the "Royal George"; that he had inquired what inns there were along the coast, and hearing ours well spoken of, I suppose, and described as lonely, had chosen it from the others for his place of residence. And that was all we could learn of our guest.

He was a very silent man by custom. All day he hung round the cove, or upon the cliffs, with a brass telescope; all evening he sat in a corner of the parlor next the fire, and drank rum and water very strong. Mostly he would not speak when spoken to; only look up sudden and fierce, and blow through his nose like a fog-horn; and we and the people who came about our house soon learned to let him be. Every day, when he came back from his stroll, he would ask if any seafaring men had gone by along the road. At first we thought it was the want of company of his own kind that made him ask this question; but at last we began to see he was desirous to avoid them. When a seaman put up at the "Admiral Benbow" (as now and then some did, making by the coast road for Bristol), he would look in at him through the curtained door before he entered the parlor; and he was always sure to be as silent as a mouse when any such was present. For me, at least, there was no secret about the matter; for I was, in a way, a sharer in his alarms. He had taken me aside one day, and promised me a silver fourpenny on the first of every month if I would only keep my "weather-eye open for a seafaring man with one leg," and let him know the moment he appeared. Often enough, when the first of the month came round, and I applied to him for my wage, he would only blow through his nose at me, and stare me down; but before the week was out he was sure to think better of it, bring me my fourpenny piece, and repeat his orders to look out for "the seafaring man with one leg."

How that personage haunted my dreams, I need scarcely tell you. On stormy nights, when the wind shook the four corners of the house, and the surf roared along the cove and up the cliffs, I would see him in a thousand forms, and with a thousand diabolical expressions. Now the leg would be cut off at the knee, now at the hip; now he was a monstrous kind of a creature who had never had but the one leg, and that in the middle of his body. To see him leap and run and pursue me over hedge and ditch was the worst of nightmares. And altogether I paid pretty dear for my monthly fourpenny piece, in the shape of these abominable fancies.

But though I was so terrified by the idea of the seafaring man with one leg, I was far less afraid of the captain himself than anybody else who knew him. There were nights when he took a deal more rum and water than his head would carry; and then he would sometimes sit and sing his wicked, old wild sea-songs, minding nobody; but sometimes he would call for glasses round, and force all the trembling company to listen to his stories or bear a chorus to his singing. Often I have heard the house shaking with "Yo-ho-ho, and a bottle of rum"; all the neighbors joining in for dear life, with the fear of death upon them, and each singing louder than the other, to avoid remark. For in these fits he was the most over-riding companion ever known; he would slap his hand on the table for silence all round; he would fly up in a passion of anger at a question, or sometimes because none was put, and so he judged the company was not following his story. Nor would he allow anyone to leave the inn till he had drunk himself sleepy and reeled off to bed.

His stories were what frightened people worst of all. Dreadful stories they were; about hanging, and walking the plank, and storms at sea, and the Dry Tortugas, and wild deeds and places on the Spanish Main. By his own account he must have lived his life among some of the wickedest men that God ever allowed upon the sea; and the language in which he told these stories shocked our plain country people almost as much as the crimes that he described. My father was always saying the inn would be ruined, for people would soon cease coming there to be tyrannized over and put down, and sent shivering to their beds; but I really believe his presence did us good. People were frightened at the time, but on looking back they rather liked it; it was a fine excitement in a quiet country life; and there was even a party of the younger men who pretended to admire him, calling him a "true sea-dog," and a "real old salt," and such-like names, and saying there was the sort of man that made England terrible at sea.

In one way, indeed, he bade fair to ruin us; for he kept on staying week after week, and at last month after month, so that all the money had been long exhausted, and still my father never plucked up the heart to insist on having more. If ever he mentioned it, the captain blew through his nose so loudly, that you might say he roared, and stared my poor father out of the room. I have seen him wringing his hands after such a rebuff, and I am sure the annoyance and the terror he lived in must have greatly hastened his early and unhappy death.

All the time he lived with us the captain made no change whatever in his dress but to buy some stockings from a hawker. One of the cocks of his hat having fallen down, he let it hang from that day forth, though it was a great annoyance when it blew. I remember the appearance of his coat, which he patched himself upstairs in his room, and which, before the end, was nothing but patches. He never wrote or received a letter, and he never spoke with any but the neighbors, and with these, for the most part, only when drunk on rum. The great sea-chest none of us had ever seen open.

He was only once crossed, and that was towards the end, when my poor father was far gone in a decline that took him off. Dr. Livesey came late one afternoon to see the patient, took a bit of dinner from my mother, and went into the parlor to smoke a pipe until his horse should come down from the hamlet, for we had no stabling at the old "Benbow." I followed him in, and I remember observing the contrast the neat, bright doctor, with his powder as white as snow, and his bright, black eyes and pleasant manners, made with the coltish country folk, and above all, with that filthy, heavy, bleared scarecrow of a pirate of ours, sitting far gone in rum, with his arms on the table. Suddenly he—the captain, that is—began to pipe up his eternal song:

> *"Fifteen men on the dead man's chest—*
> *Yo-ho-ho, and a bottle of rum!*
> *Drink and the devil had done for the rest—*
> *Yo-ho-ho, and a bottle of rum!"*

At first I had supposed "the dead man's chest" to be that identical big box of his upstairs in the front room, and the thought had been mingled in my nightmares with that of the one-legged seafaring man. But by this time we had all long ceased to pay any particular notice to the song; it was new, that night, to nobody but Dr. Livesey, and on him I observed it did not produce an agreeable effect, for he looked up for a moment quite angrily before he went on with his talk to old Taylor, the gardener, on a new cure for the rheumatics. In the meantime, the captain gradually brightened up at his own music, and at last flapped his hand upon the table before him in a way we all knew to mean—silence. The voices stopped at once, all but Dr.

Livesey's; he went on as before, speaking clear and kind, and drawing briskly at his pipe between every word or two. The captain glared at him for a while, flapped his hand again, glared still harder, and at last broke out with a villainous low oath: "Silence, there, between decks!"

"Were you addressing me, sir?" says the doctor; and when the ruffian had told him, with another oath, that this was so, "I have only one thing to say to you, sir," replies the doctor, "that if you keep on drinking rum, the world will soon be quit of a very dirty scoundrel!"

The old fellow's fury was awful. He sprang to his feet, drew and opened a sailor's clasp-knife, and, balancing it open on the palm of his hand, threatened to pin the doctor to the wall.

The doctor never so much as moved. He spoke to him, as before, over his shoulder, and in the same tone of voice; rather high, so that all the room might hear, but perfectly calm and steady:

"If you do not put that knife this instant in your pocket, I promise, upon my honor, you shall hang at next assizes."

Then followed a battle of looks between them; but the captain soon knuckled under, put up his weapon, and resumed his seat, grumbling like a beaten dog.

"And now, sir," continued the doctor, "since I now know there's such a fellow in my district, you may count I'll have an eye upon you day and night. I'm not a doctor only; I'm a magistrate; and if I catch a breath of incivility like to-night's, I'll take effectual means to have you hunted down and routed out of this. Let that suffice."

Soon after Dr. Livesey's horse came to the door, and he rode away; but the captain held his peace that evening, and for many evenings to come.

from *The Memoirs of Gen. W. T. Sherman, Written By Himself*

GENERAL WILLIAM TECUMSEH SHERMAN

(1 8 2 0 – 1 8 9 1)

> General William Tecumseh Sherman began his military life
> when he received an appointment to West Point in 1836 and
> eventually became commander-in-chief of United States troops
> from 1869 to 1883. After taking possession of Atlanta in
> September 1864, Sherman began his March to the Sea. As
> recounted in his memoirs of 1890, excerpted here, Sherman
> invaded Savannah just before Christmas 1864.

The city of Savannah was an old place, and usually accounted a
handsome one. Its houses were of brick or frame, with large yards,
ornamented with shrubbery and flowers; its streets perfectly regular,
crossing each other at right angles; and at any of the intersections
were small inclosures in the nature of parks. These streets and parks
were lined with the handsomest shade-trees of which I have knowledge, viz., the willow-leaf live-oak, evergreens of exquisite beauty;
and these certainly entitled Savannah to its reputation as a handsome
town more than the houses, which, though comfortable, would
hardly make a display on Fifth Avenue or the Boulevard Haussmann
of Paris. The city was built on a plateau of sand about forty feet
above the level of the sea, abutting against the river, leaving room
along its margin for a street of stores and warehouses. The custom-
house, courthouse, post office, etc., were on the plateau above. In
rear of Savannah was a large park, with a fountain, and between it
and the courthouse was a handsome monument, erected in the memory of Count Pulaski, who fell in 1779 in the assault made on the city
at the time it was held by the English during the Revolutionary War.
Outside of Savannah there was very little to interest a stranger,

except the cemetery of Bonaventure, and the ride along the Wilmington Channel by way of Thunderbolt, where might be seen some groves of the majestic live-oak trees, covered with gray and funereal moss, which were truly sublime in grandeur, but gloomy after a few days' campaign under them.

Within an hour of taking up my quarters in Mr. Green's house, Mr. A.G. Browne, of Salem, Massachusetts, United States Treasury agent for the Department of the South, made his appearance to claim possession, in the name of the Treasury Department, of all captured cotton, rice, buildings, etc. Having use for these articles ourselves, and having fairly earned them, I did not feel inclined to surrender possession, and explained to him that the quartermaster and commissary could manage them more to my liking than he; but I agreed, after the proper inventories had been prepared, if there remained anything for which we had no special use, I would turn it over to him. It was then known that in the warehouses were stored at least twenty-five thousand bales of cotton, and in the forts one hundred and fifty large, heavy sea-coast guns; although afterward, on a more careful count, there proved to be more than two hundred and fifty sea-coast or seige guns, and thirty-one thousand bales of cotton. At that interview Mr. Browne, who was a shrewd, clever Yankee, told me that a vessel was on the point of starting for Old Point Comfort, and, if she had good weather off Cape Hatteras, would reach Fortress Monroe by Christmas Day, and he suggested that I might make it the occasion of sending a welcome Christmas gift to the President, Mr. Lincoln, who peculiarly enjoyed such pleasantry. I accordingly sat down and wrote on a slip of paper, to be left at the telegraph office at Fortress Monroe for transmission, the following:

SAVANNAH, GEORGIA, *December* 22, 1864.

To His Excellency President LINCOLN, *Washington, D.C.:*

I beg to present you as a Christmas-gift the city of Savannah, with one hundred and fifty heavy guns and plenty of ammunition, also about twenty-five thousand bales of cotton.

W. T. SHERMAN, *Major General.*

"The Cotton Gin"

JOEL CHANDLER HARRIS (1848–1908)

Joel Chandler Harris is best known for his Uncle Remus tales, featuring the allegorical Brer Fox and Brer Rabbit characters. But his distinguished literary life is also marked by roles as editor of the *Atlanta Constitution*, problematic recorder of African American folklore, significant local colorist, and author of children's literature. Fellow humorist and *Savannah Morning News* editor William Tappan Thompson hired Harris in 1870 as a columnist and associate editor for the newspaper. The "Affairs in Georgia" column, by "Jinks" Harris, drew attention throughout the South, and especially among editors of the *News*'s largest competitor, the *Atlanta Constitution*. When Harris and his young family fled to Atlanta from Savannah's yellow fever epidemic of 1876, the *Constitution*'s editor, Evan Howell, and associate editor, Henry Grady, hired him immediately. Harris's books include *Uncle Remus: His Songs and His Sayings* (1880); *Mingo, and Other Sketches in Black and White* (1884); *Free Joe and Other Georgian Sketches* (1887); and *Uncle Remus and Brer Rabbit* (1907). The selection below, "The Cotton Gin," is taken from *Stories of Georgia* (1896). Eli Whitney's (1765–1825) "uniformity system" of interchangeable parts, developed through his work with the cotton gin and U.S. Army muskets, is the basis of modern mass production.

Brief mention has been made of Whitney's invention of the cotton gin. The event was of such world-wide importance that the story should be told here. Whitney, the inventor of the gin, was born in Massachusetts in 1765, in very poor circumstances. While the War of the Revolution was going on, he was earning his living by making nails by hand. He was such an apt mechanic that he was able to make and save enough money to pay his way through Yale College, where he graduated in 1792. In that year he engaged himself to come to Georgia as a private tutor in the family of a gentleman of Savannah; but when he reached that city, he found that the place had been filled.

While in Savannah, Whitney attracted the attention of the widow of General Nathanael Greene, who lived at Mulberry Grove, on the river at no great distance from the city. Mrs. Greene invited the young man to make his home on her plantation. He soon found opportunity to show his fine mechanical genius, and Mrs. Greene became more interested in him than ever.

The story goes, that soon after the young man had established himself on the Mulberry Grove Plantation, several Georgia planters were dining with Mrs. Greene. During their conversation the difficulty of removing the seed from the cotton fiber was mentioned, and the suggestion was made that this might be done by machinery. At this Mrs. Greene mentioned the skill and ingenuity of young Whitney, and advised her guests that he should be given the problem to solve. This advice was followed. The planters had a talk with the young man, and explained to him the difficulty which they found in separating the seed from the lint.

At that time one pound of lint cotton was all that a negro woman could separate from the seed in a day; and the more cotton the planters raised, the deeper they got in debt. The close of the war had found them in a state of the utmost poverty, so that they had been compelled to mortgage their lands in order to get money on which to begin business. Cotton was the only product of the farm for which there was any constant demand; but, owing to the labor of separating the lint from the seed, it could not be raised at a profit. Thus, in 1791, the number of pounds exported from the South to Europe amounted to only about 379 bales of 500 pounds each.

When the planters went to Whitney with their problem, he was entirely ignorant of the whole matter. He knew nothing of cotton or of cotton planting; but he at once set himself at work. He made a careful study of the cotton plant. He shut himself in a room with some uncleaned cotton, and worked at his task during a whole winter. He made his own tools at the plantation blacksmith shop; and all day long, and sometimes far into the night, he could be heard hammering and sawing away.

In 1793 he called together the planters who had asked him to solve the problem, and showed them the machine, which he called a cotton gin. When they saw it work, their surprise and delight knew no bounds. They knew at once that the problem had been solved by the young genius from Massachusetts. Little calculation was needed to show them that the cotton gin could clean as much cotton in a day as could be cleaned on a plantation during a whole winter. What before had been the work of a hundred hands for several months could now be completed in a few days.

But it seems to be the fate of the majority of those who make wonderful inventions never to enjoy the full benefits of the work of their genius. Eli Whitney was not an exception to the general rule. While he was working on his cotton gin, rumors of it went abroad and by the time it was completed, public expectation was on tiptoe. When the machine was finished, it was shown to only a few people; but the fact, of such immense importance to the people of the State, was soon known throughout the State, and the planters impatiently waited for the day when they would be able to put it in use.

One night the building in which Whitney's cotton gin was concealed was broken into, ransacked, and the machine carried off. It was a bold robbery, and a very successful one. The inventor made haste to build another gin; but before he could get his model completed, and obtain a patent right to the invention, the machine had been manufactured at various points in the South by other parties, and was in operation on several plantations. Whitney formed a partnership with a gentleman who had some capital, and went to Connecticut to manufacture his gin; but he was compelled to spend all the money he could make, fighting lawsuits. His patent had been infringed, and those who sought to rob him of the fruits of his labor took a bold stand. The result of all this was, that the inventor never received any just compensation for a machine that revolutionized the commerce of the country, and added enormously to the power and progress of the Republic. Lord Macaulay said that Eli Whitney did more to make the United States powerful than Peter the Great did to make the Russian Empire dominant. Robert Fulton declared that Arkwright, Watt, and Whitney were the three men that did more for mankind than any of their contemporaries. This is easy to believe, when we remember that while the South shipped six bags of cotton to England in 1786, and only 379 in 1791, ten years after the cotton gin came into use, 82,000 bales were exported. The very importance of Whitney's invention made it immensely profitable for the vicious and the depraved to seize and appropriate the inventor's rights. These robberies were upheld by those who were anxious to share in the profits; and political demagogues made themselves popular by misrepresenting Whitney, and clamoring against the law that was intended to protect him. It was only by means of this clamor, half political and wholly dishonest, that the plain rights of Whitney could be denied and justice postponed. His invention was entirely new. It was distinct from every other. It had no connection with and no relation to any other invention that had been made. It stood alone, and there could be no difficulty whatever in identifying it. And yet Whitney had just this difficulty. In his efforts to prove that he was the inventor of the cotton gin, and that he was entitled to a share of the immense profits that those who used it were reaping, he had to travel thousands of miles, and spend thousands of dollars in appearing before Legislatures and in courts that denied him justice. The life of his patent had nearly expired before any court finally enforced his right, and Congress refused to grant him an extension beyond the fourteen years that had then nearly expired.

Associations and combinations had been formed for the purpose of defrauding Whitney, and these were represented by the ablest lawyers that could be hired. It is no wonder that Whitney, in writing to Robert Fulton, a brother inventor, declared that the troubles he had to contend with were the result of a lack of desire on the part of mankind to see justice done. The truth is, his invention was of such prime importance that the public fought for its possession, and justice and honesty were for the moment lost sight of. At one time but a few men in Georgia were bold enough to go into court and testify to the simplest facts within their knowledge; and Whitney himself says, that in one instance he had the greatest difficulty in proving that the machine had been used in Georgia, although at that very moment three separate gins were at work within fifty yards of the building in which the court sat. They were all so near, that the rattle and hum of the machinery could be heard from the courthouse steps.

In December, 1807, a judge was found to affirm the rights of Whitney under his patent. The judge's name was Johnson; and in his decision he said, "The whole interior of the Southern States was languishing, and its inhabitants emigrating for want of some object to engage their attention and employ their industry, when the invention of this machine at once opened views to them which set the whole country in active motion. From childhood to age it has presented to us a lucrative employment. Individuals who were depressed with poverty, and sunk in idleness, have suddenly risen to wealth and respectability. Our debts have been paid off. Our capital has increased, and our lands have trebled themselves in value. We cannot express the weight of the obligation which the country owes to this invention. The extent of it cannot now be seen."

The language of the learned judge was high-flown; but he was a just judge, and he had a faint and glimmering idea of the real importance of this remarkable invention. It was a very simple affair. The principle came to Whitney in a flash, and he had a model constructed within ten days after the despairing planters had gone to him with their problem. But it may be doubted whether any other individual, by one simple invention, ever did so much for the progress and enrichment of human interests, and for the welfare and the comfort of the human race. This little machine made the agriculture of the South the strongest and the richest in the world, and gave to this section a political power that was for years supreme in the nation, and was only surrendered as the result of a long and exhausting war. By means of the cotton gin, towns and cities have sprung up, and a vast network of railways has been built; and yet the most that Whitney received was a royalty on his gin in North Carolina, and a donation of fifty thousand dollars from the State of South Carolina. In Georgia his right to his invention was stolen, and all that he got out of it was a number of costly lawsuits.

After struggling for five years against the overwhelming odds that avarice and greed had mustered to aid them, Whitney turned his attention in another direction, and made a still more remarkable display of his genius. This part of his career does not belong directly to the history of Georgia, but it is interesting enough to be briefly recorded here. The United States Government was in want of arms, and this want various con-tractors had failed to meet. Through the influence of the secre-tary of the treasury, Whitney was given a contract to make ten thousand muskets at $13.40 apiece. He had no capital, no works, no machinery, no tools, no skilled workmen, no raw material. In creating a part of these and commanding the rest, he called into play an inventive genius, the extent of which must always excite wonder and admiration.

Within ten years he created his own works, and invented and made his own tools, invented and made his own machinery. More than this, he invented and applied a wholly new principle of manufacture, a principle that has done more to advance human industry and increase wealth all over the world than any other known effort of the human mind to solve material prob-lems. He invented and developed the principle or system of mak-ing the various parts of a musket or any other complex manufactured article, such as the sewing machine, so absolutely uniform as to be interchangeable. This principle has been carried out in hundreds of thousands of different ways. It has entered into and become a feature of a vast range of manufactures. The principle was established by a series of inventions as wonderful as any that the human mind ever conceived, so that Whitney has been aptly called the Shakespeare of invention. His inventions remain practically unchanged. After ninety years of trial, they are found to be practically perfect.

It was his peculiar gift to be able to convey into inanimate machinery the skill that a human being could acquire only after years of study and practice. It is almost like belittling the greatest of marvels to call it a stroke of genius. He made it possible for the most ordinary laborer to accomplish a hundred times as much in an hour, and with the most exquisite perfection, as a skilled laborer could accomplish in a day.

On these wonderful inventions Whitney took out no patents. He gave them all to the public. In this way be revenged himself on those who had successfully robbed him of the fruits of his labor and genius in the invention of the cotton gin. Perhaps if he had been more justly treated in Georgia, he might have set up his works in this State, and this fact might have made the South the seat of great manufacturing industries. Who knows?

from *The American Scene*

HENRY JAMES (1843–1916)

> Henry James was the youngest son of noted theologian Henry James, and brother to psychologist and philosopher William James. James lived much of his life in Europe, particularly London and Paris. After completing his best-known novels, *The Wings of the Dove* (1902), *The Ambassadors* (1903), and *The Golden Bowl* (1904), James made one of his infrequent visits to his homeland. This trip produced James's most perceptive travel book, *The American Scene* (1907). The book is an admonition to value old local color and the excerpt here is a rare bit of lightness in an otherwise pessimistic take on American life.

It was absurd what I made of Savannah—which consisted for me but of a quarter of an hour's pause of the train under the wide arch of the station, where, in the now quite confirmed blandness of the Sunday noon, a bright, brief morning party appeared of a sudden to have organized itself. Where was the charm?—if it wasn't already, supremely, in the air, the latitude, the season, as well as in the imagination of the pilgrim capable not only of squeezing a sense from the important city on these easy terms and with that desperate economy, but of reading heaven knows what instalment of romance into a mere railroad matter. It is a mere railroad matter, in the States, that a station should appear at a given moment to yield to the invasion of a dozen or so of bareheaded and vociferous young women in the company of young men to match, and that they should all treat the place, in the public eye, that of the crowded contemplative cars, quite as familiar, domestic, intimate ground, set apart, it might be, for the discussion and regulation of their little interests and affairs, and for that so oddly, so innocently immodest ventilation of their puerile privacies at which the moralizing visitor so frequently gasps. I recall my fleeting instants of Savannah as the taste of a cup charged to the brim; I recall the swarming, the hatless, pretty girls, with their big-boned cues, their romping swains, their inveterate suggestion of their having more to say about American manners than any other single class; I recall the thrill produced by the hawkers of scented Southern things, sprigs and specimens of flower and fruit that mightn't as yet be of the last exoticism, but that were native and fresh and overpriced, and so all that the traveler could ask.

But most of all, I think, I recall the quite lively resolve not to give way, under the assault of the beribboned and "shirtwaisted" fair, to the provocation of their suggestiveness—even as I had fallen, reflectively speaking, straight into the trap set for me by the Charleston bagmen; a resolve taken, I blush to say, as a base economic precaution only, and not because the spectacle before me failed to make reflections swarm. They fairly hummed, my suppressed reflections, in the manner of bees about a flowerbed, and burying their noses as deep in the corolla of the subject. Had I allowed myself time before the train resumed its direction, I should have thus found myself regarding the youths and the maidens—but especially, for many reasons, the maidens—quite in the light of my so earnestly-considered drummers, quite as creatures extraordinarily disconcerting, at first, as to the whole matter of their public behavior, but covered a little by the mantle of charity as soon as it became clear that what, like the poor drummers, they suffer from, is the tragedy of their social, their cruel exposure, that treachery of fate which has kept them so out of their place.

from *A Thousand Mile Walk to the Gulf*

JOHN MUIR (1838–1914)

John Muir was born in Scotland and moved to Wisconsin at age eleven. After a stint at the University of Wisconsin, Muir left on foot for the Gulf of Mexico. Along the way he recorded his impressions and observations in a journal, excerpted here, which was posthumously published in 1916 as *A Thousand Mile Walk to the Gulf*. The acuity and transcendentalist ardor of his widely-read magazine articles spurred the United States government to adopt forest conservation programs that resulted in the creation of the Sequoia and Yosemite national parks. This, along with his founding of the Sierra Club in 1892, make him a leader of the modern preservation movement.

October 9. After going again to the express office and post office, and wandering about the streets, I found a road which led me to the Bonaventure graveyard. If that burying ground across the Sea of Galilee, mentioned in Scripture, was half as beautiful as Bonaventure, I do not wonder that a man should dwell among the tombs. It is only three or four miles from Savannah, and is reached by a smooth white shell road.

There is but little to be seen on the way in land, water, or sky, that would lead one to hope for the glories of Bonaventure. The ragged desolate fields, on both sides of the road, are overrun with coarse rank weeds, and show scarce a trace of cultivation. But soon all is changed. Rickety log huts, broken fences, and the last patch of weedy rice-stubble are left behind. You come to beds of purple liatris and living wild-wood trees. You hear the song of birds, cross a small stream, and are with Nature in the grand old forest graveyard, so beautiful that almost any sensible person would choose to dwell here with the dead rather than with the lazy, disorderly living.

Part of the grounds was cultivated and planted with live-oak, about a hundred years ago, by a wealthy gentleman who had his country residence here. But much the greater part is undisturbed. Even those spots which are disordered by art, Nature is ever at work to reclaim, and to make them look as if the foot of man had never known them. Only a small plot of ground is occupied with graves and the old mansion is in ruins.

The most conspicuous glory of Bonaventure is its noble avenue of live-oaks. They are the most magnificent planted trees I have ever seen, about fifty feet high and perhaps three or four feet in diameter, with broad spreading leafy heads. The main branches reach out horizontally until they come together over the driveway, embowering it throughout its entire length, while each branch is adorned like a garden with ferns, flowers, grasses, and dwarf palmettos.

But of all the plants of these curious tree-gardens the most striking and characteristic is the so-called Long Moss (*Tillandsia usneoides*). It drapes all the branches from top to bottom, hanging in long silvery-gray skeins, reaching a length of not less than eight or ten feet, and when slowly waving in the wind they produce a solemn funereal effect singularly impressive.

There are also thousands of smaller trees and clustered bushes, covered almost from sight in the glorious brightness of their own light. The place is half surrounded by the salt marshes and islands of the river, their reeds and sedges making a delightful fringe. Many bald eagles roost among the trees along the side of the marsh. Their screams are heard every morning, joined with the noise of crows and the songs of countless warblers, hidden deep in their dwellings of leafy bowers. Large flocks of butter-flies, all kinds of happy insects, seem to be in a perfect fever of joy and sportive gladness. The whole place seems like a center of life. The dead do not reign there alone.

Bonaventure to me is one of the most impressive assemblages of animal and plant creatures I ever met. I was fresh from the Western prairies, the garden-like openings of Wisconsin, the beech and maple and oak woods of Indiana and Kentucky, the dark mysterious Savannah cypress forests; but never since I was allowed to walk the woods have I found so impressive a company of trees as the tillandsia-draped oaks of Bonaventure.

I gazed awe-stricken as one new-arrived from another world. Bonaventure is called a graveyard, a town of the dead, but the few graves are powerless in such a depth of life. The rippling of living waters, the song of birds, the joyous confidence of flowers, the calm, undisturbable grandeur of the oaks, mark this place of graves as one of the Lord's most favored abodes of life and light.

On no subject are our ideas more warped and pitiable than on death. Instead of the sympathy, the friendly union, of life and death so apparent in Nature, we are taught that death is an accident, a deplorable punishment for the oldest sin, the arch-enemy of life, etc. Town children, especially, are steeped in this death orthodoxy, for the natural beauties of death are seldom seen or taught in towns.

Of death among our own species, to say nothing of the thousand styles and modes of murder, our best memories, even among happy deaths, yield groans and tears, mingled with morbid exultation; burial companies, black in cloth and countenance; and, last of all, a black box burial in an ill-omened place, haunted by imaginary glooms and ghosts of every degree. Thus death becomes fearful, and the most notable and incredible thing heard around a death-bed is, "I fear not to die."

But let children walk with Nature, let them see the beautiful blendings and communions of death and life, their joyous inseparable unity, as taught in woods and meadows, plains and mountains and streams of our blessed star, and they will learn that death is stingless indeed, and as beautiful as life, and that the grave has no victory, for it never fights. All is divine harmony.

Most of the few graves of Bonaventure are planted with flowers. There is generally a magnolia at the head, near the strictly erect marble, a rose-bush or two at the foot, and some violets and showy exotics along the sides or on the tops. All is enclosed by a black iron railing, composed of rigid bars that might have been spears or bludgeons from a battlefield in Pandemonium.

It is interesting to observe how assiduously Nature seeks to remedy these labored art blunders. She corrodes the iron and marble, and gradually levels the hill which is always heaped up, as if a sufficiently heavy quantity of clods could not be laid on the dead. Arching grasses come one by one; seeds come flying on downy wings, silent as fate, to give life's dearest beauty for the ashes of art; and strong evergreen arms laden with ferns and tillandsia drapery are spread over all—Life at work everywhere, obliterating all memory of the confusion of man.

In Georgia many graves are covered with a common shingle roof, supported on four posts as the cover of a well, as if rain and sunshine were not regarded as blessings. Perhaps, in this hot and insalubrious climate, moisture and sun-heat are considered necessary evils to which they do not wish to expose their dead.

The money package that I was expecting did not arrive until the following week. After stopping the first night at the cheap, disreputable-looking hotel, I had only about a dollar and a half left in my purse, and so was compelled to camp out to make it last in buying only bread. I went out of the noisy town to seek a sleeping-place that was not marshy. After gaining the outskirts of the town toward the sea, I found some low sand dunes, yellow with flowering solidagoes.

I wandered wearily from dune to dune sinking ankle-deep in the sand, searching for a place to sleep beneath the tall flowers, free from insects and snakes, and above all from my fellow man. But idle negroes were prowling about everywhere, and I was afraid. The wind had strange sounds, waving the heavy panicles over my head, and I feared sickness from malaria so prevalent here, when I suddenly thought of the graveyard.

"There," thought I, "is an ideal place for a penniless wanderer. There no superstitious prowling mischief maker dares venture for fear of haunting ghosts, while for me there will be God's rest and peace. And then, if I am to be exposed to unhealthy vapors, I shall have capital compensation in seeing those grand oaks in the moonlight, with all the impressive and nameless influences of this lonely beautiful place."

By this time it was near sunset, and I hastened across the common to the road and set off for Bonaventure, delighted with my choice, and almost glad to find that necessity had furnished me with so good an excuse for doing what I knew my mother would censure; for she made me promise I would not lie out of doors if I could possibly avoid it. The sun was set ere I was past the negroes' huts and rice fields, and I arrived near the graves in the silent hour of the gloaming.

I was very thirsty after walking so long in the muggy heat, a distance of three or four miles from the city, to get to this graveyard. A dull, sluggish, coffee-colored stream flows under the road just outside the graveyard garden park, from which I managed to get a drink after breaking a way down to the water through a dense fringe of bushes, daring the snakes and alligators in the dark. Thus refreshed I entered the weird and beautiful abode of the dead.

All the avenue where I walked was in shadow, but an exposed tombstone frequently shone out in startling whiteness on either hand, and thickets of sparkleberry bushes gleamed like heaps of crystals. Not a breath of air moved the gray moss, and the great black arms of the trees met overhead and covered the avenue. But the canopy was fissured by many a netted seam and leafy-edged opening, through which the moonlight sifted in auroral rays, broidering the blackness in silvery light. Though tired, I sauntered a while enchanted, then lay down under one of the great oaks. I found a little mound that served for a pillow, placed my plant press and bag beside me and rested fairly well, though somewhat disturbed by large prickly-footed beetles creeping across my hands and face, and by a lot of hungry stinging mosquitoes.

When I awoke, the sun was up and all Nature was rejoicing. Some birds had discovered me as an intruder, and were making a great ado in interesting language and gestures. I heard the screaming of the bald eagles, and of some strange waders in the rushes. I heard the hum of Savannah with the long jarring hallos of negroes far away. On rising I found that my head had been resting on a grave, and though my sleep had not been quite so sound as that of the person below, I arose refreshed, and looking about me, the morning sunbeams pouring through the oaks and gardens dripping with dew, the beauty displayed was so glorious and exhilarating that hunger and care seemed only a dream.

Eating a breakfast cracker or two and watching for a few hours the beautiful light, birds, squirrels, and insects, I returned to Savannah, to find that my money package had not yet arrived. I then decided to go early to the grave-yard and make a nest with a roof to keep off the dew, as there was no way of finding out how long I might have to stay. I chose a hidden spot in a dense thicket of sparkleberry bushes, near the right bank of the Savannah River, where the bald eagles and a multitude of singing birds roosted. It was so well hidden that I had to carefully fix its compass bearing in my mind from a mark I made on the side of the main avenue, that I might be able to find it at bedtime.

I used four of the bushes as corner posts for my little hut, which was about four or five feet long by about three or four in width, tied little branches across from forks in the bushes to support a roof of rushes, and spread a thick mattress of Long Moss over the floor for a bed. My whole establishment was on so small a scale that I could have taken up, not only my bed, but my whole house, and walked. There I lay that night, eating a few crackers.

Next day I returned to the town and was disappointed as usual in obtaining money. So after spending the day looking at the plants in the gardens of the fine residences and town squares, I returned to my graveyard home. That I might not be observed and suspected of hiding, as if I had committed a crime, I always went home after dark, and one night, as I lay down in my moss nest, I felt some cold-blooded creature in it; whether a snake or simply a frog or toad I do not know, but instinctively, instead of drawing back my hand, I grasped the poor creature and threw it over the tops of the bushes. That was the only significant disturbance or fright that I got.

In the morning everything seemed divine. Only squirrels, sunbeams, and birds came about me. I was awakened every morning by these little singers after they discovered my nest. Instead of serenely singing their morning songs they at first came within two or three feet of the hut, and, looking in at me through the leaves, chattered and scolded in half-angry, half-wondering tones. The crowd constantly increased, attracted by the disturbance. Thus I began to get acquainted with my bird neighbors in this blessed wilderness, and after they learned that I meant them no ill they scolded less and sang more.

After five days of this graveyard life I saw that even with living on three or four cents a day my last twenty-five cents would soon be spent, and after trying again and again unsuccessfully to find some employment began to think that I must strike farther out into the country, but still within reach of town, until I came to some grain or rice field that had not yet been harvested, trusting that I could live indefinitely on toasted or raw corn, or rice.

By this time I was becoming faint, and in making the journey to the town was alarmed to find myself growing staggery and giddy. The ground ahead seemed to be rising up in front of me, and the little streams in the ditches on the sides of the road seemed to be flowing up hill. Then I realized that I was becoming dangerously hungry and became more than ever anxious to receive that money package.

To my delight this fifth or sixth morning, when I inquired if the money package had come, the clerk replied that it had, but that he could not deliver it without my being identified. I said, "Well, here! read my brother's letter," handing it to him. "It states the amount in the package, where it came from, the day it was put into the office at Portage City, and I should think that would be enough." He said, "No, that is not enough. How do I know that this letter is yours? You may have stolen it. How do I know that you are John Muir?"

I said, "Well, don't you see that this letter indicates that I am a botanist? For in it my brother says, 'I hope you are having a good time and finding many new plants.' Now, you say that I might have stolen this letter from John Muir, and in that way have become aware of there being a money package to arrive from Portage for him. But the letter proves that John Muir must be a botanist, and though, as you say, his letter might have been stolen, it would hardly be likely that the robber would be able to steal John Muir's knowledge of botany. Now I suppose, of course, that you have been to school and know something of botany. Examine me and see if I know anything about it."

At this he laughed good-naturedly, evidently feeling the force of my argument, and, perhaps, pitying me on account of looking pale and hungry, he turned and rapped at the door of a private office—probably the Manager's—called him out and said, "Mr. So and So, here is a man who has inquired every day for the last week or so for a money package from Portage, Wisconsin. He is a stranger in the city with no one to identify him. He states correctly the amount and the name of the sender. He has shown me a letter which indicates that Mr. Muir is a botanist, and that although a traveling companion may have stolen Mr. Muir's letter, he could not have stolen his botany, and requests us to examine him."

The head official smiled, took a good stare into my face, waved his hand, and said, "Let him have it." Gladly I pocketed my money, and had not gone along the street more than a few rods before I met a very large negro woman with a tray of gingerbread, in which I immediately invested some of my new wealth, and walked rejoicingly, munching along the street, making no attempt to conceal the pleasure I had in eating. Then, still hunting for more food, I found a sort of eating-place in a market and had a large regular meal on top of the gingerbread! Thus my "marching through Georgia" terminated handsomely in a jubilee of bread.

"Savannah Twice Visited"

WILLIAM DEAN HOWELLS (1837–1920)

William Dean Howells, along with his best friends Samuel Clemens and Henry James, was considered one of the foremost men of letters of his era. Although his literary achievement may be considered more modest now, his novels *A Modern Instance* (1882), *The Rise of Silas Lapham* (1885), and *A Hazard of New Fortunes* (1889) are read and respected. Howells was editor-in-chief of *The Atlantic Monthly* for a decade. He was also active in political life. His campaign biography of Abraham Lincoln (1860) was rewarded with a consulship to Venice from 1861–1865. Howells took considerable personal and professional risk with his plea for clemency for the condemned Haymarket anarchists on the grounds that they were convicted because of their political beliefs. "Savannah Twice Visited," following below, appeared first in *Harper's Magazine* in 1919. During his last winter in Savannah in 1919–1920, Howells caught a cold from which he never recovered. After returning to New York in April 1920, he died in his sleep a month later.

When James Oglethorpe wrote home to the trustees of his English Company in 1733, he gave the look of the land at Savannah in terms which graphically map it still. "The river," he said, "has formed a half moon, around the south side of which the banks are about forty feet high, and on the top a flat which they call a bluff. The plain ground extends into the country about five or six miles, and along the river for about a mile. Ships that draw near twelve feet of water can ride within ten yards of the bank. Upon the river-side, in the center of the plain, I have laid out the town, opposite to which is an island of very rich pasturage. The river is pretty wide, the water fresh, and from the quay of the town you can see its whole course to the sea. For about six miles up into the country the landscape is very agreeable, and bordered with high woods."

The river, though it still skirts the bluff in a golden tide, sweeping to the ocean so swiftly from the inland that it pushes salt savor far seaward, would hardly be recognizable by him who first described it. The wild emptiness of the shore he saw has changed to a vision of commerce and industry, and of foundries on the banks, pouring their clouds of smoke out over a far stretch of steam and sail in the river, and beyond the river a vast expanse of docks, dense with the cotton and turpentine and resin which the railroads have brought down from the fields and forests of the whole Georgian interior to form the selvedge of the salt marsh here stretching to the horizon and fading into it.

If the river banks and the expanses of its sea meadows were estranged to .he eyes of the founder, the town itself as it thickens over the plain above would be more incredible. The financial and official and commercial streets stretch eastward and westward in impressive succession, and the quays and the roadways to them are paved with blocks of lava and marble and granite brought overseas in ballast by the ships that for nearly two hundred years have ridden at anchor in the bold water of the stream below. Then begins that noble sequence of wooded and gardened squares which form the glory of the city. These lengthen and widen far beyond eyeshot over "the plain country" where, at the moment Oglethorpe wrote, the colony was chopping its place out of the primeval forest and building its houses in little formal rows along the river bluffs, but he was already imagining those open spaces of grove and lawn which lengthen at last into a park thrice their extent.

Each square of those expanding from the main avenue of the city has its pillar or statue commemorating the events of a city storied in all our wars, from the revolt against Great Britain to the reconciliation of the States after our Civil War. Count Pulaski, the Polish exile, and Sergeant Jasper who fell in the same fight in 1778, on the field where the oldest railroad station stands, has each his figure in bronze and monument in stone in the square devoted to him. But, fitly, first and finest is the figure of Oglethorpe, where, in the somewhat swagger presence of a cavalier of the Second George's time, one of the truest Christians overlooks in the shadow of the live-oaks the rude monolith of the Indian chief whom Oglethorpe made and kept his friend life-long. The statue, as Mr. French has imagined it, and the whole gardened ground, with its curving marble seats, are of a respective charm which I suppose I must not say is surpassed by that of the lovely little children who play about in all the city squares under the fostering neglect of their kind black nurses, but seem to superabound in this, as if for the peculiar pleasure of the good and brave Oglethorpe. I may as well also say here as elsewhere that the children of Savannah are the best of Savannah; but if their mothers will not allow this, then I think no one will dispute the primacy of the beautiful young girls, of the flapper age, who seem to be perpetually going to and from the many occasions of ice-cream soda along the wide, well-shaded pavements, after the pretty schoolgirls have flocked home. Still, however I submit openly in this matter, I shall always secretly cling to my preference for the little of littlest people, who, with their nurses, or in their own personal safekeeping, abound from early morning to early nightfall; and for all reason I allege the instance of three small girls going along at twilight well outside the sidewalk in a quiet talk about school, and leaving the many whirring motors to take care of themselves. By day the children are of course safe from the electric phaetons of their mothers, grandmothers, and aunts who drive these over the smooth levels of the well-kept, and well-bricked, or well-asphalted streets; and I suppose that in the early dark a kind Providence is equally mindful of the children, even if their little steps should stray beyond the vast suburbs to the forest where along the horizon its engulfing green hides the multitudinous housetops and countless church spires and factory chimneys.

We had come to Savannah for our second visit in the earliest spring when the leaves were at their palest green, and we saw the foliage harden and thicken and darken till at last the mellow walls and roofs were almost hidden to the eye looking down on them from a high place, and the chimes from the belfry of a neighboring church seemed to peal from the heart of some dense and lofty tree, possibly one of those vast live-oaks which were letting their small leaves drip earthward in a belated autumn consciousness. Then the green tops mixed and sank together, till at last the whole thickly wooded city billowed spaciously away to a sunset sky and carved itself in a Greek bordering of black along the golden horizon. Our first visit was timed for the famous freeze of February, 1917, when we saw the buds and blossoms perish in the public grounds and dooryards, which now triumphed through an unbroken warmth with a wealth of the white dooryard roses and the milky streaming of the dog-wood flowers in the other wooded squares and avenues. There is nothing of our Northern grass in Savannah, but there is the green of Italian rye which must be sown every spring but with-ers away toward the end of the long summer, and meantime forms an admirable camouflage of our lawns, which we now saw in its tenderest prime.

Perhaps the affection of the noble founder of the Georgian state was prophetically dedicated to its best future interests; for above everything Oglethorpe was devoted to the love of his fel-low man, though this did not prevent his being a valiant soldier and a very gallant gentleman. He served in the great wars under Prince Eugene with splendid courage, and he knew so well how to defend his own dignity that, when a silly Swabian princeling once flipped some wine from his glass on him at table, Oglethorpe, aware that he could not challenge royal blood for the insult though he could not ignore it, said, quietly, "Ah, that's very well; but we do it much better in England," and flung his whole glassful in the prince's face. It was a very Thackerayan incident which might have come out of *Henry Esmond*, where Oglethorpe's Jacobitish opinions or any of the fine qualities which went with them in him, would not have found themselves amiss. Thackeray might have followed him with love and praise in his whole career, and would have known how to honor him for the philanthropy which, before Howard's, moved Oglethorpe to visit the prisons and to rescue the hopeless debtors in the abominable jails where they languished. He would have liked in him the manly poetry of helping these captives to life, liberty, and the pursuit of happiness in a new world, and he would have found a peculiar relish in this generous royalist's being the first Englishman of his class to call upon the first American ambassador to England, and hail him upon the success of his country, and his own happiness in coming to represent it at the court of the British sovereign whom the Americans had so Englishly outfought.

Oglethorpe had then lived to be nearly a hundred years old, and to be the generalissimo of the British armies. In this quality he was not less the friend of the envoy from the rebel America nation than if Mr. Adams had brought our submission to his sovereign, and he was equally the friend of every worthy Englishman who needed one. He was more eminently but not more gladly the friend of Samuel Johnson, and Oliver Goldsmith, and Doctor Johnson's henchman and superior, James Boswell. These last celebrities urged Oglethorpe to write his life, but Oglethorpe urged the work upon Johnson, who so far consented as to say that he might send him the materials for it. Oglethorpe never did so, or, if he did so, Johnson did nothing with them, but left it open for me to write it if I should live to the ripe leisure of Oglethorpe's ninety-seven years. I could desire nothing better than such an employment, for to my mind no better or greater man has lived. But life is short and in one's eighty-first year one cannot promise anything positively.

Oglethorpe not only brought to Savannah many sorts and conditions of capable and incapable colonists besides those hopeless debtors whom he delivered from prison, but he duly attracted apostles for the salvation of the colonists' souls. Chief among these were John Wesley and George Whitefield, and Wesley preached his first sermon on the one of the stateliest structures of the stately business section; but I shall not betray its identity because I cannot remember it, and the traveler can easily find it by the tablet in its wall. Wesley was, as his journals show, a saint of a troubled and troublesome mind, and he presently involved himself in a love affair, or near-love, with a very lively young lady whom some of his friends advised him not to go further with. He took their advice, but when he wished to retire from this likeness of lovemaking, neither the lively young lady nor her family liked it, and when Wesley, after her marriage with another, forbade her the communion because of her levity of make and manner, her brother-in-law took up the matter in the courts of law; and then Wesley departed out of the gates of Savannah, such as the gates were. Whitefield was of more fortunate experience in the colony, and the traveler who goes to visit the earliest and greatest of American charities at the Orphan House of Bethesda several miles out of the town, will do well to remember Whitefield as its founder and the first great preacher there. Later Bethesda enjoyed the beneficence of Lady Selina Huntingdon, who made Whitefield her chaplain when she established that "Connexion," so called, of the English Church which promoted the cause of the early Methodists in England. Her portrait, quite impossibly attributed to Sir Joshua Reynolds, hangs in the Historical Library in Savannah, and represents a lady of rather hard-favored countenance, but of iron resolution such as could very well face down the Duchess of Buckingham, who wrote her: "I thank your ladyship for the information concerning the Methodist preaching. Their doctrines are strongly tinctured with impertinence towards their superiors, in perpetually trying to level all ranks. It is monstrous to be told that you have a heart as sinful as the common wretches that crawl on the earth. I wonder your ladyship should relish any sentiments so at variance with high rank and good breeding."

The prevailing faith of colonial Savannah was evangelical, but all faiths, except the Roman Catholic, were tolerated, and Oglethorpe found among his followers some forty Portuguese Jews, who at once took a leading part in the smaller commerce and a rank in society still conceded to at least one family of them. Their synagogue can scarcely claim distinction in ecclesiastical architecture, and only the beautiful church of St. John can be called dear to both ear and eye. Its spire rises from the sea of foliage which sweeps the plain to the horizon, and at the appointed hours its chimes fill the air through and over all the other city noises, on weekdays as on Sundays. Especially on the memorable Saturday when the first Liberty Loan was inaugurated, there was such burst of patriotic tunes after the pious hymns from the bells of St. John's that the hearer's love of country might well have known a consecration to his hope of heaven. It was something that spiritualized the financial moment and gave the church a primacy which in architecture must be yielded, above every other religious edifice, to the famous Presbyterian church rebuilt in exact form after its destruction by fire. The structure on the outside is of such Sir Christopher Wrennish renaissance that one might well seem to be looking at it in a London street; but the interior is of such unique loveliness that no church in London may compare with it. Whoever would realize its beauty must go at once to Savannah and forget for one beatific moment in its presence the ceilings of Tiepolo and the roofs of Veronese.

If this is the end of our praise for sacred or civil structures, the beholder will have pleasure enough in the many lovely old mansions in the heart of the city, or where the heart once was before its life went to find other residence in the ever-enlarging suburbs. It was a fancy we cherished from the first of our first visit to the last of our last that these old houses reminded us of certain dear old English towns like, say, Leamington or Cheltenham, though it would be hard to say how or why. Perhaps it was because of their gardened keeping, oftenest glimpsed over garden walls, with roses clambering or climbing upon them, and other blossoms like azaleas and wistarias within them, and even now and then a mesh of ivy covering the whole side of a house. But we could not claim for association with Leamington or Cheltenham the mellow red-brown or the softened pink of other old houses at once so stately and so kindly. These colors brought back the sense of Latin sojourn, and perhaps it is not too extravagant to imagine the early returning from their forays into the Spanish neighborhoods below with a liking for the coloring of the old

Spanish houses of St. Augustine. I do not insist; I only say that these old mansions are lovable, if not always lovely, and that the soft damp, coolish air of late March which clung about them after rain was undeniably English, if not Bostonian, and sometimes specialized itself as Liverpoolish. One of the best of them, or which earliest took our fancy, is the house where Thackeray stayed when he was in Savannah and immensely liked staying, in 1855. It was built for Mr. Andrew Low, an Englishman, and it is of the general presence of an Italian villa, or some *palazzino* in a subordinate Italian city. . . . Another house of supreme interest and beauty was the Owens house, famous for the visit of Lafayette when he came to Savannah in 1825. The interior . . . is more French than Italian and is suggestive of the sort of hotel which is native in Paris, where its like may have been studied by the English architect Jay who built the Owens house and many another sympathetic mansion of such as give Savannah that effect of an English town which I have imagined. Such houses abound chiefly in and about that sequence of squares which follow up from the business streets along the handsome length and breadth of Bull Street. One of these, but not one of the most characteristic, is the Green mansion built by yet another Englishman, who left his name to it, and left it to be chiefly famed for becoming the headquarters of General Sherman in 1864. The gardened space about this is more open to the public eye than the grounds of most other similar houses, and it keeps itself less an allure to the fancy for that reason; instead of a high, solid wall, it has an iron grille about it, graceful enough, but not so English in effect, or even so Spanish.

These very characteristic and memorable mansions can still be counted by scores, but every now and then one of them disappears through natural causes, as well as through that effect of bad taste which asserts itself everywhere, or from some real or imaginary public demand. Only last year one was pulled down to free a site for an Auditorium, but now and then one is dedicated to the general advantage with little or no change, as in the case of the Telfair mansion. As if in response to the sympathetic tenderness with which this has been done, the Telfair Art Gallery remains a collection of pictures which no other American city of Savannah's age or population can invite the traveler to visit.

The former slaves quarters in the rear of these mansions front on the narrow streets or alleys where you may see colored people coming and going, though whether they are still the servants of the resident quality I do not know. Sometimes, but rather rarely, you find in Savannah an aged black with frosty wool who boasts himself slave-born, and counts from "before the Freedom," as they call the emancipation. The phrase is touching, and in the case of one at least of these bondsmen-born, the pathos went with both respect and self-respect and with those good manners which all men seem to have in Savannah, or for that matter the whole South in comparison with our Northern unceremoniousness. Perhaps I shall here be reminded of the savagery of the lynchings which goes along with the Southern good manners, especially in Georgia; but there has been no more powerful protest against this savagery than the paper which Judge Samuel B. Adams, the most distinguished jurist of the state, delivered a few years ago. It is a pity that his paper should not be known throughout the North where the abhorrence of the Georgian lynchings most insists. These have their causes, if not their reasons, in the jungle-lust of the criminals, but in relation to our slave-born friend (he liked to speak of our "friendship") such abominations are unimaginable, and even an infraction of good manners could not be supposed of him. I should call him a gentleman if gentlemen were not often such poor things, but as it is I will call him a man, more than manly in his moments of such extreme courtesy as always lifting his hat when he spoke to us, and of first assenting to whatever we said until he could gather himself for necessary dissent. He was a most intelligent guide to the city and its objects of interest, and if his top phaeton, which we preferred to any hireling automobile, left at last, as at first, something to be desired in style and repair, it somehow grew to seem newer and handsomer. If it had been at its worst somewhat tattered in its leathern and linen appointments, the presence of our friend on the front seat constituted it an establishment of prime quality, especially with those whose social rank he recognized, when he said, one day after a round of calls with us, "You seem to know *all* our best people."

His delicate recognition of our good fortune in this was a finer compliment than could have been paid to our merit and it kept our regard for our slave-born friend untainted by suspicion of flattery. In fact, there was no suspicion of this in the intercourse of the races, so far as I noticed it. What was apparent was the absolute submission of the colored people in all public matters to the rule of segregation. I never witnessed any attempt to transgress it, but the compliance was for me so nearly painful that when I got back to New York it was a relief to sit down next to a chocolate-colored fellow-man in the first streetcar I took. Yet I am bound to say that in the very wide-mindedly imagined city which Oglethorpe founded there seemed no abuse of their superiority by the white people, and there was no apparent willingness to keep the blacks ignorant or intellectually inferior. The Georgia Industrial College is one of the several institutions which testify to this fact, and if I speak especially of the Cuyler Street School for the training of boys in the manual, and the colored girls in the domestic arts, it is because the visit I paid to it in the company of certain Savannah gentlefolks was practical proof of what I say. I heard the pupils of both sexes read and sing excellently; I saw the boys working at carpentry through the school windows, and I sat down with my friends to a tasteful and admirably appetizing lunch which the girls had cooked. It would not have been possible for the near-white teacher who talked with us over our shoulders to sit at table with us, but neither would this have been probable in Boston, and I think several of these kindly Southern gentry felt with me the irk of that modest man's obvious inferiority; but then I do not like to have a pure white man wait behind my chair in the character of servant. I have no right to suppose any great parity of feeling in myself and my commensals concerning our conventionally enforced superiority, but I may at least own my sympathy with one of our company when he said, in noting several of the children who looked as Caucasian as either of us, but were black in reality, "Yes, that is the tragedy."

It is useless to deny a sense of the situation which remains for the South from the enslavement of blacks in the obscure, beginnings of colonial life. Here as elsewhere, slavery was not desired at first; Oglethorpe did not want it, nor his Trustees, but the easing of labor to the colonists by the toil of the slaves was insidious, and even the good Whitefield could justify slavery as a providential means of civilizing the Africans. When the cotton gin gave its touch to the pecuniary profit of the cotton culture, and the institution ended in the chaos of "the Freedom," the North madly took a part in it, and turned the slaves with all their unfitness into sovereigns. This could not last, and then nothing but patience remained, the patience of the whites with the black masters changing back into servants, and the patience of the blacks with their old masters doing them the civil wrong, which seems to be the only possibility of the impossible situation. How long this can endure no one thinks or dreams; there is no tangible or imaginable outcome. . .

His tenderness of feeling for the past transmits to the young Southerner a faith in the prehistoric kindness of the slaveholding days, but no trace of it appears to the traveler. If he deals honestly with himself, he finds only ugliness and hatefulness, which in such a relic as The Hermitage becomes monumental. People motor out of Savannah to see this famous place and return to suffer from the thought of it unless they can rejoice over the shame that has befallen its pride. The mansion which was once so stately and beautiful is now a dismal presence of barred windows, and verandas flocked over and defiled by goats, with a rabble of black boys scattering over what was the lawn and assembling to mob the stranger with a clamor for money and afflict him with their shapeless dances and their version of the variety-show songs instead of the "spirituals" which he may have hoped for from them. Behind them scatter a few lank black girls with babies on their hips, and then beyond the squalid dwelling of these lies the desolation of what had been a walled garden. On the river front of the mansion stretch the grounds of what had been its flowery pleasaunce, but the wilderness has stolen back upon it all and the waters of the swollen river have leaked among the paths which once led to it. Beside it an autumnal cotton field shows the husks of the gathered bolls on its withered stems, and to the landward of the mansion, under the boughs of the moss-hung live oaks, stretches a row of slave huts built of brick, with each a hearth and a single window to light its only room. The things have the effect of having been boastfully shown as the homes of the happy slaves who must have always groveled in them. I suppose they are now the nightly lairs of those rabble boys who were waiting our return to our motor; but only one of the huts showed any sign of habitation; and the gloom of the hovering live-oaks, with their funeral wreaths of moss, seemed to swoop down upon them.

Possibly I might have found gainlier memorials of the past if I had duly sought them, but the traveler must take his chances, and I had chosen The Hermitage as the most typical. I wished to forget it as soon as I could in my return to the charming city, where I found nothing to remind me of slavery except the slaves' quarters opening in the alleys behind those mansions which I can never be tired of praising. Out of their doors sometimes issued elderly uncles or aunties laden with whatever burden they were bearing to or from the great house or their own, wrapped in the gloom of their habitual black which I never saw relieved in either sex except once when one of the aunties suffered herself to wear a gay handkerchief turban-wise. I have the belief that this, so universal in the times "before the Freedom," could hardly have been well seen by her neighbors; and I have a like doubt for a like reason that the only surviving street-cry was not heard with pleasure as a voice from the past. Every morning, however, we had our own pleasure in it as it issued from the ample lips of an ample hucksteress who bore a wide, flat basket on her head, in the classic manner, and cried the wares which we never could be sure of till we stopped her and bribed her to tell.

What she seemed very nasally to call was: "A *crab*! Buyer! *A crab*!" and we had our difficulty in convincing her that we did not wish to buy the crabs which she took down her basket to show us; but eventually we prevailed, to her joy in our absurd curiosity as great as if she had sold us all her crabs.

These crab-women and the children's nurses, of various dusks and pallors, and those elderly uncles and aunties were the black folk whom we saw oftenest; but probably we might have seen the coming and going of the domestic servants, who as in other Southern cities could not be persuaded to "sleep in," but had their custom of abandoning their mistresses' household at nightfall, and "sleeping out" wherever their own shelter was, with such basketfuls as remained to them from the meal they may not otherwise have fully shared with their employing families. They may have gone with this provision for their own families as far as the quarter called Yamacraw, now given almost wholly up to them, after being first the tribal capital of the Indians whom Oglethorpe placed there, and then the home of some of the proudest and finally the poorest of the white colonists. It is a very dismal quarter now, little enlivened by the aspect of leisure in the inhabitants hanging from their doors and windows or sprawling over the steps of their porches.

Yamacraw is not so squalid as it might be, but it is very dispiriting from the gloom of the unpainted, weather-worn wooden houses which partake of the dismal coloring, voluntary and involuntary, of the inhabitants in their persons and clothing. One could wish they wore flaming scarlets or flaring blues, but they do not, and they probably would not think such dyes respectable. Even the young girls who wore a semblance of the modern fashion in the better quarters of the town subdued them to a quieter taste even than that of some white ladies; and expressed the abeyance of their race in all outward things.

The city seemed largely given over to the white children and the young girls who kept their supremacy well into maturity. We fancied an absolute deference to their sex which it might have been mortally perilous for any one of the other sex to default in, if such a thing had not apparently been impossible; and here again I wish to testify my pleasure and comfort in the good manners of the Southern men of all classes. This Southern courtesy did not wear away with use; it was as if the men always had time for it, and I chose to believe that if I had been young or middle-aged I should have met the same politeness which soothed and reassured my senility. I could not say whether it was ever based upon the danger of reprisal. The violence of some "lewd fellows of the baser sort" among Georgians toward blacks is notorious, but if there was ever anything homicidal in the resentments of gentlemen among themselves, the duel is now apparently quite extinct. There is a record of it incomparably touching in an epitaph of that beautiful old cemetery which the city keeps for a playground of the neighboring schoolchildren, and the resort of sympathetic frequenters. In rural graveyards everywhere the grief of the survivor is apt to express itself with unsparing passion, but here, beyond elsewhere it imparted the pang of indignant anguish. "He fell," this epitaph said of the dead below, "by the hand of a man who a short time before would have been friendless but for him. By his untimely death the prop of a mother's age is broken, the hope and consolation of sisters is destroyed, the pride of brothers is humbled in the dust, and a whole family, happy until then, is overwhelmed with affliction." The words must have been primarily meant for the eye of the homicide, but they wrung my heart with abhorrence for the custom which wronged him and his victim alike and made me feel its atrocity and stupidity as never before. There were other touching records in the place, but perhaps no other so personal as one which was impersonal to the point of leaving the gravestone without any inscription. A serpent coiled in the symbol of eternity, with no name or date in the circle, tacitly offered a choice of legendary sins and shames to the credence of the stranger, where time had often obliterated an epitaph or left a headstone to fall upon the grave like some desperate mourner prostrated there. Often the stone was broken, but where this had happened the fragments were piously gathered up and set in a boundary wall of the cemetery with other fallen memorials to the effect of tablets in a church. Constantly I was impressed by the youth of the dead, whose ages were oftenest under thirty and seldom beyond forty, and I easily accepted the theory that they were victims to the pestilential air of the river flats in the time when these were the flooded rice fields. But one day when I noted this youthful mortality to another stranger whom I met in the old graveyard, he opposed the theory, and made me observe how commonly the early dead were from the North. In the ignorant old days as soon as consumption intimated itself to the victim he was hurried to the South, and especially to Savannah, where the soft climate was fatally imagined beneficial in the white plague when the wiser science of our day would have prescribed the pure rigor of his native cold. I believe that people live as long in Savannah now as anywhere, but I am not versed in the statistics, and know only from hearsay that the long summer is exhausting chiefly because it is so very long, and the winter is never what we Northerners would find severe in the lowest of its habitual temperatures.

The old cemetery is now given up to the school children for a playground, and in the adjoining common they have their games unmolested by the kindly ghosts who would not resent the forays of the boys among their tombs (often built in a grotesque likeness to brick ovens), but could not like the marauders breaking the limbs of the low trees that embowered their strange roofs, though at the worst they seemed to make no spectral reprisals. The marauders were, in fact, comparatively few, and were probably truants from a distance; the other frequenters of the place were young mothers with their babies in perambulators, and young lovers sitting hand in hand on the benches, or sauntering through the aisles under the level boughs of the milky-blossomed dogwoods. The children from the schoolhouse next their playground were drilled one morning by a lady teacher in civil and military exercises, the girls eagerly responsive to her commands, and the boys, as their nature is, reluctantly and grotesquely, if finally, obedient. To our ignorance she

seemed an excellent disciplinarian, and so did a young lady tip-
toed and high-heeled who taught them old-fashioned English
folk games and dances. I remember nothing pleasanter than the
times we gave in all practicable weather to this old burial ground
in both our first and second visit. In the first we felt the tourist's
obligation to see the famous Bonaventure cemetery, with its
grandeur of live oaks and solemnity of moss-hung aisles, but I
thought its fame exaggerated and went to it only once. I forget
just where on the way coming or going we passed one of those
negro graveyards which seem of a conventional pattern in the
South, with on a fantastic decoration of bottles and tumblers
holding feathers and flowers in whatever tradition of ancestral
Africa, and wildly expressing the grief of the wild hearts that
broke in compliance with it.

Our second visit included Easter Sunday, which is an especial
feast of Savannah, but was now spoiled for outward show by the
rain that lasted far into the afternoon. The bright summer things
to have been worn by the young girls and little girls, whom
bright summer things are meant for by nature, had mostly to be
left at home with their wearers. But no malice of the elements
could quite extinguish them, and curls and flapping hats tardily
dared the best of the bad weather. The clouds broke and then in
the cool air youth came forth, sometimes in the company of
khaki-clad figures which were so often finding their way into
town from the nearest camps. A moment of vivid expression
devoted itself to the white of two intensely black little girls
whom no one could have had the heart to deny it, and who
looked glad enough for a whole cityful of gratified children.

I am trying to believe that I know more of the social life of
Savannah than the facts justify. One of the things I have heard is
that receptions for ladies, especially young ladies, are often given
in the forenoon, and are followed by lunches which do not prevent the ladies from going home to dinner at two o'clock, with
supper at seven, when the gentlemen of their families come from
business to join them. The office hours of the city, whose chief
business is that of cotton, are much governed by the hours of

Liverpool, where the difference of time makes itself felt in this domestic derangement. But the like derangement prevails elsewhere in the South, and fifty years ago in Boston where very little cotton is grown, I remember people used to dine at two, and half past two.

Since the world war involved us, the ladies of Savannah have been devoted to the duties of the Red Cross, and the Gordon house, one of the most memorable and beautiful old mansions, was given up to its various work. The wonted amusements of the town were relinquished though perhaps not totally; but I must recur to the experiences of our first visit if I would give an idea of the gay abandon of the young people in amusing themselves and delighting the public. There was then a whole evening of colored song and dance and conundrum, in the conventional ideal of negro minstrelsy, when they took part in the only form of drama which America has invented. They exhausted the resources of this, and then they added events studied from the colored life of their own town or country homes and remembered with affectionate fun in what may often have been the portrayal of actual character. As strangers, we were necessarily on the outside of much and could only guess at the truth of the hits from the pleasure of an audience which filled to the roof the friendly old theater (the oldest in the country), but was more wont to yawn over the drama of one-night stands.

I hope I am not very guilty in so far omitting mention of those intellectual clubs which largely occupy the Savannah ladies, as well as the ladies of our whole land. I can only plead that this paper is a less serious study than I should like to make it if I could, and that I must seem to neglect many facts of interest, when I am merely ignorant of them. We heard vague mention of picnics which young people enjoyed when the cold of the early winter made the woods safe in the torpor of the rattlesnakes; there were friends who drove us in their automobiles in widening circumferences beyond the city and showed us the reach of its ambition and prosperity everywhere; and there was one excursion down the river to the sea which was a revelation of the enterprises and industries promising a business future far beyond the great business present. Not every visitor has the luck or the leisure for a sail beyond Tybee Light, but no one need fail of seeing the expanse of the freight sheds with their cotton and turpentine in the shore across from the city, or on the city side the magnificent dock of the coastwise steamers, which is the last and loudest word of dockage in the whole world, a thing absolutely so fitted to its vast use as to be as much a thing of beauty as a painting or a flower.

As the river seeks the sea both shores and the same level with a like low boscage and the same reaches of reedy swampland, which cease as the yellow current ceases in the ocean tides. There is at one place an old fort of the Vauban design which does not succeed in being very historical, but in another there is a human event which makes a more dramatic impression. "Now, watch, and you will see her," we were promised as we drew abreast a house with a veranda opening toward the river; and in fulfilment a woman came out and waved a white kerchief in salute. "She waves the cloth by day to every ship that passes, and by night she waves a lantern, and she has done it ever since she was a little girl." The sailors remember her in every sea, and when they come near always return her salute. It was a poetic impulse, and it was one-half possible, but for the other half, the nightly half, the tradition had its difficulties for a mind perplexed with the details of waking up, or keeping awake for the moment of romantic drama.

The lure of the great river was not seaward, but inland; and I longed to take a steamboat for Augusta, but I was warned against the too great simplicity of the life on board, and eventually I contented myself with that excursion in a government yacht. The yellow waters were practicable as far as Florida, I heard, but again I denied myself and went only so far as the Isle of Hope in a friend's motor. There we visited the famous terrapin farm (a roofed-in space of the native swamp), which supplies Baltimore terrapin to the whole world and to the visitor is accompanied by a lecture from the "farmer," which does not well transport entire. One of the most portable jokes was his scientific explanation of the difference between a mud-turtle and a terrapin of the same size; the terrapin is worth three dollars and the mud-turtle is worth nothing. Another difference appeared experimentally in the course of the lecture when the farmer made a low chirping noise to the terrapin lurking by hundreds, perhaps thousands, in their oozy beds, when they cast off their covering and started toward him chortling in tender affection or expectation of food, while the mud-turtles in their haunts outside remained mute if not motionless.

The terrapin farm is what mostly attracts the stranger, even if he cannot afford to eat terrapin, but the Isle of Hope adds the attraction of dancing and dining for the Savannah youth, or perhaps the lower middle class. The suburb of Thunderbolt has a restaurant of peculiar merit for its fish, rolls, and coffee; and the whole region is of suburban residence and resort throughout the year and in the summer months, when the activity of the rattlesnake forbids the neighboring groves to the picnicker. Throughout the South, indeed, you must count with the rattlesnake in your love of nature, and I should be loath to give an exaggerated notion of peculiar peril in the neighborhood of Savannah. I suspected that in its season the mosquito would be a far more constant and insistent enemy even in the city itself, but in neither springtime of our visits had I any experience of it. I saw nothing even of the alligators which in the earliest colonial times are said to have come up from the river and prowled the streets after nightfall to the terror of the inhabitants, until the paternal Oglethorpe caught a monster twenty feet long and invited the boys to beat it to death with sticks. The boys liked the sport so much and the alligators so little that the sole incident of record sufficed to end the peculiar danger.

So much cannot be said of the annoyance which the colonists suffered for a long series of years from the Spaniards who came up out of Florida and put to proof the effectiveness of Georgia as a buffer for Carolina, which valued it mainly for that use. There was no trouble with the Indians from the first, for the simple reason that Oglethorpe made friends with them by justice and mercy; but the Spaniards were another matter. They claimed the whole country round about where he had settled his humanitarian colony, and he had to fight them everywhere in the wilderness, which their men-at-arms infested. He always beat them, but this did not avail, and even his siege of St. Augustine was in vain, perhaps because it had to be raised after the bombardment of the great fortress of San Marco, which still remains perfect there, but his campaigns served for the comfort of Carolina till a general peace between the mother-countries could be made to include their colonies.

In the meantime divers experiments were tried at Savannah for the material and spiritual prosperity of the settlers. Every form of Christian faith except the Roman Catholic was welcomed in its missionaries, while slavery was established for the release of the white settlers from the heavier labors of the field and in the several forms of experiment. It was supposed that with the gentle climate the grape would flourish and the best wines be made, but the sandy soil did not second the sun in its favor, and the olive shared the fate of the grape. From the beginning it was hoped that the silkworm would prosper, and experienced Italians were imported for its care, while it was fed from the mulberry trees which promptly took root and produced an inexhaustible abundance of foliage for its food. It is not clear why the silk culture followed the disuse of the wine and oil culture; it was almost universally attempted, and within the memory of men still living the silkworms remained in the warm attics where they were fostered, and attested in death their attempt to justify the wisdom of the experiment made in their introduction. The cotton culture, which is now the supreme industry of Georgia, and is incomparably the greatest commercial interest of Savannah, far excelling the famous Georgia pine and its resin, was the reason why the silk culture began to decay, and forbade all competition. The cotton exchange of Savannah is not quite the cotton exchange of Manchester, but it was of a presence equally interesting as it evoked itself from the clouds of tobacco smoke, and was of a certain authority as being a main cause of the Lancastrian consequence. I cannot say that I found it so impressively housed in Savannah, but it was incomparably more magnificently placed. A window of it hospitably lent its outlook over the river . . . and the obliging host realized to the author the difference between the long-fiber cotton of the Sea Islands and the short-fiber of the Georgian uplands as it showed in the comparative samples put side by side on his coat-sleeve, as I suppose they are shown to actual customers. I yielded my highest admiration for the silky Sea Island fiber with some such regard as one pays to rank in society, and viewed with the lessening consideration which one pays to middle and lower middle class merit, the shorter and shortest fibers of the decline from the aristocratic filaments. Cotton is still king in the South as it was before the states went to war with one another in our great civil contest, but its sovereignty is founded now upon the industry which is not bought and sold; but is practiced in free competition by black as well as white planters. This seems to me an advance, and it is a comfort which I like to think Oglethorpe would share with me in his generous humanity.

I am always coming back to him, and I do not wish to leave him again in these inadequate notices of the city he founded. Of all the fathers of our American civilization, I think him the kindest, and the wisest because the kindest, and I offer to the visitor Savannah for all and full proof. There is a very Roman legend of a local Fountain of Trevi (by whatever other name it is known) and a superstition that any one who drinks of it will be sure to come again. For my own part I do not think I need drink of Tomochichi's magic source; I shall hope to return without the draught, unless something among things here ventured should spoil my welcome; but I shall trust that Oglethorpe where he looks down from his column on the Indian's monolith will invoke a friendly spirit in my behalf. I will not turn from Mr. French's brave statue of the good hero, the true gentleman, without trying again for fit recognition of its inspiration, and I will say that if Oglethorpe is not the highest praise of Savannah, then at least Savannah is a supreme honor to the Jacobite philan-thropist, of whom it could be said far beyond the Jacobite prince and martyr—"He nothing common did or mean."

"Memories of My Girlhood"

JULIETTE GORDON LOW (1860–1927)

> Juliette Gordon Low began and ended her peripatetic life in
> Savannah: she was born at 142 Bull Street and died at 329
> Abercorn Street. After many years of devotion to her loveless
> marriage and playing hostess to the highest levels of interna-
> tional society, Low began to seek a central purpose and a legacy
> for her life. While pursuing her lifelong interest in art by study-
> ing in Paris, Low met General Sir Robert Baden-Powell, a
> retired British Army officer and founder of the Boy Scouts. She
> learned that 6,000 girls had joined his new group. Aware that
> her traditional feminine upbringing had left her ill-prepared for
> many of the practical necessities of life, she enlisted her sister
> Agnes to form the Girl Guides, later the Girl Scouts of the
> U.S.A. The first meeting of the group was March 12, 1912, in
> Low's Savannah home. Low was buried in her green serge uni-
> form in her family plot in Laurel Green Cemetery. The follow-
> ing memoir of her girlhood appeared in *Juliette Low and the
> Girl Scouts* (1928). The Savannah Theatre Company, men-
> tioned here, is located on Chippewa Square and is the longest
> continuously operated theater site in North America.

The first recollection of my childhood takes me back to the age
of two years, when I appeared on the stage of the Savannah
Theater, in some charity tableaux, in the role of Puck. I recollect
distinctly pulling the donkey ears of Bottom, and, clothed only
in a pair of gauze wings and a Roman sash, I was given such an
ovation of applause that, frightened by the unexpected noise, I
wept and had to be hastily banished from the scene!

But I remember the year 1864 as vividly as if I had been fourteen instead of three years old. In that year Savannah, which had
been besieged for months, surrendered to the enemy, and
Sherman's army marched through the city. I can even now feel
the thrill and hear the tramp of the tired troops. My colored

nurse waked me from sound sleep and wrapped me in the blanket of my crib bed.

Here we peeped through the green jalousies, and I saw for the first time real live Yankees, thousands of thousands of them! My "Mormer" (nurse) admired the blue uniforms and the music of the band, but I indignantly said, "They's playing 'When This Cruel War Is Over' and they's doing it all themselves!"

Later in the week General Sherman called on my mother. He had known her before her marriage. He asked if he could be of use to her, and I remember that he had with him an officer who had lost his arm. He took me on his knee, and with childish curiosity I inquired about the loss of that gentleman's arm.

"Got it shot off by a Rebel!" was the laconic explanation.

"I s'pose my father did it," I artlessly exclaimed. "He shot lots of Yankees." My mother hurried me from the room!

One of our old slaves, Nancy, without my grandmother's knowledge, hastily made Bene cakes, molasses candy, and wafers, and took the tray of dainties into the street, where she sold them to the soldiers. Triumphantly, she brought the money to my grandmother, for we had been nearly starved during the siege. And although her orders had been that no servant was to communicate with the troops, Nancy excused herself to Granny.

"Mars Sherman can't tell dat I give you de money, ole Miss," she said. "You leave Mars Sherman 'lone. De Debil knows who b'longs to him and he'll take care of his own!"

A military proclamation ordered every white woman and child to leave Savannah within a limited time. The country was swarming with disbanded troops, and railroad trains were crammed with soldiers. The journey from Savannah to Chicago was undertaken by my mother, for her only refuge was with her own people in Chicago. And under escort of her young brother, a Northern officer, we traveled for days and days without rest or proper food.

The privations and strain of this journey brought on an attack of brain fever, and for weeks I was delirious and at death's door. We three little sisters were so much more like scarecrows than human beings that one of my mother's girlhood friends said to another, "Have you seen Nelly Kinzie's children? They have tow-colored hair and clay-colored skins, and they look like the poor white trash of the South."

When this criticism was repeated to my mother, she remarked, "Well, this is the first time I ever heard So-and-so speak the truth." With better food and rest, however, we improved.

I remember the Indians who used to pass through Chicago en route to Washington, for they always camped on Grandfather John Kinzie's grounds, and my Grandmother Kinzie always gave them refreshments—lemonade, chocolate, cakes, and other dainties. Grandfather was the government agent for the Indians, and because he paid them in silver they named him "Shawniawkie," which means Silver Man. My grandmother was called by them "Little Ship Under Full Sail," a name that my family sometimes applies to me!

My next recollections skip over a number of years and bring me to the summers we used to spend on the plantation in the north of Georgia. There were three adjoining estates, and the cousins who lived on these three plantations made up a group of twenty boys and girls. We had one governess, who taught us all in the grove, where we had a schoolhouse under the walnut trees, and along the side of this grove was the peach orchard. Our greatest game was to play that the schoolhouse was a hotel where "Peach Gobble," a sort of puree of peach and mulberry wine, was sold for paper money. Our two eldest boy cousins pretended they were streetcar conductors; one drove the goat cart with two handsome cashmere goats, and the other streetcar was the donkey cart with a gray and lazy donkey. In turns we drove to the river and paid paper money for the fares, and our game usually ended in a hilarious swim through the rapids of the Etowah River.

The first organization I ever founded was a club that we formed in the winter of 1876. The cousins who lived next door to us in Savannah rigged up a telephone (this was long before the invention of the real telephone, and we called it our telegraph), which consisted of two tomato cans covered with vellum and with a string passed through them. One can was kept in our house, the other next door, and when any important business of the club was transacted, we took the greatest care first to send the message over the way by a servant, then to telephone it. So it came to pass that what was shouted through the tin cans was always understood!

The name of the club was Helpful Hands; its object was to help others. The first job we found for ourselves was to make garments for an Italian family who had a fruit stall and whose children were in rags. I arranged to give the club instructions in sewing, and collected the members in a circle about me, each one facing me. By some curious mischance I forced them all to thread their needles with their left hands! So we get the name of "Helpless Hands." Unfortunately, our work was not a complete success, because the Italians were of very warlike tempers, and in one battle which took place in our lane the sleeves of the watermelon pink calico garment came completely out, and the boy discarded the garment altogether, racing home *sans culottes*, pursued by the policeman.

We had great fun in our club, but it was broken up in the summer of 1876, when the yellow fever epidemic came to Savannah. My father remained to nurse the people, but he sent my mother and us children away. We left a perfectly silent, almost deserted city, nothing to be seen in the streets except hearses carrying away the dead. Our little Italian protégés fell the first victims, and one of our club members, a beautiful girl of ten years, also died of the scourge.

When I was fourteen years old and was staying at the plantation, I had my first grown-up callers. I had traveled South with two young West Point cadets, who represented themselves as being Yankees and bitter enemies of Rebels! They were in reality both Southerners and lived on a plantation about ten miles from Etowah. One summer's day I had climbed a high tree in the park and was perched on a seat in the top-most branch reading the exciting book *Uncle Silas*, by Justin Le Fanu, when I saw a buggy drive beneath me. I did not, however, recognize its occupants. I thought they were, of course, calling on my aunt. Presently Janette, a sprightly young negress, called me. I was rushed back to the house, clothed in a clean pique dress heavily embroidered in white braid, finished on the edge of the basque with Tom Thumb fringe. My hair, which was bobbed, was slicked down and I was ushered into the drawing room.

For the first time in my life I felt shy and self-conscious! I remembered that on the train one of these boys had told me that I had "liquid brown eyes" and the other had declared that a scar which disfigured my brow was really "a great beauty spot." I also remembered that they had represented themselves as sworn enemies of the South, so it swept over me that my two would-be admirers were two very untruthful, dangerous men, and I must have sadly disappointed them if they expected the same lively sallies and caustic repartee with which I had entertained them on the voyage South! For I was tongue-tied, and thus the first glimpse of grown-up life was for me a dismal failure.

After the cadets had departed my brother tried to reassure me when I asked him if I looked very ugly. He said: "Sister, you looked so nice none of us recognized you."

"Adrift in Georgia: Savannah"

SHERWOOD ANDERSON (1876–1941)

> Sherwood Anderson has been recognized as one of America's most
> important short-story writers based on his stories "The Egg,"
> "Death in the Woods," "The Man Who Became a Woman," and
> "Brother Death." He was born and raised in Ohio where he
> received little formal education and never attended college. His
> best-known novels, *Winesburg, Ohio* (1919) and *Horses and Men*
> (1923), earned him membership among the modernists of the
> Chicago Renaissance. Anderson spent most of his last sixteen years
> living and traveling in the South. "Adrift in Georgia: Savannah"
> first appeared in the *Marion (Va.) Democrat* in 1930. Anderson
> owned and edited the two weekly newspapers—one Democratic,
> one Republican—in that town.

Savannah—an old city, beside a red river, with old houses, not
unlike those in the old French quarter of New Orleans. The
streets are filled with Negroes. Ocean-going ships come up the
red Savannah River to the docks lying below but facing the city.

The city is built about little squares, heavily wooded and with
benches under the trees. There is everywhere a feeling of leisure.
No one seems in a hurry. Many wealthy people from the North
have come here, have bought old houses and live here through
the winter months.

The city is some sixteen miles up-river from the sea and at the
river's mouth are many islands. They build big country houses
on the islands.

I did not go down river to any of the great houses owned by
the northern rich men. None of them asked me to.

This is the land for your sunsets. Even when it has been raining all day down here the sky has a way of clearing in the late
afternoon—as though to say—"Hello, Yank. Stand by. We will
put on the daily show now."

It is sure a gorgeous show. There is the red land, the red Savannah River and the flaming red sky. Once I tried to paint such a sunset and when I had finished my canvas a friend looked at it. It was, beyond a doubt, a pool of blood. My friend shook his head. The secret of all modern art is to do something that no one understands. I had him there.

"It's pretty sad," he said, "who got murdered here?"

"Art," I said.

Negro boys are on the Savannah River in their row boats. They take people across the river for five cents a ride. A half dozen boats rush eagerly to meet each passenger. The Negro boys, from rowing all day against the stiff current, have become strong of arm and body. Strong men are graceful. Some of them sing as they row the passengers across the river.

Your river bank in your late afternoon—anywhere, any river—is your grand place for your idlers. I sit on the end of a pile, see the red water of the river, see a majestic ship coming slowly upstream, see the sun going down in a sea of blood.

I hear Negroes singing. I see gulls flying. "This is the place for me," I say to myself, "this suits me."

I have become like an old Negro man, walking on the big road. I talk aloud to myself. I burn cigarettes and throw the ends into the river.

The gulls are circling and diving, the water in the red river is running swiftly, Negro boys are rowing their boats and singing, a fat wench with a basket on her head comes down a flight of stone steps to the river's edge.

I should be at work. I should be writing smart magazine articles. I should be earning money.

"However," I tell myself, "if I do not patronize swell hotels, if I eat fish stews in riverside restaurants, I'll bet I can survive without working for a long time yet.

"Money will come in. Don't worry, boy. Take it easy. My own books—there are seventeen of them sailing the seas now—every now and then some poor fish will buy one.

"People in towns and cities, all over America and all over

Europe, will go into book stores. They will buy books and every now and then one of them will buy a book of mine.

"Books are like ships, sailing the ports of the world. They sail into a port here and one there. They pick up little cargoes of nice, round shining nickels and dimes."

I sit thus on the end of a pile on the shore of the red Savannah River and think of myself as the master of a whole fleet of ships.

The sun sets quickly, with a strange, abrupt quickness. This is a characteristic of the sun when he goes south. There is no evening twilight. There is broad daylight, this gaudy show—the evening sun going down—and then, suddenly night.

I saw a night coming as I stood on one of the little public squares in Savannah. I was reading the stately sentences carved on the monument erected to Oglethorpe, who founded the state of Georgia.

Did you know that George II gave to Oglethorpe and his pals in that adventure all the land lying between the Savannah River and a river to the south called the Altamaha, and "westward to the South Seas?" He did.

"A gaudy stretch of country, surely," I said to myself as I stood reading the words of the charter, carved in the stone.

I turned westward, facing the setting sun, thinking now of the South Seas, thinking of all that stretch of land and sea lying between me and the South Seas, thinking of Alabama and Texas, of the deserts of the movie-makers in Hollywood, of the calm and wide Pacific with whales besporting themselves, of the Hawaiian Islands and girls dancing on the beaches.

"Onward! Onward!" I cried. "On to Hawaii!"

King George gave it all away. He didn't care. "Take it," he said.

As I stood thus, wishing, as a man will wish sometimes, with large loose simplicity, that I could be King George II, giving to my friends islands and continents, rivers, forest and deserts, saying to this one, "Here, Jimmy Jones, take this hundred thousand square miles of land, plow it, plant it to crops, keep yourself warm"; and to that one, "Here, Charlie, have a Pacific Ocean, put some of these islands into your pockets—you may need them—they may come in handy."

I say as I was thinking all this, standing in the city of Savannah and reading over the old Georgia state charter, and as night came on, I saw, or imagined I saw, a woman running through the street.

Before her was the day and back of her the brown night. She was nude, a slender thing. She ran bare-footed on the stones of the city street and—at first—I could not see her clearly. She passed and I myself stood in darkness. I could not read the words on Oglethorpe's monument now.

It was the figure of the night, the southern night, coming and passing. Of course, it couldn't have been a white woman, being Night.

It wasn't a black woman either. It was a brown woman, a high-brown, so I walked off singing a little song I know:

"It takes a long, slim, high-brown gal,
To make a preacher lay his Bible down,"

I sang.

There isn't any question but that, being in Savannah, being a loafer here, seeing red rivers and red lands, starts something down inside me singing again.

"Foreword" to Harriet Ross Colquitt's *The Savannah Cook Book*

OGDEN NASH (1902–1971)

Ogden Nash is known as a consummate New Yorker, but his Southern roots run deep. Both his parents were Southerners; his great-great grandfather was governor of North Carolina during the Revolutionary War; and Nashville, Tennessee, was named for his ancestor, General Francis Nash. Nash spent some of his nomadic childhood in the Andrew Low house at 329 Abercorn Street in Savannah and described his own peculiar accent as "clam chowder of the East Coast—New England with a little Savannah at odd moments." Nash's numerous books of poetry, screenplays, and children's literature include *Hard Lines* (1931), *Happy Days* (1933), and *The Bad Parent's Garden of Verse* (1936). The following untitled poem was written as the foreword to Harriet Ross Colquitt's *The Savannah Cook Book* (1933).

Pilgrim's Progress is a good book, and so, I am told, is
  Deuteronomy,
But neither is to be compared with this epic of gastronomy.
Some people have to die to get to heaven, and others hitch-
  hike in fiery chariots,
But really intelligent people stay home alive and have heaven
  served to them out of this volume of Miss Harriet's,
For as everybody knows, life on Savannah victuals
Is just one long round of Madeira and skictuals.
Certainly every schoolboy knows that famous remark made
  by the late Mark Hanna:
"I care not who makes our Presidents as long as I can eat in
  Savannah."

If you like dishes made out of a piece of lettuce and ground-
    up peanuts and a maraschino cherry and marshmallow
    whip and a banana
You will not get them in Savannah,
But if you seek something headier than nectar and tastier
    than ambrosia and more palatable than manna,
Set your teeth, I beg you, in one of these spécialitiés
    de Savannah.
Everybody has the right to think whose food is the most
    gorgeous,
And I nominate Georgia's.

from *The Damned Don't Cry*

HARRY HERVEY (1900–1951)

Harry Hervey was educated at the Georgia Military Academy.
Although a native Texan, Hervey's connections to Savannah
are many and he spent a good part of his life in the city. His
mother was a Savannahian by birth and Hervey lived in
Savannah from 1938 until an eventually fatal illness precipitated his hospitalization in New York. Ten of his thirteen novels became best sellers, among them *Where Strange Gods Call*
(1924), *Congai* (1927, later adapted for the stage with native
Savannahian Carleton Hildreth), and *The Iron Widow* (1931).
His autobiographical *Ethan Quest* (1925) is partially set in
Savannah. Hervey was a globe-trotting traveler who wrote travel
pieces for popular magazines and the screenplay for *Shanghai
Express* (1932). Most significantly, during travel in northern
Vietnam in the 1930s, he discovered previously unknown Khmer
ruins. *The Damned Don't Cry* (1939), excerpted here, was
locally controversial because of its indictment of the social structure of Savannah, where the novel is set. (The piece mentions the
indigenous Savannah child's game, halfrubber. The three-team
off-shoot of baseball is played by sidearm pitching half a sponge
rubber ball and batting it with a heavy-duty mop handle.) Later
in the novel, the protagonist Zelda opens a disreputable house in
the mansion she admires in this excerpt.

It stands facing an arid little square, in a city where most of the
squares are exuberantly green. Its bolted shutters give it a blank
stare. About the formal entranceway, dead magnolia leaves clus-
ter like warped parchment. Somber, ruddy-brown, it half hides
behind medallions of Chinese yews; and giant magnolia trees,
flanked by sycamores, shade its scabby face. Easily the most
magnificent house in the neighborhood, it lifts its ponderous
three stories from a half-sunk cellar, maintaining, even in its
desertion, a haggard dignity, an imperturbable aloofness from

its surroundings. At night, plunged into a rich depth of shadow, it broods, its attic, like a tired brain, aroused to wan nostalgia. But in daylight, it has a cultured grimness, as though disapproving the intrusion that has visited its urban quiet. For, once a select quarter, Savannah's Old Fort district has crept westward and encroached, bringing with it the noisy vitality of shanty Irish and Negroes; and a bastard architecture. The square seems to share the reserve of the house. Once it dreamed to the murmur of well-bred voices. Now, in the still summer evenings, the whining of radios incites the heat; auto horns, rupturing backfire, blast out from behind the mansion, where in past years a walled garden breathed gently, but where now a filling station exhales gas fumes and the cloying disinfectant from a restroom. The attendants, slow-talking low-country boys, willingly discuss the house. Only the erudite among them may recite that it was built by a French Huguenot family; that, architecturally, it is brazenly Greek Revival and discreetly Victorian; that the mansard roof, a comparatively recent addition, is an abomination. . . . But all are likely to mention the name of Zelda O'Brien.

II

Zelda was seven when she first saw the house.

It was a hot July afternoon. Storm clouds bellied in from Tybee, pressing humidly upon the city.

Ostensibly, her mother was taking her and Lathe for a walk. But Zelda knew that, really, Katie was looking for Gil, who was lying off somewhere drunk. Katie hated walking, unless for a reason.

Zelda thought her mother looked very pretty that afternoon; excepting, of course, her hair, which was always disheveled, and a little stringy. Katie's hair bothered Zelda, who was born with an instinct for the completely right in appearance. Without being able to define it as such, she recognizes it as an utter vindication of Callie Mullis' repeated contention that Katie O'Brien was a slut. What Zelda did not recognize was that, in a few years, that knot of hair slightly askew on the back of her mother's neck, would, still askew, find itself atop her head; and that Katie, her bland pink cheeks puffing with maturity, her already ample breasts and thighs considerably augmented, would suggest, to those inclined toward ribald observation, a malicious caricature of a Watteau shepherdess.

Lathe had lagged behind, crayon in hand, to write a dirty word on the brick pavement. Zelda's interest in what his imagination would produce on the sidewalk dissipated as she became aware of the house.

A gracious iron fence rose from sandstone coping, enclosing a small, sparsely planted front yard. Beside the two tall, symmetrically placed gates, within, were twin gas lamp-posts, guarding identical curving stairways. The thick Chinese yews, their shadows deepened by the twilight falling from the larger trees, thrust the colonnade into verdant dusk, in which the four fluted pillars, with their attendant square columns, rose like the massive guardians of some dingy temple. The iron balcony over the door was all but lost in dank gloom.

The house suddenly loomed over Zelda, at once monstrously forbidding and incredibly splendid.

She stared.

Particularly fascinating was the stretch of basement wall beneath the colonnade. In it were three iron grilles, grim as prison windows. Below them mold spread a green mucous.

It became, in that instant, an awesome and enchanted fortress, behind whose walls her future lay battlemented.

Impulsively, she hopped up on the stepping-stone, pretended to lift a long skirt, then tripped airily across the brick pavement.

Katie eyed her with lackadaisical suspicion. "What you doin'?" she demanded. That child certainly was peculiar, she reflected. Always acting like something she wasn't. And using fancy words. She guessed it was a mistake letting Zelda be one of the angels in Father Caspar's Easter pageant last year. Her feet hadn't touched the ground since then. Some of the things that child did were a caution—enough to provoke the Saints. Like that time they went to White Bluff on a picnic, and she found Zelda lying, naked as a jaybird, in a clump of wild honeysuckle. Said she was playing angel. Well, Katie observed, she had certainly given her celestial little bottom a good tanning. . . .

"What you doin'?" she repeated.

"Practicin'," Zelda answered. "Some day"—and she pointed toward the house, her eyes glowing with a solemn light—"I'm gonna live there."

That struck Katie as bitterly amusing. She laughed. "You, right!" she mocked. And as an afterthought she added, more to herself than to the child: "Get that good-for-nothin' drunken ol' man uh yours t' make you a present of it!" Then, entirely to herself, she muttered: "Catch that low-down sonabitch, I'll brain 'im!"

Then she crossed herself. Katie always crossed herself after indulging in profanity.

She grabbed Zelda's hand. "Come on," she said impatiently Glancing around, she saw Lathe stooped over the sidewalk. "Get up from there, you hear?" she shrilled; "an' stop writin' them filthy words or I'll slap you side the head, Lathe O'Brien!"

Grinning impudently, the boy printed another word, in bigger letters, then rose and skipped after his mother and sister. As he came up behind Zelda, he made a rude gesture under the rear of her petticoat. Zelda was too entranced by her discovery of the house to do more than slap perfunctorily at his hand. But her mother, seeing what Lathe did, and being in no such exalted mood, cuffed him severely.

"You nasty-minded li'l' buzzard!" she scolded, becoming raucously maternal. In the first place, she was unbearably hot: perspiration stung her eyes and ran down over her lips; and, in spite of her shields, stains were creeping out from under her armpits. Secondly, she was furious with Gil; he hadn't been home since yesterday. And, finally, she had not failed to see that word Lathe scrawled on the bricks. It outraged her low-class sense of decency; and generated a subtly illicit sensation in her loins. "You stop doin' them nasty things, hear?" she fumed on. "You gonna be jus' like yo' nasty-minded ol' man!" She paused, then, with a species of ecstatic contempt, summed up: "Ev'y man is jus' plain nasty-minded, 'at's all!"

Yanking her children after her, she resumed her militant walk, continuing to admonish Lathe:

"Where's yo' respec' for yo' sister? You jus' no good, 'at's all." She whined a little as she proclaimed her fortitude and grieved her lot. "God knows I try t' learn you decent ways—God knows I do! Sometimes I think my burden's too heavy t' bear—a drunk, chippy-crazy ol' man—a dirty little brat for a son—an'—an'—" She hesitated, then pronounced emphatically: "An' a daughter 'at puts on crazy airs!"

When Katie's fretting subsided, Zelda commenced to pester her with questions.

"Who lives in 'at house, mama?"

"Some uppity 'ristocrats—who you reckon?" retorted Katie, enviously.

"Is it worth a million dollars, 'at house, mama?"

Katie laughed derisively. "They ain't a million dollars in Savannah!" she declared with contempt. "Po' 'ristocrats, 'at's all 'at's here—an' po'er white trash—an' niggers. 'At's what's here. Where I come from, they got nice folks—nothin' but hospitable quality folks."

Katie was from Mobile.

A little Negro boy came skipping around a corner. As he saw the three whites approaching, he slowed down abruptly, then sidled over to a fence and leaned there, one bare, squirming foot thrust into his hock.

Lathe tossed him a superior grin. "Hi there, Pincus."

Solemnly the little Negro returned: "Hi, Lathe."

Katie scowled at her son. "You let 'at li'l' nigger call you Lathe?" she demanded. Belligerently she said to the piccaninny "Boy, you call him *Mista* Lathe—you un'erstan'?"

The Negro child rolled his eyes, then looked down at the side walk. "Yasum." Without lifting his eyes, he asked Lathe: "You wanna come wid me, Lathe—uh—Mista Lathe? I gwine T'une'e'bolt wid mah Pa—"

"Sure," Lathe responded enthusiastically.

"You don't do no sucha thing," Katie declared. "Why you always runnin' 'roun with niggers? Ain't you got no—"

"Aw, Ma," Lathe protested, "lemme go—"

"No, siree! You been real bad today. You goin' home."

"Aw, Christ!" said Lathe.

Katie grabbed his shoulder and slapped at him, but he dodged wrenching free.

"You, Lathe! You stay here now! Don't you go run away. You do, I'll tell yo' ol' man, an' he'll wear you out!"

Sullenly, reluctantly, Lathe obeyed; at the back of his eye lurked a hint of cunning that belied submission. Although instinctively Zelda disapproved, she did not even bother to give him a glance of censure. She was in another region, aloof, utterly remote, an almost mystical vacancy in her childish eyes. Anyway this wrangling was part of the daily routine. She had come to accept it without distress.

Katie took a firm hold on Lathe's arm. "You come along now an' behave yo'self, hear?"

Lathe did not reply. There was a furtive, impudent glimmer in his eyes. . . .

Katie grimly convoyed her two offspring across the street, into a square.

The heavy air was shrill with the shouting of many boys. They were pitching ball, playing "half-rubber," wrestling, or picking fights and otherwise tormenting one another. All those running, shrieking, superheated bodies lent a feverish pregnancy to the atmosphere, already swollen with impending storm, and filled Katie with enervating irritation. A truant baseball rolled across the sidewalk in front of her. She experienced a perverse disappointment: if that had hit her or the children . . . !

A muffled, splintering crash of thunder drew her eyes upward. The sky was the color of dirty smoke, and had a weird yellowish cast.

Suddenly Katie became aware of a new animation in the air. It was both warning and caressing. A stealthy wind, sick with the smell of marshes, sighed treacherously. It had wandered inland from the ocean, pervading the swamps, taking from them their miasmal offering, then followed the broad, muddy river up to Bay Street, spreading slyly over the town. Now it sent the fallen leaves, in this and other squares, scratching over the sidewalks; shook flakes of sound from the trees; brought a harsh sibilance from the palmettos as their fronds swayed and scraped.

Swiftly, almost imperceptibly, an immaculate coolness had purified the stagnant humidity.

For an instant Savannah, like a soggy West Indian seaport, shuddered ecstatically in this release from heat. Then the rain fell, in great drenching splashes.

In a few seconds the park was evacuated.

Katie, in a mood to feel there was something personally humiliating in the abrupt downpour, took refuge, with Zelda and Lathe, in Christo Pellegrino's corner fruit-stand. She had intended to stop by anyhow—Christo "aged" and sold corn-whiskey in the back, and Gil might be there or the Greek might know his whereabouts—but she had hardly counted on rushing in, overheated, breathless, and wet. Somehow she didn't like that Greek, whom she considered inferior, seeing her ruffled or bedraggled.

Christo was an enormous man in whose slow-moving body a swart, voluptuous vitality slept. He had long, thick, black wavy hair which he was always combing. He was combing it when Katie and the children entered. His hot liquid eyes took her in with impersonal desire; it was a look he gave every woman. She understood the implication of it, and a flush of what she chose to believe was resentment mounted through her breasts into her throat. The sour-sweet smell of ripe fruit, of dry herbs and spilled syrups—the scent of a saloon without the added pungency of alcohol—invariably disturbed her.

"Seen my ol' man?" she asked, trying to be casual.

"No, ma'am," the Greek answered indifferently; insolently, she thought.

She shifted her eyes quickly as she caught herself staring at the great mass of black hair showing through his thin shirt.

"I wanna soda," said Lathe.

"Give 'im one," Kane told Christo curtly.

"A cream soda," Lathe instructed.

Katie watched the Greek's thickly veined forearm as it dipped into the icebox. Christo lifted two bottles tentatively. "W'at about the li'l' girl?" he asked.

"Zelda, you wanna soda?" Katie demanded. "Zelda! You pay 'tention to me—I said you wanna soda?"

The little girl, startled out of exquisite dreaming, nodded quickly. "Yes, ma'am."

"Give her cream soda," Katie ordered; "same as her brother."

"I want sa's'p'rilla," Zelda asserted.

"Well, give 'er that," said Katie impatiently. "Always have to be ornery, don't you?"

While the children were drinking their sodas, Christo, his black eyes unsmiling, invited Katie into the rear "for a li'l' one on the house." She went with a show of sulky reluctance. As he shoved aside the soiled flowered curtain for her to pass, a glimmer of virile contempt slipped into his phlegmatic gaze. Something electric flared out and charged the woman.

If 'at greasy Greek touches me, she thought vigorously, I'll make Gil skin 'im alive!

In a dim space behind the portieres were two tables covered with checkered cloths. A gaudy icon hung above littered shelves. The rain, flooding down the fly-specked panes, made blurred, fluid patterns. It was incredibly hot, and musty.

"Lawdy," Katie breathed heavily, "this heat sure is terrible. . ."

Christo made no comment. He indicated a chair, and Katie sat uneasily. As he reached up for a jar of whiskey, he leaned forward slightly and pressed his hard, flexed thigh against her shoulder. Her muscles contracted. But she did not move. She'd show him he couldn't scare her. . . .

In the front of the stand, Lathe had gulped down his soda. Zelda was still sipping hers through a straw, staring, dreamy-eyed, out at the rain. The sky had become a dark slate upon which lightning chalked livid scribbles. A sound drew her gaze back to Lathe. Watching the curtains, he quickly thrust his hand into a jar of candy, scooped up several pieces, and stuffed them into his pocket. He returned Zelda's look defiantly. Her expression was silent reproof. It never occurred to her to call her mother. That would be "telling on" Lathe, which she had been taught, through her elementary training among the children of the neighborhood, was a low form of treason. Nor did she think of trying to stop him. Lathe always had his way, whether by consent or otherwise. What was not granted, he took. And, although he was slapped and beaten by both Katie and Gil, he invariably was forgiven—because of the hurt look he could summon into his startlingly black eyes, and because of the naive guilelessness of his thin, oval little face.

As he darted toward the doorway, Zelda asked: "Where you goin'?"

"Ssh!" he cautioned, glowering. "None your business!"

"You goin' T'un'e'bolt with Pincus," she divined.

"Think you're smart, don't you?" he parried.

"It's rainin' hard," she warned. "An' you'll get a lickin'."

Lathe put his thumb to his nose and, with a mocking smile, ducked out into the rain.

Zelda was vaguely upset. Her mother would be boiling mad. And rightfully, she reasoned. Lathe shouldn't be going around with nigger children. Suddenly Zelda felt sorry for Katie. Why, she wondered, didn't her father come home? And why was Lathe always running off?

With noticeable abruptness, Katie appeared from behind the portieres. There was a glazed, unnatural look in her eyes; they seemed too brilliant. Christo sauntered after her, one hand thrust into his trouser-pocket. . . . His appearance, for some reason she could not understand, generated a faint hostility in Zelda.

Incendiary thoughts scorched Katie's brain: Greasy Greek! 'At's 'e kind 'at rapes you, 'em Greeks. An' niggers. He better not put his han' on me again, 'at greasy Greek!

A moment passed before she observed Lathe's absence.

"Where's yo' brother?"

Zelda looked blank and shook her head.

"You lyin'," Katie accused.

Striding to the doorway, she leaned out, shading her eyes from the rain, and peered right and left, then, in a gesture of exasperation, placed her hands on her hips and muttered: "Well, damn his hide. . . ."

For several seconds she stood there, scowling, her brain functioning with hot, insistent sluggishness. She tried to think of Lathe, but his face, in her mind, took on a mask of Christo Pellegrino; became, fantastically, an offspring of his, as though this sudden, almost overpowering carnality that shook her, conceived and reproduced the boy in the image of her desire. She caught her breath sharply, nauseated, startled by this absurd illusion, this twisted vagary of her imagination. She felt as if, in some thoroughly unnatural way, she had been violated and the indignation engendered by this assault resolved into a stubborn, persistent denial of her lust.

Zelda, starting at the silhouette of her against the gray slackening rain, was puzzled. She had expected an outburst. Presently, when her mother turned, the expression in her eyes further perplexed the child. Anger was there, to be sure; but, somehow, she sensed it did not entirely have to do with Lathe. She looked as though she had something on her mind, something secret and troubling.

Katie kept her gaze away from Christo. He had busied himself with some indefinite task in the rear, taciturnly dismissing her presence. She wished it would stop raining. . . . It did, just as abruptly as it commenced. A damp coolness sighed up from the wet bricks. The square looked incredibly green. Out of hibernation swarmed the little boys, resuming their frantic exertions. Katie's voice was deliberately harsh as she said to Zelda: "Come on. It's let up now." The Greek evinced no interest as they went out. . . .

When they reached East Broad, where they lived, the street, figuratively speaking, was airing itself on its respective stoops. In the wake of the rain had come a faint, muggy haze. through which the somber, brassy light in the sky glared weirdly. Again the air was still, insidiously secretive, as though sharing with the heavens some mysterious pact, of which that violent shower was but an indication. In this unnatural citron twilight, the people looked malarial and unhealthy. This atmospheric tension, so familiar to the lush islands and keys closer to the Gulf but less prevalent along this coast, always scared Katie. It was unearthly. It promised some indefinite doom. She felt it all about her, even in the street. East Broad moved to its customary rhythm. Negroes called to one another from the mephitic interiors of adjoining houses; at intervals shrill African laughter split the quiet; phonographs whined and scraped perpetually; a few soldiers drifted by from the Tybee station; women in wrappers swept off their doorsteps and screeched at brats playing in the parkway; up from the Bay sauntered seamen or fishermen, hands thrust into dungarees, or swinging a string of dead fish. But, somehow, this afternoon all this, enclosed in that eerily luminous haze, and intensified by the inert air, had for Katie more than its usual lazy stridence: in it was a sense of muffled panic.

This elusive uneasiness urged her to quicken her step. She had to hurry home, why she didn't know, unless it was that Gil might be there. Huh, fat chance, she sniffed. . . .

She approached the Abrahams Home—for old ladies—this true necessity for haste suffered a brief interruption. She saw that Essie and Erna Flaherty, or "the Flaherty girls" as they were called, had brought their rockers out onto the sidewalk, and sat fanning themselves and harkening avidly as Mrs. Palmeri held forth. Mrs. Palmeri ran a grocery store on lower Broughton Street, and knew all the gossip of the Old Fort. It might be worthwhile to stop and speak, Katie decided.

The three women returned her greeting with polite suspicion.

"The Flaherty girls" were about sixty, and twins; scrawny gray little creatures, who always sat hunched forward, arms pressed primly to their sides, in identical attitudes, looking for all the world like a pair of plucked sparrows. Over them, Mrs. Palmeri, with her dark Sicilian ripeness, presided like a plump, self-satisfied guinea fowl.

"Real nice shower, wasn't it?" chirped Essie. "Cooled things off a mite."

"Did no sucha thing," contradicted Erna spiritedly. "Miz Palmeri here was jus' tellin' us 'bout the killin' las' night." Impatiently: "Go on, Miz Palmeri. . . ."

Katie knew what she was referring to: she had read about it in the paper that morning—some cop had shot his woman, over on Price Street.

For Katie's benefit, Mrs. Palmeri, with oily tolerance, repeated part of her recital: she'd been passing the house at the very instant of the murder, and she had heard the shots—yes, indeed, three of them, just like the paper said! And what's more, it was she who had called the ambulance. Always glad to be useful. She'd waited around until they brought the body out, but she didn't get to see it because it was covered with a sheet; so today when she went over to the undertaking-parlor, and—would you believe it?—at least fifty people were there. Most of them she knew: Mrs. Monohan, Mrs. Pheney, Mrs. Lubiski, Mrs. Kumpf, Mrs. Oberhoffer. . . . And, my, had they fixed that girl up wonderful!—she looked at least ten years younger. . . .

"'Ese men sho shoots lotsa wimmin 'roun' Savannah," ventured Essie with a certain wistful relish.

Dismissing this as paltry comment, Erna declared: "I seen six of 'em 'at was shot by they men. An' they sho looked purty laid out. You wouldn't 'a' thought they was bad. . . ."

Essie was determined not to be completely overshadowed by Erna. "I seen one myself once," she maintained; "'member, Erna? 'Ey had the nicest glass eye where her'n were shot out. Couldn't 'a' tol' the difference. . . ."

Zelda, who had been listening wide-eyed, spoke up: "I never seen a corpse."

Katie snatched at her hand. "You come on, Zelda," she said virtuously. "This ain't no talk for chirrun."

Mrs. Palmeri looked mildly annoyed, and a bit hurt, at the suggestion that any conversation she participated in was not fit for any ears, even the youngest.

As Katie moved off with the reluctant Zelda, Erna squinted after them and smirked "Well," she observed tardy, "I ain't no spring chicken, but I don't min' tellin' you *I'd* hate t' hav' t' lis'en t' all '*at* chile hears at *home*!"

Essie cackled. "You right!"

Meanwhile, Katie was having her say. "Don't think 'bout nothin' but men an' shootin' an' lovin'," she muttered, "nasty-minded ol' crows!"

"Mama," asked Zelda, "why do men shoot wimmin?"

"'Cause wimmin ain't no good," Katie retorted. And she added: "Not 'at men is any better. Fact, they a sight worse."

"Ain't you good, mama?" queried Zelda.

Katie yanked at her arm. "You oughta be 'shamed uh yo'self, askin' questions like 'at!" she scolded. "Co'se yo' mama's good!" Then she demanded sharply: "You ever hear anybody say she wasn't?"

"No, ma'am. Nobody 'cept Callie Mullis."

That chippy! Katie thought. She should talk! Ev'ybody knows Denny Mullis ain't the father of her brat! He ain't got it in 'im! To the child she said: "You jus' min' yo' business, an' don't pay no 'tention to what people say—least, till you grow up. You hear?"

"Yes, ma'am." But Zelda was not satisfied. "Mama," she pursued, "why ain't wimmin an' men good—I mean, all 'cept you an' papa?"

Katie laughed humorlessly. "'At's a question you hafta ask God," she advised.

Looking ahead, she saw Callie Mullis sitting on her stoop, nursing her six-months-old baby, Jenvie; and her face set in grim lines. Zelda, too, saw Callie Mullis, but her interest went beyond, to her home, which was next door to Callie's. Why, she wondered, dimly ashamed and unhappy, didn't they live in a mansion, like the one she'd seen this afternoon?

The gas-plant was directly behind the O'Brien house. It rose from a sprawling mound of ancient breastworks called the Old Fort—a name loosely applied to the district. On the highest bastion, in futile boast, two impotent eighteenth-century cannon sent a bogus threat toward the river. Below them, brick ramparts, soiled white, and stained with the spewings of drains, crept down a hill in blanched shame, only to find themselves further mortified by the adjacency of railway tracks and vulgar ironworks. Thus debased, this venerable shell of a fortification seemed glumly submissive, shoddily humiliated, like a warrior stripped without spectacle. Once Fort Wayne, its brick and mortar groin had ejected shell and flame; now these petrified loins, with weary indifference, vented their flatulence somewhat in the manner of social Savannah, upon the surrounding area.

Katie's house was on a corner, near the end of Bay Street and the river—a low, hybrid little house, squatting almost against the gas-works. The basement was of old brick from which the whitewash had practically disappeared; the upper portion, unpainted clapboard. Faded green blinds sagged open at the screenless windows. It had an air of passive dejection, as though no longer oppressed by the giant black tanks looming over it, but completely resigned to the tyranny of them and the panting smokestacks that day and night emptied their lungs upon it.

Zelda, approaching her home, was depressed for the first time in her brief life by the neighborhood in which she lived. A little bewildered, she looked up at her mother to see if she gave any sign of this feeling. But Katie's face showed only her hostility toward Callie Mullis.

Callie's waist was undone, her infant held listlessly against one breast. As the child sucked and dribbled, she gazed out vaguely, sulkily, at nothing in particular. She had a thin white face which should have been frail but which was hard with the brittle hardness of a china egg. Seated there on her stoop, nursing her baby, she was a slovenly, indifferent madonna, faintly irked by what she was doing yet too lazy to arouse any rebellion; therefore content to fulfill this duty half-heartedly, slatternly, wherever and whenever the necessity arose. Callie was frustrated, without comprehending it as that; all she knew was that, in plain words, she had a "hell of a life." Callie wanted to go out; to have fun. But Denny was always too tired to do anything except stuff his lean, hard-muscled body with Callie's greasy cooking and then go to sleep, stark naked, a sunburnt, good-looking, and thoroughly useless shell of a man. Callie had heard that Denny habitually "fixed up" other women. But she didn't believe it. God, she ought to know, oughtn't she? "Lis'en, 'oman," Denny would say to her, "if you wanna go out, an' you can fin' somebody t' take you, go on. But, by Jesus, if I ever catch you cheatin' on me, I'll break that goddamned neck of yours. . . ." And so Callie, who had no resources within herself, was slowly shriveling inside; and because she was a coward, she vented her thwarted desire in lustful, hungry looks at men and petty meanness toward her own sex.

Callie, aware of Katie's approach, watched her and the child with a kind of animal curiosity, mixed with torpid enmity. Idly, a bit resentfully, she wondered where Zelda got her looks. Certainly not from that flowsy mother of hers—nor from red-nosed Gillian O'Brien! Funny eyes that kid had. Callie guessed they really were gray, but sometimes they seemed green, sometimes blue. They were sort of "foreign." Slanty, like a Chink's. They bothered you. They . . . well, they just bothered you, that was all. What Callie did not understand was that they were almost breathtakingly honest, with a candor and directness that stemmed from more than mere childish innocence.

Katie pretended not to see Callie and in a loud voice declared: "Some folks don't min' where they do *anything*."

Callie took up the challenge. Spitefully she asked: "Find Gil?"

"Who's lookin' for 'im?" Katie retorted, without stopping.

"Well," said Callie guilelessly, "I jus' thought maybe you'd like to know where he's at."

Katie managed to remain outwardly indifferent until she mounted her stoop, then she turned abruptly. "Where is he at?" she demanded.

Pleased, Callie pushed her baby's face away from her pap and adjusted her waist before she answered. "Denny seen 'im 'bout 'n hour ago—down t' Nick's place." The baby commenced crying; she shook it. "You hush, hear?" Then, with a snicker, she relayed to Katie: "Said he sure looked three sheets in the wind!"

Some day, thought Katie, I'm gonna slap the livin' daylights outa 'at woman!

She put her hands on her hips and glowered across at Callie.

"Lis'en, Callie Mullis—I'm tired uh you 'sinuatin' 'roun'—"

Callie, who was afraid of Katie, countered in hurt tones: "Who said anything?"

"You did! An' lemme tell you somethin' right now—Gil O'Brien's a damn sight better man 'an Denny Mullis—an' I got two kids 'at's *his* t' prove it!"

With that she stomped inside, jerking Zelda after her and slamming the door. Instantly she realized it was suffocatingly hot, and opened the door. She could hear Callie's voice. Now that she was in the house, Callie had taken courage, and was "blessing her out." Katie knew, with vicious satisfaction, that she had but to show herself and Callie would stop. She was tempted to, but it seemed a useless exertion; it was enough to know that Callie was "yellow."

Zelda hung about the door, listening. Katie shot her a disapproving look.

"Get away from 'ere," she ordered irritably. "Go wash yo' face an' hands, an' I'll getcha some supper." A sharp sigh escaped her. "Guess it ain't any use waitin' f' Lathe an' 'e ol' man."

As Zelda passed her mother's room, the crucifix hanging above the bed caught her eye. In the dimness, the ivory Christ made a slim, tortured flame against the black cross. It seemed to speak gently out of the shabby room, to remind her what Katie, with bawdy cynicism, had admonished. And as she went into the bathroom and filled the washbasin, she said aloud, solemnly:

"God, why ain't men and wimmin good? . . . An', God, when I grow up, will I be good—like mama an' papa? . . . An' please, God, can I live in 'at nice house? It's such a nice house, God. . . ."

"Strange Moonlight"

CONRAD AIKEN (1889–1973)

Conrad Aiken was born at 503 Whitaker Street in Savannah and lived in his natal town until age eleven. After his parents' murder-suicide in 1901, he lived with an aunt in Massachusetts. Aiken studied at Harvard University with Heywood Broun, Walter Lippmann, Van Wyck Brooks, and T. S. Eliot, to whom he gave his poetry for criticism. His more than fifty books of fiction, poetry, autobiography, criticism, and drama earned him many awards, most notably a Pulitzer Prize in 1930 for his *Selected Poems* and a National Book Award in 1954 for his *Collected Poems*. Governor Jimmy Carter named him Georgia Poet Laureate in 1973. Aiken wintered in Savannah in the last years of his life in a row house at 230 East Oglethorpe Avenue, next door to his boyhood home, and it later became his full-time residence. Like his poem, *The Coming Forth By Day of Osiris Jones* (1931), and autobiographical essay, *Ushant* (1952), the short story "Strange Moonlight" (1925), reprinted here, recount his views of his hometown.

It had been a tremendous week—colossal. Its reverberations around him hardly yet slept—his slightest motion or thought made a vast symphony of them, like a breeze in a forest of bells. In the first place, he had filched a volume of Poe's tales from his mother's bookcase, and had had in consequence a delirious night in inferno. Down, down he had gone with heavy clangs about him, coiling spouts of fire licking dryly at an iron sky, and a strange companion, of protean shape and size, walking and talking beside him. For the most part, this companion seemed to be nothing but a voice and a wing—an enormous jagged black wing, soft and drooping like a bat's; he had noticed veins in it. As for the voice, it had been singularly gentle. If it was mysterious, that was no doubt because he himself was stupid. Certainly it had sounded placid and reasonable, exactly, in fact, like his father's explaining a problem in mathematics; but, though he had noticed the orderly and logical structure, and felt the inevitable approach toward a vast and beautiful or terrible conclusion, the nature and meaning of the conclusion itself always escaped him. It was as if, always, he had come just too late. When, for example, he had come at last to the black wall that inclosed the infernal city, and seen the arched gate, the voice had certainly said that if he hurried he would see, through the arch, a far, low landscape of extraordinary wonder. He had hurried, but it had been in vain. He had reached the gate, and for the tiniest fraction of an instant he had even glimpsed the wide green of fields and trees, a winding blue ribbon of water, and a gleam of intense light touching to brilliance some far object. But then, before he had time to notice more than that every detail in this fair landscape seemed to lead toward a single shining solution, a dazzling significance, suddenly the infernal rain, streaked fire and rolling smoke, had swept it away. Then the voice had seemed to become ironic. He had failed, and he felt like crying.

He had still, the next morning, felt that he might, if the opportunity offered, see that vision. It was always just round the corner, just at the head of the stairs, just over the next page. But other adventures had intervened. Prize-day, at school, had come upon him as suddenly as a thunderstorm—the ominous hushed gathering of the entire school into one large room, the tense air of expectancy, the solemn speeches, all had reduced him to a state of acute terror. There was something unintelligible and sinister about it. He had, from first to last, a peculiar physical sensation that something threatened him, and here and there, in the interminable vague speeches, a word seemed to have eyes and to stare at him. His prescience had been correct—abruptly his name had been called, he had walked unsteadily amid applause to the teacher's desk, had received a small black pasteboard box; and then had cowered in his chair again, with the blood in his temples beating like gongs. When it was over, he had literally run away—he didn't stop till he reached the park. There, among the tombstones (the park had once been a graveyard) and trumpet-vines, he sat on the grass and opened the box. He was dazzled. The medal was of gold, and rested on a tiny blue satin cushion. His name was engraved on it—yes, actually cut into the gold; he felt the incisions with his fingernail. It was an experience not wholly to be comprehended. He put the box down in the grass and detached himself from it, lay full length, resting his chin in his wrist, and stared first at a tombstone and then at the small gold object, as if to discover the relation between them. Humming-birds, tombstones, trumpet-vines, and a gold medal. Amazing. He unpinned the medal from its cushion, put the box in his pocket, and walked slowly homeward, carrying the small, live, gleaming thing between fingers and thumb as if it were a bee. This was an experience to be carefully concealed from mother and father. Possibly he would tell Mary and John. . . . Unfortunately, he met his father as he was going in the door, and was thereafter drowned, for a day, in a glory without significance. He felt ashamed, and put the medal away in a drawer, sternly forbidding Mary and John to look at it. Even so, he was horribly conscious of it—its presence there burned him unceasingly. Nothing afforded escape from it, not even sitting under the peach tree and whittling a boat.

II. The oddest thing was the way these and other adventures of the week all seemed to unite, as if they were merely aspects of the same thing. Everywhere lurked that extraordinary hint of the enigma and its shining solution. On Tuesday morning, when it was pouring with rain, and he and Mary and John were conducting gigantic military operations in the back hall, with hundreds of paper soldiers, tents, cannon, battleships, and forts, suddenly through the tall open window, a goldfinch flew in from the rain, beat wildly against a pane of glass, darted several times to and fro above their heads, and finally, finding the open window, flashed out. It flew to the peach tree, rested there for a moment, and then over the outhouse and away. He saw it rising and falling in the rain. This was beautiful—it was like the vision in the infernal city, like the medal in the grass. He found it impossible to go on with the Battle of Gettysburg and abandoned it to Mary and John, who instantly started to quarrel. Escape was necessary, and he went into his own room, shut the door, lay on his bed, and began thinking about Caroline Lee.

John Lee had taken him there to see his new air-gun and a bag of BB shot. The strange house was dim and exciting. A long winding dark staircase went up from near the front door, a clock was striking in a far room, a small beautiful statue of a lady, slightly pinkish, and looking as if it had been dug out of the earth, stood on a table. The wallpaper beside the staircase was rough and hairy. Upstairs, in the playroom, they found Caroline, sitting on the floor with a picture book. She was learning to read, pointing at the words with her finger. He was struck by the fact that, although she was extraordinarily strange and beautiful, John Lee did not seem to be aware of it and treated her as if she were quite an ordinary sort of person. This gave him courage, and after the air-gun had been examined, and the bag of BB shot emptied of its gleaming heavy contents and then luxuriously refilled, he told her some of the words she couldn't make out. "And what's this?" she had said—he could still hear her say it, quite clearly. She was thin, smaller than himself, with dark hair and large pale eyes, and her forehead and hands looked curiously transparent. He particularly noticed her hands when she brought her five-dollar goldpiece to show him, opening a little jewel box which had in it also a necklace of yellow beads from Egypt and a pink shell from Tybee Beach. She gave him the goldpiece to look at, and while he was looking at it put the beads round her neck. "Now, I'm an Egyptian!" she said, and laughed shyly, running her fingers to and fro over the smooth beads. A fearful temptation came upon him. He coveted the goldpiece, and thought that it would be easy to steal it. He shut his hand over it and it was gone. If it had been John's, he might have done so, but, as it was, he opened his hand again and put the goldpiece back in the box. Afterwards, he stayed for a long while, talking with John and Caroline. The house was mysterious and rich, and he hadn't at all wanted to go out of it, or back to his own humdrum existence. Besides, he liked to hear Caroline talking.

But although he had afterwards for many days wanted to go back to that house, to explore further its dim rich mysteriousness, and had thought about it a great deal, John hadn't again suggested a visit, and he himself had felt a curious reluctance about raising the subject. It had been, apparently, a vision that was not to be repeated, an incursion into a world that was so beautiful and strange that one was permitted of it only the briefest of glimpses. He had, almost, to reassure himself that the house was really there, and for that reason he made rather a point of walking home from school with John Lee. Yes, the house was there—he saw John climb the stone steps and open the huge green door. There was never a sign of Caroline, however, nor any mention of her; until one day he heard from another boy that she was ill with scarlet fever, and observed that John had stayed away from school. The news didn't startle or frighten him. On the contrary, it seemed just the sort of romantic privilege in which such fortunate people would indulge. He felt a certain delicacy about approaching the house, however, to see if the red quarantine sign had been affixed by the door, and carefully avoided Gordon Square on his way home from school. Should he write her a letter or send her a present of marbles? For neither action did there seem to be sufficient warrant. But he found it impossible to do nothing, and later in the afternoon, by a very circuitous route which took him past the county jail— where he was thrilled by actually seeing a prisoner looking out between the gray iron bars—he slowly made his way to Gordon Square and from a safe distance, more or less hiding himself behind a palmetto tree, looked for a long while at the wonderful house, and saw, sure enough, the red sign.

Three days later he heard that Caroline Lee was dead. The news stunned him. Surely it could not be possible? He felt stifled, frightened, and incredulous. In a way, it was just what one would expect of Caroline, but none the less he felt outraged. How was it possible for anyone, whom one actually knew, to *die*? Particularly anyone so vividly and beautifully remembered! The indignity, the horror, of death obsessed him. *Had* she actually died? He went again to Gordon Square, not knowing precisely what it was that he expected to find, and saw something white hanging by the green door. But if, as it appeared, it was true that Caroline Lee, somewhere inside the house, lay dead, lay motionless, how did it happen that he, who was so profoundly concerned, had not at all been consulted, had not been invited to come and talk with her, and now found himself so utterly and hopelessly and forever excluded—from the house, as from her? This was a thing which he could not understand. As he walked home, pondering it, he thought of the five-dollar goldpiece. What would become of it? Probably John would get it, and, if so, he would steal it from him. . . . All the same, he was glad he hadn't taken it.

To this reflection he came back many times, as now once more with the Battle of Gettysburg raging in the next room. If he had actually taken it, what a horror it would have been! As it was, the fact that he had resisted the temptation, restored the goldpiece to the box, seemed to have been a tribute to Caroline's beauty and strangeness. Yes, for nobody else would he have made the refusal—nobody on earth. But, for her, it had been quite simple, a momentary pang quickly lost in the pleasure of hearing her voice, watching her pale hands twisting the yellow beads, and helping her with her reading. "And what's this?" she had said, and "Now I'm an Egyptian!" . . . What was death that could put an end to a clear voice saying such things? . . . Mystery was once more about him, the same mystery that had shone in the vision of the infernal city. There was something beautiful which he could not understand. He had felt it while he was lying in the grass among the tombstones, looking at the medal; he had felt it when the goldfinch darted in from the rain and then out again. All these things seemed in some curious way to fit together.

III. The same night, after he had gone to bed, this feeling of enormous and complicated mystery came upon him again with oppressive weight. He lay still, looking from his pillow through the tall window at the moonlight on the white outhouse wall, for everything was extraordinarily near at hand if he could only find it. The mystery was like the finest of films, like the moonlight on the white wall. Surely, beneath it, there was something solid and simple. He heard someone walk across the yard, with steps that seemed astoundingly far apart and slow. The steps ceased, a door creaked. Then there was a cough. It was old Selena, the Negro cook, going out for wood. He heard the sticks being piled up, then the creak of the door again, and again the slow steps on the hard baked ground of the yard, æons apart. How did the peach tree look in the moonlight? Would its leaves be dark, or shiny? And the chinaberry tree? He thought of the two trees standing there motionless in the moonlight, and at last felt that he must get out of bed and look at them. But when he had reached the hall, he heard his mother's voice from downstairs, and he went and lay on the old sofa in the hall, listening. Could he have heard aright? His mother had just called his father "Boy!" Amazing!

"It's two parties *every* week, and sometimes three or four, that's excessive. You know it is."

"Darling, I *must* have *some* recreation!"

His father laughed in a peculiar angry way that he had never heard before—as strange, indeed, as his mother's tone had been.

"Recreation's all right," he said, "but you're neglecting your family. If it goes on, I'll have another child—that's all."

He got off the sofa and went softly down the stairs to the turn of the railing. He peered over the bannisters with infinite caution, and what he saw filled him with horror. His mother was sitting on his father's knee, with her arms about his neck. She was kissing him. How awful! . . . He couldn't look at it. What on earth, he wondered as he climbed back into bed, was it all about? There was something curious in the way they were talking, something not at all like fathers and mothers, but more like children, though he couldn't in the least understand it. At the same time, it was offensive.

He began to make up a conversation with Caroline Lee. She was sitting under the peach tree with him, reading her book. What beautiful hands she had! They were transparent, some-how, like her forehead, and her dark hair and large pale eyes delighted him. Perhaps she *was* an Egyptian!

"It must be nice to live in your house," he said.

"Yes, it's very nice. And you haven't seen half of it, either."

"No, I haven't. I'd like to see it all. I liked the hairy wallpaper and the pink statue of the lady on the table. Are there any others like it?"

"Oh, yes, lots and lots! In the secret room downstairs, where you heard the silver clock striking, there are fifty other statues, all more beautiful than that one, and a collection of clocks of every kind."

"Is your father very rich?"

"Yes, he's richer than anybody. He has a special carved ivory box to keep his collars in."

"What does it feel like to die—were you sorry?"

"Very sorry! But it's really quite easy—you just hold your breath and shut your eyes."

"Oh!"

"And when you're lying there, after you've died, you're really just pretending. You keep very still, and you have your eyes *almost* shut, but really you know everything! You watch the people and listen to them."

"But don't you want to talk to them, or get out of bed, or out of your coffin?"

"Well, yes, at first you do—but it's nicer than being alive."

"Why?"

"Oh, I don't know! You understand everything so easily!"

"How nice that must be!"

"It is."

"But after they've shut you up in a coffin and sung songs over you and carried you to Bonaventure and buried you in the ground, and you're down there in the dark with all that earth above you—isn't that horrible?"

"Oh, no! . . . As soon as nobody is looking, when they've all gone home to tea, you just get up and walk away. You climb out of the earth just as easily as you'd climb out of bed."

"That's how you're here now, I suppose."

"Of course!"

"Well, its very nice."

"It's lovely. . . . Don't I look just as well as ever?"

"Yes, you do."

There was a pause, and then Caroline said:

"I know you wanted to steal my goldpiece—I was awfully glad when you put it back. If you had asked me for it, I'd have given it to you."

"I like you very much, Caroline. Can I come to Bonaventure and play with you?"

"I'm afraid not. You'd have to come in the dark."

"But I could bring a lantern."

"Yes, you could do that."

. . . It seemed to him that they were no longer sitting under the peach tree, but walking along the white shell-road to Bonaventure. He held the lantern up beside a chinquapin tree, and Caroline reached up with her pale, small hands and picked two chinquapins. Then they crossed the little bridge, walking carefully between the rails on the sleepers. Mossy trees were all about them; the moss, in long festoons, hung lower and lower, and thicker and thicker, and the wind made a soft, seething sound as it sought a way through the gray ancient forest.

IV. It had been his intention to explore, the next morning, the vault under the mulberry tree in the park—his friend Harry had mentioned that it was open, and that one could go down very dusty steps and see, on the dark floor, a few rotted boards and a bone or two. At breakfast he enlisted Mary and John for the expedition; but then there were unexpected developments. His father and mother had abruptly decided that the whole family would spend the day at Tybee Beach. This was festive and magnificent beyond belief. The kitchen became a turmoil. Selena ran to and fro with sugar sandwiches, pots of deviled ham, cookies, hard-boiled eggs, and a hundred other things; piles of beautiful sandwiches were exquisitely folded up in shining, clean napkins, and the wicker basket was elaborately packed. John and Mary decided to take their pails with them, and stamped up and downstairs, banging the pails with the shovels. He himself was a little uncertain what to take. He stood by his desk wondering. He would like to take Poe's tales, but that was out of the question, for he wasn't supposed to have the book at all. Marbles, also, were dismissed as unsuitable. He finally took his gold medal out of its drawer and put it in his pocket. He would keep it a secret, of course.

All the way to the station he was conscious of the medal burning in his pocket. He closed his fingers over it, and again felt it to be a live thing, as if it were buzzing, beating invisible wings. Would his fingers have a waxy smell, as they did after they'd been holding a June bug, or tying a thread to one of its legs?

. . . Father carried the basket, Mary and John clanked their pails, everybody was talking and laughing. They climbed into the funny, undignified little train, which almost immediately was lurching over the wide, green marshes, rattling over red-iron bridges enormously complicated with girders and trusses. Great excitement when they passed the gray stone fort, Fort Pulaski. They'd seen it once from the river, when they were on the steamer going to the cotton islands. His father leaned down beside Mary to tell her about Fort Pulaski, just as a cloud shadow, crossing it, made it somber. How nice his father's smile was! He had never noticed it before. It made him feel warm and shy. He looked out at the interminable green marshes, the flying clouds of rice-birds, the channels of red water lined with red mud, and listened intently to the strange complex rhythm of the wheels on the rails and the prolonged melancholy wail of the whistle. How curious it all was! His mother was sitting opposite him, very quiet, her gray eyes turned absently toward the window. She wasn't looking at things—she was thinking. If she had been looking at things, her eyes would have moved to and fro, as Mary's were doing.

"Mother," he said, "did you bring our bathing suits?"

"Yes, dear."

The train was rounding a curve and slowing down. They had suddenly left the marshes and were among low sand dunes covered with tall grass. He saw a man, very red-faced, just staggering over the top of one of the dunes and waving a stick. . . . It was hot. They filed slowly off the train and one by one jumped down into the burning sand. How strange it was to walk in! They laughed and shrieked, feeling themselves helpless, ran and jumped, straddled up the steep root-laced sides of dunes and slid down again in slow, warm avalanches of lazy sand. Mother and father, picking their way between the dunes, walked slowly ahead, carrying the basket between them—his father pointed at something. The sunlight came down heavily like sheets of solid brass and they could feel the heat of the sand on their cheeks. Then at last they came out on the enormous white dazzling beach with its millions of shells, its black-and-white-striped lighthouse, and the long, long sea, indolently blue, spreading out slow, soft lines of foam, and making an interminable rushing murmur like trees in a wind.

He felt instantly a desire, in all this space and light, to run for miles and miles. His mother and father sat under a striped parasol. Mary and John, now barefooted, had begun laborious and intense operations in the sand at the water's edge, making occasional sallies into the sliding water. He began walking away along the beach close to the waves, keeping his eye out for any particularly beautiful shell, and taking great care not to step on jellyfish. Suppose a school of flying fish, such as he had seen from the ship, should swim in close to the beach and then, by mistake, fly straight up onto the sand? How delightful that would be! It would be almost as exciting as finding buried treasure, a rotten chest full of goldpieces and seaweed and sand. He had often dreamt of thrusting his hand into such a sea-chest and feeling the small, hard, beautiful coins mixed with sand and weed. Some people said that Captain Kidd had buried treasure on Tybee Beach. Perhaps he'd better walk a little closer to the dunes, where it was certainly more likely that treasure would have been hidden. . . . He climbed a hot dune, taking hold of the feathery grass, scraping his bare legs on the coarse leaves, and filling his shoes with warm sand. The dune was scooped at the top like a volcano, the hollow all ringed with tall, whistling grass, a natural hiding place, snug and secret. He lay down, made excessively smooth a hand's breadth of sand, then took the medal out of his pocket and placed it there. It blazed beautifully. Was it as nice as the five-dollar goldpiece would have been? He liked especially the tiny links of the little gold chains by which the shield hung from the pin-bar. If only Caroline could see it! Perhaps if he stayed here, hidden from the family, and waited till they had gone back home, Caroline would somehow know where he was and come to him as soon as it was dark. He wasn't quite sure what would be the shortest way from Bonaventure, but Caroline would know—certainly. Then they would spend the night here, talking. He would exchange his medal for the five-dollar goldpiece, and perhaps she would bring, folded in a square of silk, the little pink statute. . . . Thus equipped, their house would be perfect. . . . He would tell her about the goldfinch interrupting the Battle of Gettysburg.

V. The chief event of the afternoon was the burial of his father, who had on his bathing suit. He and Mary and John all excitedly labored at this. When they had got one leg covered, the other would suddenly burst hairily out, or an arm would shatter its mold, and his father would laugh uproariously. Finally they had him wholly buried, all except his head, in a beautiful smooth mound. On top of this they put the two pails, a lot of pink shells in a row, like the buttons of a coat, and a collection of seaweeds. Mother, lying under her parasol, laughed lazily, deliciously. For the first time during the day she seemed to be really happy. She

began pelting small shells at father, laughing in an odd, delightful, teasing way, as if she was a girl, and father pretended to be
furious. How exactly like a new grave it looked! It was singularly as Caroline had described it, for there he was all alive in it,
and talking, and able to get up whenever he liked. Mary and
John, seeing mother throw shells, and hearing her teasing laughter, and father's comic rage, became suddenly excited. They
began throwing things wildly—shells, handfuls of seaweed, and
at last sand. At this, father suddenly leapt out of his tomb, terri-
fying them, scattered his grave clothes in every direction, and
galloped gloriously down the beach into the sea. The upturned
brown soles of his feet followed him casually into a long, curl-
ing green wave, and then his head came up shaking like a dog's
and blowing water, and his strong white arms flashed slowly
over and over in the sunlight as he swam far out. How magnificent! . . . He would like to be able to do that, to swim out and
out and out, with a sea-gull close beside him, talking.

Later, when they had changed into their clothes again in the
salty-smelling wooden bathhouse, they had supper on the
veranda of the huge hotel. A band played, the colored waiters
bowed and grinned. The sky turned pink, and began to dim; the
sea darkened, making a far sorrowful sound; and twilight deepened slowly, slowly into night. The moon, which had looked like
a white thin shell in the afternoon, turned now to the brightest
silver, and he thought, as they walked silently toward the train,
of which they could see the long row of yellow windows, that
the beach and dunes looked more beautiful by moonlight that by
sunlight. . . . How mysterious the flooded marshes looked, too,
with the cold moon above them! They reminded him of something, he couldn't remember what. . . . Mary and John fell asleep
in the train; his father and mother were silent. Someone in the
car ahead was playing a concertina, and the plaintive sound
mingled curiously with the clacking of the rails, the rattle of
bridges, the long, lugubrious cry of the whistle. Hoo-o! Hoo-o!
Where was it they were going—was it to anything so simple as
home, the familiar house, the two familiar trees, or were they,

rather, speeding like a fiery comet toward the world's edge, to plunge out into the unknown and fall down and down forever?

No, certainly it was not to the familiar. . . . Everything was changed and ghostly. The long street, in the moonlight, was like a deep river, at the bottom of which they walked, making scattered, thin sounds on the stones, and listening intently to the whisperings of elms and palmettos. And their house, when at last they stopped before it, how strange it was! The moonlight, falling through the two tall swaying oaks, cast a moving pattern of shadow and light all over its face. Slow swirls and spirals of black and silver, dizzy gallops, quiet pools of light abruptly shattered, all silently followed the swishing of leaves against the moon. It was like a vine of moonlight, which suddenly grew all over the house, smothering everything with its multitudinous swift leaves and tendrils of pale silver, and then as suddenly faded out. He stared up at this while his father fitted the key into the lock, feeling the ghostly vine grow strangely over his face and hands. Was it in this, at last, that he would find the explanation of all that bewildered him? Caroline, no doubt, would understand it; she was a sort of moonlight herself. He went slowly up the stairs. But as he took the medal and a small pink shell out of his pocket, and put them on his desk, he realized at last that Caroline was dead.

"The King of the Birds"

FLANNERY O'CONNOR (1925–1964)

Flannery O'Connor was born and lived at 207 East Charlton Street on Savannah's Lafayette Square until age twelve. She was educated at Sacred Heart School at 209 East Thirty-eighth Street and St. Vincent's Academy at 207 East Liberty Street, both in Savannah, before attending what is now Georgia College, in Milledgeville, Georgia. She earned a master's degree from the University of Iowa. Her life was relatively short, her output of work small, and her range somewhat narrow. Yet O'Connor ranks as one of the immortals of American fiction. The piece presented below was originally published in *Holiday* magazine under the title "Living with a Peacock" (1961). It was collected in her posthumous reader of essays, lectures, and criticism, *Mystery and Manners* (1976). Although it does not illustrate her most recognized technique and most common theme—her use of violent or shocking imagery to jar her readers into recognition of an intensely Roman Catholic vision of God's redemption—it is illustrative of her extremely fine prose styling. O'Connor's novels include *Wise Blood* (1952) and *The Violent Bear It Away* (1960). Her letters were collected in *The Habit of Being* (1979), and her collected short stories won a posthumous National Book Award in 1971. Along with numerous other honors, O'Connor won the O. Henry Award three times.

When I was five, I had an experience that marked me for life. Pathé News sent a photographer from New York to Savannah to take a picture of a chicken of mine. This chicken, a buff Cochin Bantam, had the distinction of being able to walk either forward or backward. Her fame had spread through the press, and by the time she reached the attention of Pathé News, I suppose there was nowhere left for her to go—forward or backward. Shortly after that she died, as now seems fitting.

If I put this information in the beginning of an article on pea-cocks, it is because I am always being asked why I raise them, and I have no short or reasonable answer.

From that day with the Pathé man I began to collect chickens. What had been only a mild interest became a passion, a quest. I had to have more and more chickens. I favored those with one green eye and one orange or with overlong necks and crooked combs. I wanted one with three legs or three wings but nothing in that line turned up. I pondered over the picture in Robert Ripley's book, *Believe It or Not*, of a rooster that had survived for thirty days without his head; but I did not have a scientific temperament. I could sew in a fashion and I began to make clothes for chickens. A gray bantam named Colonel Eggbert wore a white pique coat with a lace collar and two buttons in the back. Apparently Pathé News never heard of any of these other chickens of mine; it never sent another photographer.

My quest, whatever it was actually for, ended with peacocks. Instinct, not knowledge, led me to them. I had never seen or heard one. Although I had a pen of pheasants and a pen of quail, a flock of turkeys, seventeen geese, a tribe of mallard ducks, three Japanese silky bantams, two Polish Crested ones, and sev-eral chickens of a cross between these last and the Rhode Island Red, I felt a lack. I knew that the peacock had been the bird of Hera, the wife of Zeus, but since that time it had probably come down in the world—the Florida *Market Bullet* advertised three-year-old peafowl at sixty-five dollars a pair. I had been quietly reading these ads for some years when one day, seized, I circled an ad in the *Bulletin* and passed it to my mother. The ad was for a peacock and hen with four seven-week-old peabiddies. "I'm going to order me those," I said.

My mother read the ad. "Don't those things eat flowers?" she asked.

"They'll eat Startena like the rest of them," I said.

The peafowl arrived by Railway Express from Eustis, Florida, on a mild day in October. When my mother and I arrived at the station, the crate was on the platform and from one end of it protruded a long, royal-blue neck and crested head. A white line above and below each eye gave the investigating head an expression of alert composure. I wondered if this bird, accustomed to parade about in a Florida orange grove, would readily adjust himself to a Georgia dairy farm. I jumped out of the car and bounded forward. The head withdrew.

At home we uncrated the party in a pen with a top on it. The man who sold me the birds had written that I should keep them penned up for a week or ten days and then let them out at dusk at the spot where I wanted them to roost; thereafter, they would return every night to the same roosting place. He had also warned me that the cock would not have his full complement of tail feathers when he arrived; the peacock sheds his tail in late summer and does not regain it fully until after Christmas.

As soon as the birds were out of the crate, I sat down on it and began to look at them. I have been looking at them ever since, from one station or another, and always with the same awe as on that first occasion; though I have always, I feel, been able to keep a balanced view and an impartial attitude. The peacock I had bought had nothing whatsoever in the way of a tail, but he carried himself as if he not only had a train behind him but a retinue to attend it. On that first occasion, my problem was so greatly what to look at first that my gaze moved constantly from the cock to the hen to the four young peachickens, while they, except that they gave me as wide a berth as possible, did nothing to indicate they knew I was in the pen.

Over the years their attitude toward me has not grown more generous. If I appear with food, they condescend, when no other way can be found, to eat it from my hand; if I appear without food, I am just another object. If I refer to them as "my" peafowl, the pronoun is legal, nothing more. I am the menial, at the beck and squawk of any feathered worthy who wants service. When I first uncrated these birds, in my frenzy I said, "I want so many of them that every time I go out the door, I'll run into one." Now every time I go out the door, four or five run into me—and give me only the faintest recognition. Nine years have passed since my first peafowl arrived. I have forty beaks to feed. Necessity is the mother of several other things besides invention.

For a chicken that grows up to have such exceptional good looks, the peacock starts life with an inauspicious appearance. The peabiddy is the color of those large objectionable moths that flutter about light bulbs on summer nights. Its only distinguished features are its eyes, a luminous gray, and a brown crest which begins to sprout from the back of its head when it is ten days old. This looks at first like a bug's antennae and later like the head feathers of an Indian. In six weeks green flecks appear in its neck, and in a few more weeks a cock can be distinguished from a hen by the speckles on his back. The hen's back gradually fades to an even gray and her appearance becomes shortly what it will always be. I have never thought the peahen unattractive, even though she lacks a long tail and any significant decoration. I have even once or twice thought her more attractive than the cock, more subtle and refined; but these moments of boldness pass. The cock's plumage requires two years to attain its pattern, and for the rest of his life this chicken will act as though he designed it himself. For his first two years he might have been put together out of a rag bag by an unimaginative hand. During his first year he has a buff breast, a speckled back, a green neck like his mother's, and a short gray tail. During his second year he has a black breast, his sire's blue neck, a back which is slowly turning the green and gold it will remain; but still no long tail. In his third year he reaches his majority and acquires his tail. For the rest of his life—and a peachicken may live to be thirty-five—he will have nothing better to do than manicure it, furl and unfurl it, dance forward *and backward* with it spread, scream when it is stepped upon, and arch it carefully when he steps through a puddle.

Not every part of the peacock is striking to look at, even when he is full-grown. His upper wing feathers are a striated black and white and might have been borrowed from a Barred Rock fryer; his end wing feathers are the color of clay; his legs are long, thin, and iron-colored; his feet are big; and he appears to be wearing the short pants now so much in favor with playboys in the summer. These extend downward, buff-colored and sleek, from what might be a blue-black waistcoat. One would not be disturbed to find a watch chain hanging from this, but none does. Analyzing the appearance of the peacock as he stands with his tail folded, I find the parts incommensurate with the whole. The fact is that with his tail folded, nothing but his bearing saves this bird from being a laughingstock. With his tail spread, he inspires a range of emotions, but I have yet to hear laughter.

The usual reaction is silence, at least for a time. The cock opens his tail by shaking himself violently until it is gradually lifted in an arch around him. Then, before anyone has had a chance to see it, he swings around so that his back faces the spectator. This has been taken by some to be insult and by others to be whimsey. I suggest it means only that the peacock is equally well satisfied with either view of himself. Since I have been keeping peafowl, I have been visited at least once a year by first-grade school children, who learn by living. I am used to hearing this group chorus as the peacock swings around, "Oh, look at his underwear!" This "underwear" is a stiff gray tail, raised to support the larger one, and beneath it a puff of black feathers that would be suitable for some really regal woman—a Cleopatra or a Clytemnestra—to use to powder her nose.

When the peacock has presented his back, the spectator will usually begin to walk around him to get a front view; but the peacock will continue to turn so that no front view is possible. The thing to do then is to stand still and wait until it pleases him to turn. When it suits him, the peacock will face you. Then you will see in a green-bronze arch around him a galaxy of gazing, haloed suns. This is the moment when most people are silent.

"Amen! Amen!" an old Negro woman once cried when this happened, and I have heard many similar remarks at this moment that show the inadequacy of human speech. Some people whistle; a few, for once, are silent. A truck driver who was driving up with a load of hay and found a peacock turning before him in the middle of the road shouted, "Get a load of that bastard!" and braked his truck to a shattering halt. I have never known a strutting peacock to budge a fraction of an inch for truck or tractor or automobile. It is up to the vehicle to get out of the way. No peafowl of mine has ever been run over, though one year one of them lost a foot in the mowing machine.

Many people, I have found, are congenitally unable to appreciate the sight of a peacock. Once or twice I have been asked what the peacock is "good for"—a question which gets no answer from me because it deserves none. The telephone company sent a lineman out one day to repair our telephone. After the job was finished, the man, a large fellow with a suspicious expression half hidden by a yellow helmet, continued to idle about, trying to coax a cock that had been watching him to strut. He wished to add this experience to a large number of others he had apparently had. "Come on now, bud," he said, "get the show on the road, upsy-daisy, come on now, snap it up, snap it up."

The peacock, of course, paid no attention to this.

"What ails him?" the man asked.

"Nothing ails him," I said. "He'll put it up terreckly. All you have to do is wait."

The man trailed about after the cock for another fifteen minutes or so; then, in disgust, he got back in his truck and started off. The bird shook himself and his tail rose around him.

"He's doing it!" I screamed. "Hey, wait! He's doing it!"

The man swerved the truck back around again just as the cock turned and faced him with the spread tail. The display was perfect. The bird turned slightly to the right and the little planets above him hung in bronze, then he turned slightly to the left and they were hung in green. I went up to the truck to see how the man was affected by the sight.

He was staring at the peacock with rigid concentration, as if he were trying to read fine print at a distance. In a second the cock lowered his tail and stalked off.

"Well, what did you think of that?" I asked.

"Never saw such long ugly legs," the man said. "I bet that rascal could outrun a bus."

Some people are genuinely affected by the sight of a peacock, even with his tail lowered, but do not care to admit it; others appear to be incensed by it. Perhaps they have the suspicion that the bird has formed some unfavorable opinion of them. The peacock himself is a careful and dignified investigator. Visitors to our place, instead of being barked at by dogs rushing from under the porch, are squalled at by peacocks whose blue necks and crested heads pop up from behind tufts of grass, peer out of bushes, and crane downward from the roof of the house, where the bird has flown, perhaps for the view. One of mine stepped from under the shrubbery one day and came forward to inspect a carful of people who had driven up to buy a calf. An old man and five or six white-haired, barefooted children were piling out the back of the automobile as the bird approached. Catching sight of him they stopped in their tracks and stared, plainly hacked to find this superior figure blocking their path. There was silence as the bird regarded them, his head drawn back at its most majestic angle, his folded train glittering behind him in the sunlight.

"Whut is thet thang?" one of the small boys asked finally in a sullen voice.

The old man had got out of the car and was gazing at the peacock with an astounded look of recognition. "I ain't seen one of them since my grandaddy's day," he said, respectfully removing his hat. "Folks used to have 'em, but they don't no more."

"Whut is it?" the child asked again in the same tone he had used before.

"Churren," the old man said, "that's the king of the birds!"

The children received this information in silence. After a minute they climbed back into the car and continued from there to stare at the peacock, their expressions annoyed, as if they disliked catching the old man in the truth.

The peacock does most of his serious strutting in the spring and summer when he has a full tail to do it with. Usually he begins shortly after breakfast, struts for several hours, desists in the heat of the day, and begins again in the late afternoon. Each cock has a favorite station where he performs every day in the hope of attracting some passing hen; but if I have found anyone indifferent to the peacock's display, besides the telephone lineman, it is the peahen. She seldom casts an eye at it. The cock, his tail raised in a shimmering arch around him, will turn this way and that, and with his clay-colored wing feathers touching the ground, will dance forward and backward, his neck curved, his beak parted, his eyes glittering. Meanwhile the hen goes about her business, diligently searching the ground as if any bug in the grass were of more importance than the unfurled map of the universe which floats nearby.

Some people have the notion that only the peacock spreads his tail and that he does it only when the hen is present. This is not so. A peafowl only a few hours hatched will raise what tail he has—it will be about the size of a thumbnail—and will strut and turn and back and bow exactly as if he were three years old and had some reason to be doing it. The hens will raise their tails when they see an object on the ground which alarms them, or sometimes when they have nothing better to do and the air is brisk. Brisk air goes at once to the peafowl's head and inclines him to be sportive. A group of birds will dance together, or four or five will chase one another around a bush or tree. Sometimes one will chase himself, end his frenzy with a spirited leap into the air; and then stalk off as if he had never been involved in the spectacle.

Frequently the cock combines the lifting of his tail with the raising of his voice. He appears to receive through his feet some shock from the center of the earth, which travels upward through him and is released: *Eee-ooo-ii! Eee-ooo-ii!* To the melancholy this sound is melancholy and to the hysterical it is hysterical. To me it has always sounded like a cheer for an invisible parade.

The hen is not given to these outbursts. She makes a noise like a mule's bray—*heehaw, heehaw, aa-aawww*—and makes it only when necessary. In the fall and winter, peafowl are usually silent unless some racket disturbs them; but in the spring and summer, at short intervals during the day and night, the cock, lowering his neck and throwing back his head, will give out with seven or eight screams in succession as if this message were the one on earth which needed most urgently to be heard.

At night these calls take on a minor key and the air for miles around is charged with them. It has been a long time since I let my first peafowl out at dusk to roost in the cedar trees behind the house. Now fifteen or twenty still roost there; but the original old cock from Eustis, Florida, stations himself on top of the barn, the bird who lost his foot in the mowing machine sits on a flat shed near the horse stall, there are others in the trees by the pond, several in the oaks at the side of the house, and one that cannot be dissuaded from roosting on the water tower. From all these stations calls and answers echo through the night. The peacock perhaps has violent dreams. Often he wakes and screams "Help! Help !" and then from the pond and the barn and the trees around the house a chorus of adjuration begins:

> *Lee-yon lee-yon,*
> *Mee-yon mee-yon!*
> *Eee-e-yoy eee-e-yoy!*
> *Eee-e-yoy eee-e-yoy!*

The restless sleeper may wonder if he wakes or dreams.

It is hard to tell the truth about this bird. The habits of any peachicken left to himself would hardly be noticeable, but multiplied by forty, they become a situation. I was correct that my peachickens would all eat Startena; they also eat everything else. Particularly they eat flowers. My mother's fears were all borne out. Peacocks not only eat flowers, they eat them systematically, beginning at the head of a row and going down it. If they are not hungry, they will pick the flower anyway, if it is attractive, and let it drop. For general eating they prefer chrysanthemums and roses. When they are not eating flowers, they enjoy sitting on top of them, and where the peacock sits he will eventually fashion a dusting hole. Any chicken's dusting hole is out of place in a flower bed, but the peafowl's hole, being the size of a small crater, is more so. When he dusts he all but obliterates the sight of himself with sand. Usually when someone arrives at full gallop with the leveled broom, he can see nothing through the cloud of dirt and flying flowers but a few green feathers and a beady, pleasure-taking eye.

From the beginning, relations between these birds and my mother were strained. She was forced, at first, to get up early in the morning and go out with her clippers to reach the Lady Bankshire and the Herbert Hoover roses before some peafowl had breakfasted upon them; now she has halfway solved her problem by erecting hundreds of feet of twenty-four-inch-high wire to fence the flower beds. She contends that peachickens do not have enough sense to jump over a low fence. "If it were a high wire," she says, "they would jump onto it and over, but they don't have sense enough to jump over a low wire."

It is useless to argue with her on this matter. "It's not a challenge," I say to her; but she has made up her mind.

In addition to eating flowers, peafowl also eat fruit, a habit which has created a lack of cordiality toward them on the part of my uncle, who had the fig trees planted about the place because he has an appetite for figs himself. "Get that scoundrel out of that fig bush!" he will roar, rising from his chair at the sound of a limb breaking, and someone will have to be dispatched with a broom to the fig trees.

Peafowl also enjoy flying into barn lofts and eating peanuts off peanut hay; this has not endeared them to our dairyman. And as they have a taste for fresh garden vegetables, they have often run afoul of the dairyman's wife.

The peacock likes to sit on gates or fence posts and allow his tail to hang down. A peacock on a fence post is a superb sight. Six or seven peacocks on a gate are beyond description; but it is not very good for the gate. Our fence posts tend to lean in one direction or another and all our gates open diagonally.

In short, I am the only person on the place who is willing to underwrite, with something more than tolerance, the presence of peafowl. In return, I am blessed with their rapid multiplication. The population figure I give out is forty, but for some time now I have not felt it wise to take a census. I had been told before I bought my birds that peafowl are difficult to raise. It is not so, alas. In May the peahen finds a nest in some fence corner and lays five or six large buff-colored eggs. Once a day, thereafter, she gives an abrupt *hee-haa-awww!* and shoots like a rocket from the nest. Then for half an hour, her neck ruffled and stretched forward, she parades around the premises, announcing what she is about. I listen with mixed emotions.

In twenty-eight days the hen comes off with five or six moth-like, murmuring peachicks. The cock ignores these unless one gets under his feet (then he pecks it over the head until it gets elsewhere), but the hen is a watchful mother and every year a good many of the young survive. Those that withstand illnesses and predators (the hawk, the fox, and the opossum) over the winter seem impossible to destroy, except by violence.

A man selling fence posts tarried at our place one day and told me that he had once had eighty peafowl on his farm. He cast a nervous eye at two of mine standing nearby. "In the spring, we couldn't hear ourselves think," he said. "As soon as you lifted your voice, they lifted their'n, if not before. All our fence posts wobbled. In the summer they ate all the tomatoes off the vines. Scuppernongs went the same way. My wife said she raised her flowers for herself and she was not going to have them eat up by a chicken no matter how long his tail was. And in the fall they shed them feathers all over the place anyway and it was a job to clean up. My old grandmother was living with us then and she was eighty-five. She said, 'Either they go, or I go.'"

"Who went?" I asked."

"We still got twenty of them in the freezer," he said.

"And how," I asked, looking significantly at the two standing nearby; "did they taste?"

"No better than any other chicken," he said, "but I'd a heap rather eat them than hear them."

I have tried imagining that the single peacock I see before me is the only one I have, but then one comes to join him; another flies off the roof, four or five crash out of the crepe-myrtle hedge; from the pond one screams and from the barn I hear the dairy-man denouncing another that has got into the cowfeed. My kin are given to such phrases as, "Let's face it."

I do not like to let my thoughts linger in morbid channels, but there are times when such facts as the price of wire fencing and the price of Startena and the yearly gain in peafowl all run uncontrolled through my head. Lately I have had a recurrent dream: I am five years old and a peacock. A photographer has been sent from New York and a long table is laid in celebration. The meal is to be an exceptional one: myself. I scream, "Help! Help!" and awaken. Then from the pond and the barn and the trees around the house, I hear that chorus of jubilation begin:

> *Lee-yon lee-yon,*
> *Mee-yon mee-yon!*
> *Eee-e-yoy eee-e-yoy!*
> *Eee-e-yoy eee-e-yoy!*

I intend to stand firm and let the peacocks multiply, for I am sure that, in the end, the last word will be theirs.

from "A Matter of Vocabulary"

JAMES ALAN MCPHERSON (1943–)

James Alan McPherson was born and raised in Savannah. He was educated at Morris Brown College, Harvard Law School, and the Writer's Workshop at the University of Iowa, where he currently teaches. McPherson won the Pulitzer Prize in 1978 for his short story collection *Elbow Room*. He has been the recipient of a MacArthur Foundation Award (1981), a Guggenheim Fellowship (1972–1973), and grants from the *Atlantic Monthly* (1969), the Rockefeller Foundation (1970), and the National Institute of Arts and Letters (1970). McPherson became a contributing editor of the *Atlantic* in 1969. He published *Crabcakes* in 1998. The following excerpt from his short story, "A Matter of Vocabulary," appeared in the *Atlantic* in February 1969. It draws on his experience working at the M&M Supermarket in Savannah before leaving for college in Atlanta. In this selection, thirteen-year-old Thomas Brown hears from his bed the plaintive wails of the Barefoot Lady, a neighborhood homeless woman who forages in garbage cans and cries in front of the Herbert A. Jones Funeral Parlor. In previous scenes Thomas's mother has told him he must get on the redeemed Right Side with those to be resurrected on Judgement Day and the reader has been introduced to the Brown's West Indian neighbor Mrs. Quick, a practitioner of voodoo.

Both Thomas and his brother worked at the F&F Supermarket, owned by Milton and Sarah Feinburg. Between the two of them they made a good third of a man's salary. Thomas had worked himself up from carry-out boy and was now in the Produce Department, while his brother, who was still new, remained a carry-out boy. Thomas enjoyed the status he had over the other boys. He enjoyed not having to be put outside on the street like the boys up front whenever business was slow and Milton Feinburg wanted to save money. He enjoyed being able to work all week after school while the boys up front had to wait for weekends when there would be sales and a lot of shoppers. He especially liked becoming a regular boy because then he had to help mop and wax the floors of the store every Sunday morning and could not go to church. He knew that his mother was not pleased when he had been taken into the mopping crew because now he had an excuse not to attend church. But being on the crew meant making an extra three dollars, and he knew that she was pleased with the money. Still, she made him pray at night, and especially on Sunday.

His job was bagging potatoes. Every day after school and all day Saturday he would come into the air-conditioned produce room, put on a blue smock, take a fifty-pound sack of potatoes off a huge stack of sacks, slit open the sack and let the potatoes fall into a shopping cart next to a scale, and proceed to put them into five- and ten-pound plastic bags. It was very simple; he could do it in his sleep. Then he would spend the rest of the day bagging potatoes and looking out the big window, which separated the produce room from the rest of the store, at the customers. They were mostly white, and after almost a year of this type of work, he began to realize why they did not speak to him in the street. And then he did not mind going to the bathroom, knowing, when he did go, that all of them had to go, just as he did, in the secret places they called home. Some of them had been speaking to him for a long time now, on this business level, and he had formed some small friendships grounded in this.

He knew Richard Burke, the vet who had a war injury in his back and who walked funny. Richard Burke was the butcher's helper, who made hamburger from scraps of fat and useless meat cuttings and red powder in the back of the produce room, where the customers could not see. He liked to laugh when he mixed the red powder into the ground white substance, holding gobs of the soft stuff up over the big tub and letting it drip, and then dunking his hands down into the tub again.

Sometimes he threw some of it at Thomas, in fun, and Thomas had to duck. But it was all in fun, and he did not mind it except when the red-and-white meat splattered the window and Thomas had to clean it off so that his view of the customers, as he bagged potatoes, would not be obstructed.

He thought of the window as a one-way mirror which allowed him to examine the people who frequented the store without being noticed himself. His line of vision covered the entire produce aisle, and he could see everyone who entered the store making their way down that aisle, pushing their carts and stopping, selectively, first at the produce racks, then at the meat counter, then off to the side, beyond his view, to the canned goods and frozen foods and toilet items to the unseen right of him. He began to invent names for certain of the regular customers, the ones who came at a special time each week. One man, a gross fat person with a huge belly and the rough red neck and face of a farmer, who wheeled one shopping cart before him while he pulled another behind, Thomas called Big Funk because, he thought, no one could be that fat and wear the same faded dungaree suit each week without smelling bad. Another face he called the Rich Old Lady, because she was old and pushed her cart along slowly, with a dignity shown by none of the other shoppers. She always bought parsley, and once, when Thomas was wheeling a big cart of bagged potatoes out to the racks, he passed her and for just an instant smelled a perfume that was light and very fine to smell. It did not linger in the air like most other perfumes he had smelled. And it seemed to him that she must have had it made just for her and that it was so expensive that it stayed with her body and would never linger behind her when she had passed a place. He liked that about her. Also, he had heard from the boys up front that she would never carry her own groceries to her house, no more than half a block from the store, and that no matter how small her purchases were, she would require a boy to carry them for her and would always tip a quarter. Thomas knew that there was always a general fight among the carry-out boys whenever she checked out. Such a fight seemed worthy of her. And after a while of watching her, he would make a special point of wheeling a cart of newly bagged potatoes out to the racks when he saw her come in the store, just to smell the perfume. But she never noticed him either.

"You make sure you don't go over on them scales now," Miss Hester, the Produce manager, would remind him whenever she saw him looking for too long a time out the window. "Mr. Milton would get mad if you went over ten pounds."

Thomas always knew when she was watching him and just when she would speak. He had developed an instinct for this from being around her. He knew, even at that age, that he was brighter than she was; and he thought that she must know it too because he could sense her getting uncomfortable when she stood in back of him in her blue smock, watching him lift the potatoes to the plastic bag until it was almost full, and then the plastic bag up to the gray metal scale, and then watching the red arrow fly across to ten. Somehow it almost always stopped wavering at exactly ten pounds. Filling the bags was automatic with him, a conditioned reflex, and he could do it quite easily, without breaking his concentration on things beyond the window. And he knew that this bothered her a great deal; so much so, in fact, that she continually asked him questions, standing by the counter or the sink behind him, to make him aware that she was in the room. She was always nervous when he did not say anything for a long time, and he knew this too, and was sometimes silent, even when he had something to say, so that she could hear the thud and swish of the potatoes going into the bag, rhythmically, and the sound of the bags coming down on the scale, and after a second, the sound, sputtering and silken, of the tops of the bags being twisted and sealed in the tape machine. Thomas liked to produce these sounds for her because he knew she wanted something more.

Miss Hester had toes like the Barefoot Lady, except that her nails were shorter and cleaner, and she was white. She always wore sandals, was hefty like a man, and had hair under her arms. Whenever she smiled he could not think of her face or smile as that of a woman. It was too tight. And her laugh too loud and came from too far away inside her. And the huge crates of lettuce or cantaloupes or celery she could lift very easily made her even less a woman. She had short red-brown hair, and whenever he got very close to her it smelled funny, unlike the Rich Old Lady's smell.

"What you daydreamin' about so much all the time?" she asked him once.

"I was just thinking," he had said.

"What about?"

"School and things."

He could sense her standing behind him at the sink, letting her hands pause on the knife and the celery she was trimming.

"You gonna finish high school?"

"I guess so."

"You must be pretty smart, huh, Tommy?"

"No. I ain't so smart," he said.

"But you sure do think a lot."

"Maybe I just daydream," Thomas told her.

Her knife had started cutting into the celery branches again. He kept up his bagging.

"Well, anyway, you a good worker. You a good boy, Tommy."

Thomas did not say anything.

"Your brother, he's a good worker too. But he ain't like you though."

"I know," he said.

"He talks a lot up front. All the cashiers like him."

"Eddie likes to talk," Thomas said.

"Yeah," said Miss Hester. "Maybe he talks too much. Mr. Milton and Miss Sarah are watchin' him."

"What for?"

She stopped cutting the celery again. "I dunno," she said. "I reckon it's just that he talks a lot."

On Saturday nights Thomas and his brother would buy the family groceries in the F&F Supermarket. Checking the list made out by his mother gave Thomas a feeling of responsibility that he liked. He was free to buy things not even on the list, and he liked this too. They paid for the groceries out of their own money, and doing this, with some of the employees watching, made an especially good feeling for Thomas. Sometimes they bought ice cream or a pie or something special for their mother. This made them exceptional. The other black employees, the carry-out boys, the stock clerks, the bag boys, would have no immediate purpose in mind for their money beyond eating a big meal on Saturday nights or buying whiskey from a bootlegger because they were minors, or buying a new pair of brightly colored pants or pointed shoes to wear into the store on their days off, as if to make all the other employees see that they were above being, at least on this one day, what they were all the rest of the week.

Thomas and Edward did not have days off; they worked straight through the week, after school, and they worked all day on Saturdays. But Edward did not mop on Sunday mornings, and he still went to church. Thomas felt relieved that his brother was almost certain to be on the Right Side on That Day because he had stayed in the church and would never be exposed to all the stealing the mopping crew did when they were alone in the store on Sunday mornings with Lloyd Bailey, the manager, who looked the other way when they took packages of meat and soda and cartons of cigarettes. Thomas suspected that Mr. Bailey was stealing bigger things himself, and that Milton Feinburg, a big-boned Jew who wore custom-made shoes and smoked very expensive, bad-smelling green cigars, knew just what everyone was stealing and was only waiting for a convenient time to catch certain people. Thomas could see it in the way he smiled and rolled the cigar around in his mouth whenever he talked to certain of the bigger stealers; and seeing this, Thomas never stole. At first he thought it was because he was afraid of Milton Feinburg, who had green eyes that could look as deep as Mrs. Quick's; and then he thought that he could not do it because the opportunity only came on Sunday mornings when, if he had never told that first lie, he should have been in church.

Both Milton and Sarah Feinburg liked him. He could tell it by the way Sarah Feinburg always called him up to her office to clean. There were always rolls of coins on her desk, and scattered small change on the floor when he swept. But he never touched any of it. Instead, he would gather what was on the floor and stack the coins very neatly on her desk. And when she came back into the office after he had swept and mopped and waxed and dusted and emptied her wastebaskets, Miss Sarah Feinburg would smile at Thomas and say: "You're a good boy, Tommy."

He could tell that Milton Feinburg liked him because whenever he went to the bank for money he would always ask Thomas to come out to the car to help him bring the heavy white sacks into the store, and sometimes up to his office. On one occasion, he had picked Thomas up on the street, after school, when Thomas was running in order to get to work on time. Milton Feinburg had driven him to the store.

"I like you," Milton Feinburg told Thomas. "You're a good worker."

Thomas could think of nothing to say.

"When you quit school, there'll be a place in the store for you."

"I ain't gonna quit school," Thomas had said.

Milton Feinburg smiled and chewed on his green cigar. "Well, when you finish high school, you can come on to work full time. Miss Hester says you're a good worker."

"Bagging potatoes is easy," said Thomas.

Milton Feinburg smiled again as he drove the car. "Well, we can get you in the stock room, if you can handle it. Think you can handle it?"

"Sure," said Thomas. But he was not thinking of the stock room and unloading trucks and stacking cases of canned goods and soap in the big, musty, upstairs storeroom. He was thinking of how far away he was from finishing high school and how little that long time seemed to matter to Milton Feinburg.

Thomas was examining a very ugly man from behind his window one afternoon when Miss Hester came into the produce room from the front of the store. As usual, she stood behind him. And Thomas went on with his work and watching the very ugly man. This man was bald and had a long thin red nose that twisted down unnaturally, almost to the level of his lower lip. The man had no chin, only three layers of skin that lapped down onto his neck like a red-cloth necklace. Barney Benns, one of the stock clerks who occasionally passed through the produce room to steal an apple or a banana, had christened the very ugly man "Do-funny," just as he had christened Thomas "Little Brother" soon after he had come to the job. Looking at Do-funny made Thomas sad; he wondered how the man had lost his chin. Perhaps, he thought, Do had lost it in the war, or perhaps in a car accident. He was trying to picture just how Do-funny would look after the accident when he realized that his chin was gone forever, when Miss Hester spoke from behind him.

"Your brother's in a lotta trouble up front," she said.

Thomas turned to look at her. "What's the matter?"

Miss Hester smiled at him in that way she had, like a man. "He put a order in the wrong car."

"Did the people bring it back?"

"Yeah," she said "But some folks is still missin' their groceries. They're out there now mad as hell."

"Was it Eddie lost them?"

"Yeah. Miss Sarah is mad as hell. Everybody's standin' round up there."

He looked through the glass window and up the produce aisle and saw his brother coming toward him from the front of the store. His brother was untying the knot in his blue smock when he came in the swinging door of the air-conditioned produce room. His brother did not speak to him but walked directly over to the sink next to Miss Hester and began to suck water from the black hose. He looked very hot, but only his nose was sweating. Thomas turned completely away from the window and stood facing his brother.

"What's the matter up front, Eddie?" he said.

"Nothing," his brother replied, his jaws tight.

"I heard you put a order in the wrong car and the folks cain't git it back," said Miss Hester.

"Yeah," said Eddie.

"Why you tryin' to hide back here?" she said.

"I ain't tryin' to hide," said Eddie.

Thomas watched them and said nothing.

"You best go on back up front there," Miss Hester said.

At that moment Miss Sarah Feinburg pushed through the door. She had her hands in the pockets of her blue sweater and she walked to the middle of the small, cool room and glared at Edward Brown. "Why are you back here?" Miss Sarah Feinburg asked Edward.

"I come back for some water."

"You know you lost twenty-seven dollars' worth of groceries up there?"

"It wasn't my fault," said Eddie.

"If you kept your mind on what you're supposed to do this wouldn't have happened. But no. You're always talking, always smiling around, always running your mouth with everybody."

"The people who got the wrong bags might bring them back," Eddie said. His nose was still sweating in the cool room. "Evidently somebody took my cart by mistake."

"*Evidently! Evidently!*" said Sarah Feinburg. "Miss Hester, you should please listen to *that! Evidently.* You let them go to school, and they think they know everything. *Evidently*, you say?"

"Yeah," said Eddie. Thomas saw that he was about to cry.

Miss Hester was still smiling like a man.

Sarah Feinburg stood with her hands in her sweater pockets and braced on her hips, looking Eddie in the face. Eddie did not hold his eyes down, and Thomas felt really good but sad that he did not.

"You get back up front," said Sarah Feinburg. And she shoved her way through the door again and out of the cool produce room.

"Evidently, evidently, that sure was funny," said Miss Hester when the fat woman was halfway down the produce aisle. "Lord, was she mad. I ain't never seen her git so mad."

Neither Thomas nor Eddie said anything.

Then Miss Hester stopped smiling. "You best get on back up front, Eddie."

"No," said Eddie. "I'm goin' home."

"You ain't quittin'?" said Miss Hester.

"Yeah."

"What for?"

"I dunno. I just gotta go home."

"But don't your folk need the money?"

"No," Eddie said.

He took off his blue smock and laid it on the big pile of fifty-pound potato sacks. "I'm goin' home," he said again. He did not look at his brother. He walked through the door, and slowly down the produce aisle and their out the front door, without looking at anything at all.

Then Thomas went over to the stack of unbagged potatoes and pushed the blue smock off the top sack and into a basket on the floor next to the stack. He picked up a fifty-pound sack and lugged it over to the cart and tore it open with his fingers, spilling its contents of big and small dirty brown potatoes into the cart. He could feel Miss Hester's eyes on him, on his arms and shoulders and hands as they moved. He worked very quickly and looked out the window into the store. Big Funk was supposed to come this afternoon. He had finished seven five-pound bags before Miss Hester moved from where she had been standing behind him, and he knew she was about to speak.

"You going to quit too, Tommy?"

"No," he said.

"I guess your folk *do* need the money now, huh?"

"No," he said. "We don't need the money."

She did not say anything else. Thomas was thinking about Big Funk and what could be done with the time if he did not come. He did not want to think about his brother or his mother or the money, or even the good feeling he got when Milton Feinburg saw them buying the Saturday-night groceries. If Big Funk did not come, then perhaps he could catch another glimpse of Dofunny before he left the store. The Rich Old Lady would not come again until next week. He decided that it would be necessary to record the faces and bodies of new people as they wandered, selectively, with their shopping carts beyond the big window glass. He liked it very much now that none of them ever looked up and saw him watching. That way he did not have to feel embarrassed or guilty. That way he would never have to feel compelled to nod his head or move his mouth or eyes, or make any indication of a greeting to them. That way he would never have to feel bad when they did not speak back.

In his bed that night, lying very close to his brother's back, Thomas thought again very seriously about the Judgment Day and the Left Side. Now, there were certain people he would like to have with him on the Left Side on That Day. He thought about church and how he could never go back because of the place where the deacons had made him tell his first great lie. He wondered whether it was because he did not want to have to go back to church on Sunday mornings that he had not quit. He wondered if it was because of the money or going to church or because of the window that he had not walked out of the store with his brother. That would have been good: the two of them walking out together. But he had not done it, and now he could not make himself know why. Suddenly, in the night, he heard the Barefoot Lady under the blue-and-white Herbert A. Jones neon light, screaming.

"*Mr. Jones! I love you, Mr. Jones!*"

But the sound did not frighten him now. He pushed against his brother's back.

"Eddie? *Eddie.*"

"Yeah?"

"Wonder why she does it?"

"I dunno."

"I wonder why," he said again.

Eddie did not answer. But after the sound of the woman came again, his brother turned over in the bed and said to Thomas:

"You gonna quit?"

"No."

"Why not? We could always carry papers."

"I dunno. I just ain't gonna quit. Not now."

"Well *I* ain't goin' back. I'll go back in there one day when I'm rich. I'm gonna go in and buy everything but hamburger."

"Yeah," said Thomas. But he was not listening to his brother. *"Mr. Jones! I love you, Mr. Jones!"*

"And I'm gonna learn all the big words in the world too," his brother went on. "When I go back in there I'm gonna be talking so big that fat old Miss Sarah won't even be able to understand me."

"That'll be good," said Thomas. But he was thinking to himself now.

"You'll see," said Eddie. "I'll do it too."

But Thomas did not answer him. He was waiting for the sound to come again.

"Mr. Jones! I love you, Mr. Jones!"

And then he knew why the Barefoot Lady came to that place almost every night to cry when there was no one alive in the building to hear or care about her sound. He felt what she must feel. And he knew now why the causes of the sound had bothered him and would always bother him. There was a word in his mind now, a big word, that made good sense of her sound and the burning, feeling thing he felt inside himself. It was all very clear, and now he understood that the Barefoot Lady came in the night, not because she really loved Mr. Jones, or because he had once buried someone for her for free, or even because she liked the blue-and-white neon light. She came in the night to scream because she, like himself, was in misery, and did not know what else to do.

from *Beulah Land*

LONNIE COLEMAN (1920–1982)

Lonnie Coleman was educated at the University of Alabama. Coleman worked as a magazine editor, most notably at *Collier's* and *McCall's*, and was awarded prizes for his short stories by the *Atlantic Monthly* and *Mademoiselle* magazines. With the successful publication of *Beulah Land* (1973), the first in a trilogy consisting of *Look Away, Beulah Land* (1977) and *The Legacy of Beulah Land* (1980), Coleman devoted himself exclusively to fiction writing. However, his earlier novels, *Clara* (1952) and *Ship's Company* (1955), had been better received by critics. His last novel, *Mark* (1981), is the story of a young writer who realizes and later accepts his homosexuality. Coleman died of cancer in Savannah in 1982. Following is the first chapter of *Beulah Land*.

Savannah was one of the South's great ports, acting as goods and culture broker between the land mass behind it and the world beyond its shores. Many roads led from Savannah to other, smaller centers. One of these, a town called Highboro, fifty-three miles northwest of Savannah, had its own roads leading to other, smaller towns, and to farms and plantations. The main road out of Highboro was red clay with veins of blue-black. In fair weather it was hard as stone to the hoofs of horses and mules, but when rain fell in more than a brief shower, it became a slippery bog. Two roads led from the main road to the plantation called Beulah Land.

A back road ran through cotton and corn fields that claimed the choicest of the sixteen hundred acres, through the neck of a wood of cypress, oak, and pine, watered by a creek. The road ended with barns, smoke houses, chicken yards, water wells, a kitchen garden, and the forty cabins that housed the Negroes who worked the plantation. These numbered a hundred and

fifty, more or less, depending on births and deaths rather than
sales, and were never referred to by Arnold Kendrick as slaves,
although the phrase he used, "my people," spoke ownership as
well as a kinship.

The front road to Beulah Land curved over a hill through an
orchard of plum and peach trees until it settled to a straight, dignified avenue bordered by cedar and oak trees all the way to the
front door of the house that was its end and reason for being.
The house was a large one, built mostly of wood, and owed
whatever distinction it possessed to size rather than design.

Fronting it was a broad porch with squared columns lifting the
full two-story height of the house to support the roof. The house
was painted gray, its shutters dark green. The work buildings out
in back had been left to weather gray and were a softer, warmer
shade than the house. The slave cabins were whitewashed, as
were the lower trunks of the trees nearest the big house.

The front porch opened directly into a wide center hall, off
which, on either side, were living and dining rooms. The stairway
to the next floor was in the front left living room, leaving the center hall a clear passage for whatever breezes to the kitchens and
store room where Deborah Kendrick spent much of her time.

Although Lovey, who was about her own age, acted as her
deputy, it was Deborah who had trained, or retrained, the house
servants and who indeed knew how all the male hands on the
place were occupied: who plowed and hoed, who chopped and
sawed, and who cared for which animals. Deborah and Lovey
were a strange pairing, if anyone thought about it, but no one did,
because they had been for so long the pair who ran the house.

Deborah was an erect, quick-stepping woman whose face,
because it seemed ever to be scrutinizing and weighing, held no
softness or humor. Her dark red hair was parted in the middle
and caught at the back of her neck in a bun that grew heavier
and larger every year.

Lovey was shorter than her mistress and ampler in bosom and
behind, but equally quick-stepping. Unlike Deborah, she laughed
frequently. Her gestures, like her laugh, were quick and nervous,

by temperament rather than reason, for Lovey was afraid of nothing and no one. Her independence of spirit was the thing Deborah had first noticed about her when she came to live at Beulah Land following her marriage to Arnold in 1800.

In the bill of sale that had brought her to Beulah Land a year before Deborah's arrival, Lovey's name was given as Laverne La Vey, but this was too fancy to be endured by her new fellows, who soon converted La Vey into Lovey and dropped Laverne altogether.

Laverne La Vey had been plump and attractive, and her temper delighted the other slaves, for their only entertainment was in each other and the turn of events on the plantation. One after another the unattached men made approaches to the girl, who slapped them away like so many flies, declaring that she had no time or mind for men, that, in fact, she despised every one of them and was determined that her distant but eventual grave be virginal. This was taken as an amusing display of spirit, even rebellion, since it was understood that a woman's function, in addition to performing whatever work she was set to, was to bear the children who would replace her and her man, when their time of usefulness was over. Besides, it was so obviously absurd. How could a girl as pretty and lively as Laverne hope to hold out against the pressing ardor of the young men?

Yet hold out she did for two years until, where youth had failed, age prevailed in the person of a quiet man named Ezra. He was the blacksmith, but more than that. Jobs were assigned, of course, but a man's aptitudes governed his eventual occupations. Ezra's understanding of animals other than horses and mules grew as the years passed until, in addition to being blacksmith, he was Beulah Land's animal doctor. He remembered every remedy he heard about, discarding the ones that failed to work for him and venturing to experiment with local herbs. Ezra's word was law on the treatment of all animal ills at Beulah Land, and, in time, since the bodies of men and women have much in common with those of beasts, he was consulted on human ills by the other slaves, and sometimes by the Kendricks too; and he began to be called, inevitably, Doctor.

Ezra's knowledge was held in awe and superstition by his fellow slaves. It was supposed that he knew even more than he did, and field and house gossip made legend of his spells and predictions, although his predictions were always based on clever diagnosis, and he had nothing at all to do with spells.

His attendance on the ill meant that he was sometimes present at deaths, and this led to further duties of "laying out" the dead for burial. Treating thus with the dead made him a further object of awe and superstition, set him apart. It might not have been so had he married, but he had not at the time Laverne La Vey was brought to live and work at Beulah Land, when he was near forty and had long been considered one of those whose concerns turned them away from an interest in women. Ezra was, in truth, lonely, in spite of the busy life he led. The rare times there was no call on his services he spent fishing on the creekbanks or sitting in the cabin that he tended himself. He had not even a pet dog or cat, for when every animal is a man's concern, he is unlikely to single out one for special attention.

Ezra along with the others noted Laverne's prettiness and her temper, and found himself pleased as well as amused by her when, alone in his cabin at night, he thought of her—something he had heard her say that day, her laugh, a shout of sudden, transient rage.

Lovey could not say when she first began to notice Ezra, but when she did, it was as though she had always known and trusted him. By that time she had been picked as special helper by the new bride and mistress. Since most of her waking hours were spent with, or within call of, Deborah Kendrick, and since Arnold Kendrick often found himself consulting with Ezra when the work day was done and he and Deborah drew closer for night company, so Lovey and Ezra became accustomed to each other and found themselves easy together.

On more than one dark night Ezra escorted Lovey from the big house to the cabin she shared with Widow Jane and her ugly unmarried daughters, Posie and Buttercup. When he saw that she accepted him as a familiar, that is, that she could be still in his presence, evidently feeling no need to strain and buck and break away as she did in the presence of others, he began to give her such things as were in his power to give: a perfect peach, a nicely trimmed quill to pick her teeth, and once a remedy for earache made of crushed camphor leaves and oil of cloves.

As she grew aware of him, Lovey knew what had happened and what would happen, and to her credit she did not tease the man with vagaries and protestations. Her awareness showing in her eyes emboldened Ezra to speak; and when she listened quietly, to take her hand; and when she did not withdraw, the thing was quickly settled between them.

Deborah and Arnold saw them married in the living room of the big house one Sunday in September 1801. Ezra's cabin became Lovey's, and together Lovey and Ezra were those closest to the Kendricks of all who dwelled at Beulah Land. Before her marriage, which to her raucous delight astonished the other plantation hands, Lovey had been in a position of growing, if undefined, power. After it, Ezra's own maturity extenuating her youth, she was recognized as the mistress of the house—after the Mistress.

Lovey was honest to the bone; it would not have occurred to her to be otherwise; it was part of her independence. Never shy, she found perfectly natural her new role as household harrier. She abominated dirt and laziness and understood that they came together in the persons of bad workers; so her duty was clear to her. She harried, she scolded, she trotted about seeing that work was properly done. Deborah found ease and comfort in her noisiness and nervous good humor. The work got done, and its accomplishment was the satisfaction Lovey took and gave. The girls and women who worked under her supervision resented her, of course, and occasionally, briefly, hated her. But they could not hate her long, because even the dullest of them saw that she was as just as she was relentless. Deborah might now and then choose to appear not to see a piece of slovenly work for what it was; Lovey, never. The house was hers. It would be clean.

And to comfort the sullen and the slovenly, Lovey offered one ridiculous flaw: she was a bad cook. Every other woman on the place took pride in her ability to cook certain dishes better than others could or did, for herself and her family, sometimes for the Kendricks. But Lovey knew and admitted her failing. She said herself that if she stepped through a kitchen door where cake was baking, the cake would fall. Laughing, she declared that the sound of her voice soured cream, encouraged rice to stick and burn. Her not being able to cook, and her generous appreciation of the good cooking of others, made her almost, sometimes popular.

from *A Lion's Share*

MARK STEADMAN (1930–)

> Mark Steadman took his bachelor's degree from Emory University and earned both a master's degree and a doctorate at Florida State University. His collection of twelve gothic tales, *McAfee County: A Chronicle* (1971), was followed by *A Lion's Share* (1975), set in his wife's hometown of Savannah. The following selection from *A Lion's Share*, "Kate," is part of a cycle of stories that moves from comedy to tragedy as it begins and ends with different characters' reactions to the funeral of a minor high school football star. The story takes place in one of the "little" squares of Savannah's northeast quadrant, diminished in size and status from their central city counterparts.

Kate left Johnny Curran—they left each other, against God's will—after eight years of marriage, when Jack was six years old. Johnny loved her to come home to. He really did. But the longer they were married, the more he drank like an Irishman. And the more he drank like an Irishman, the less he came home. There were some days—sometimes runs of three and four days—when she didn't see him at all, though the Lighthouse Bar was only four blocks away from the house on Warren Square. In October of 1935 he was away for a week. The sixth day went over Kate's limit, so she walked out on him.

Kate was phlegmatic in a fashion that could have been taken for patience, but the world had always appeared to her to be a certain way, and sitting around waiting six days for Johnny to come home didn't fit in with her sense of the proper disposition of things. That wasn't the kind of a marriage she had in mind, and she was never one to put up with a way of the world that wasn't to her liking.

So she moved out. Without nagging, and without discussing it with him—Kate was never much of a talker with those she had her deepest feelings for. Just—he came home and she wasn't there. Gone. With Jack and the few pieces of furniture she had brought into the house when they had gotten married. Pinned to the pillow of their bed was a note: "Enough is enough." The last words that ever passed between them.

It was a hard move that she had to make, because the Church was into her very deep, and she knew it was her immortal soul that was at stake. The family—except for her brother Donald—never forgave her for it. Nor did she ask them to. She took her husband's neglect for a long time without complaining about it. But finally, Johnny—the way he behaved—was more than she could bear, or thought she ought to, whether God expected it of her or not.

Her father died the year after she broke off her marriage, though they were never sure that was the cause of it. She went to the funeral, standing at the back with Jack, then leaving afterward without trying to speak to any of them. Kate was Mr. Lynch's favorite child, and his greatest disappointment. He never came to see her after she walked out on Johnny. The two or three times they met on the street he crossed to the other side without speaking. He didn't live to see her marry Gault Reilley. Which was just as well, or so the family thought. "It would have killed him for sure," said Jane, her ugly sister.

Kate wouldn't try to see any of them after the divorce, the more so since they had all opposed the marriage in the first place. Though she would dress Jack up and send him around to go to mass with them on Sundays.

She got a job with the Central of Georgia Railroad, in the payroll department, which is where she met Gault Reilley. They were married the year after the divorce from Johnny became final. After that, any kind of reconciliation with the family was out of the question. She never visited them, and they never visited her. They wouldn't have been able to talk about the divorce or the marriage, and there wasn't anything else to talk about. So she and Reilley went their own way, though the family was keeping up with them right along. When Susy was born, her sister Jane sent her a sympathy card with a black border on it.

Donald dropped around from time to time—usually for meals and a place to sleep when he was drying out. He brought her some of the news of her mother and Jane, but he didn't see much of her other brothers and sisters himself.

It was a willful family, and they all had a lot of what used to be called character, but Kate had the best backbone of the lot. Her marriage to Johnny was a kind of culmination of the whole tendency of her life up to that point, and the family's opposition to him was a great part of her interest in him to begin with—though after she got started she loved him mostly for herself. With a kind of blind tenacity that was beyond both explanation and understanding.

Her father wouldn't have him in the house at first, and Johnny was scared of the older man—who was also bigger. Later, when it got to be clear that his patriarchal will was going to be thwarted anyway, Mr. Lynch would go off into the bedroom upstairs the times Johnny came around, and Mrs. Lynch had to let him into the house to see Kate.

Mr. Lynch went to the wedding. The family argued him into that because of the way it would look if he didn't, though Kate wouldn't have anything to do with it—passing her plans for the wedding along to her sister Jane, who carried them back to the family. They got him to the church, but he tied his tie crooked deliberately, and wouldn't speak to say he was giving his daughter away when the time came. He just stepped back and sat down on the pew beside his wife.

The reception cost him a thousand dollars, and was held at the house. He didn't go to it himself, but after all the guests had arrived he came down from the second-floor bedroom in his shirt sleeves and got a bottle of Jameson's from the sideboard in the dining room. He opened it with flourishes, standing there in the roomful of guests, and took a long pull straight out of the bottle. Then he took it back upstairs with him without speaking.

Kate had been raised in a house on Washington Square, with fourteen-foot ceilings and windows that rose ten feet, starting at the floor. Her father was six feet five inches tall, two of her brothers were six feet four and a half, and Donald was six feet six. Her mother was five feet five, but the girls all got their growing genes from the father's side, though two of them looked like Mrs. Lynch in the face. Kate was the oldest and the biggest at five feet nine and a half inches and 155 pounds. Her dark hair was curly, different from the rest of the family, whose hair was dark and straight. Between her two front teeth was a gap, which she got from her father and passed on to her children. She wasn't a pretty woman, but she had a vitality about her that was appealing to certain kinds of men.

After they were married, Kate and Johnny lived in a house on Warren Square—two blocks away from the Lynches. They had the first-floor rooms and the use of the yard—another old house with fourteen-foot ceilings and windows up to the cornice at the ten-foot mark.

After she left Johnny, she moved into the ground floor of a slightly newer house near the Big Park, on Waldburg Street. It had twelve-foot ceilings, and bay windows on the back side, with panes of curved glass in them. She lived there for ten years, until after she sent Jack out of town to school. Then she and Reilley bought the house on Avalon Street in the Marshoaks project.

It was the first time she had ever had a whole house to herself, but most of the Marshoaks bungalow would have fitted into the living room of the place on Washington Square, and she had to make herself think about it to get used to the diminished proportions. The bedrooms were nine by eleven and eight by ten and a half. The living room was ten by seventeen, including the dining alcove at the end. The kitchen was so small that she had to back through the swinging door into the dining alcove to open the door of the refrigerator. And when she did baking and had to open the door of the oven, she banged her rear end on the cabinet under the sink.

Gault Reilley was a small, pink and gray marshmallow of a man, two inches shorter than Kate, and a total retreat from everything she had known before in the way of dimensions. The house was to a scale that suited him well enough, but it pinched and cramped her at first, and she had to go through a period of adjustment—pulling in on her gestures, and making sure she didn't make sudden movements—though she liked the coziness even from the first. Whenever she wasn't thinking about it, something got broken. Now and then she would begin to feel like the walls were closing in on her, and that if she tried to run away out the front door the whole house would stick to her like the carapace of a snail, and she would carry it off on her back.

They had to give up on floor lamps altogether. And Reilley, who was good at fixing things and handy around the house, got living room lamps with wooden bases, which he screwed down to the end tables so Kate wouldn't knock them off.

Eventually she settled into the coziness and really got to liking it. She and Reilley were happy together, and she learned to move with enough caution to keep the breakage down to a level that they could afford.

There had been a leak under the kitchen floor in front of the sink, and the flooring had rotted out. When Kate washed dishes at the sink, the spongy feeling of the floor made her nervous. Reilley didn't want to go under the house in the crawl space to repair the joists—the crawl space was only eighteen inches high, and very dark and spidery, with a soggy, damp smell to it, placenta-like, as if something fork-tongued and scaly had dropped into life down there. But he got a piece of plywood and covered it with linoleum that almost matched the kitchen floor, then nailed it over the rotten place so she wouldn't feel like she was going through when she stood there. He offered to take a turn at washing the dishes, but Kate wouldn't let him do it. Even though they were both working, she kept the woman things for herself. Reilley looked after the maintenance, which he was very good at and enjoyed.

Around the house Kate went barefoot, because she was a little sensitive about being so much taller than Reilley. But he never seemed to mind. When there were just the two of them, after Susy got married and moved out, he called her his "big hunk of woman." Which always made her shoot him with her gap-toothed smile. When she was standing on the plywood at the sink, she was nearly three inches taller than he was. He liked to watch her through the kitchen door and would come into the kitchen and hug her when she was doing the dishes, tucking his gray-fringed bald head under her chin. "You big hunk of woman," he would say.

Jack's death came down on Kate very hard—harder than anything that had happened to her since her father died.

They weren't seeing much of him at the time, but he was her firstborn, and the boy. Reilley liked him, too—he got along with big people—but, of course, it didn't come over him the way it did Kate, because he only got to know Jack well the one year he had been in the house with them, 1947–1948, when he had been at Boniface. But it upset him the way Kate took it. It upset them both.

Kate was the kind to hold it in, but the night and the day after Jack died she was having to let it out. Her crying was like a man's—whole-framed and shuddery. It took her over so much that she couldn't stand up to do it. All day long she sat around the house that way, sobbing big pumping sobs that made the floors shake, and tilted the pictures on the walls. Reilley didn't know what to do for her, and he had to sit on the side and watch. Every now and then she would pull herself together long enough to move from the chair to the couch, or from the couch to the bed. But then it would come over her again, and she would collapse in a heap, and the sobbing would start up once more.

Susy came over as soon as she had gotten her husband off to work. But she was pregnant and having morning sickness very bad. Seeing her mother that way upset her and made her sicker than ever. She stayed for about an hour, trying to get Kate to eat something and pull herself together. But she couldn't get through to her mother any more than Reilley could, so she gave up and left—afraid that too much of it might do some kind of damage to the baby.

It might have gone on longer than it did. But late Thursday afternoon Kate saw the spider, and the spider stopped it.

She was afraid of spiders. In fact, there were a lot of things she was afraid of, but spiders were one of the things she was afraid of most. They went up near the head of a list which she had made and hung on the cabinet in the kitchen. Spiders sent her into a tizzy. So did frogs, lizards, snakes, rats, cats, birds, and big cockroaches. (Cockroaches are too common in Savannah to stay upset about as a regular thing if you live there. Everybody has to put up with them. Most of the city cockroaches are little bitty things, and know how to behave themselves. When you turn on the kitchen light, they will run away under the sink, or hide in the woodwork. But their country cousins that sometimes come in from the woods are another story. They are humdingers. Monsters up to three inches long, with wings. They can't fly very well, but that's just a liability and no comfort at all, since they might just as well buzz right up your nose trying to get away. It would be a lot better if they were ace fliers, and could go just where they wanted to go.)

Kate had uncomfortable feelings about some abstract things, too, like high places and going to sleep in the dark. But mostly she was afraid of things that were really there, animals that could move in and out of the spaces around her. Seeing them sent her into a tizzy, and she wasn't the tizzying sort, because of her size.

So she tried to get on top of it by making a list of all the things that scared her from a list she found in a *Reader's Digest* article which gave the real medical names. The list in the article was a very long one, and it was comforting for her to see all of the other things that she wasn't afraid of.

She put up her list on the cabinet in the kitchen where she could see it every day, and maybe get used to the things she had written on it. It didn't really work, but it made her feel better about them in a theoretical way—when none of them were around where she could see them. Maybe it worked a little.

GOD MADE FEARFUL THINGS
Arachnephobia-Spiders
Batrachophobia-Frogs

Saurophobia-Lizards
Rodentiaphobia-Rats and Mice
Ailurophobia-Cats
Aviaphobia-Birds
Blattidaephobia-Cockroaches (big)
Acrophobia-High Places
Claustrophobia-Close Places
Achluophobia-Dark Places

After she hung it up, Reilley put stars beside Ophidiophobia, Arachnephobia, and Claustrophobia. Then he put a star at the bottom of the page, and beside it wrote, "Me Too!"

Seeing the spider—it had gotten into the bathtub and was trying to climb out—brought her back into herself in a strong familiar way, stopping the sobbing.

She came out of the bathroom and into the living room where Reilley sat slumped in a chair. "There's a spider in the tub," she said. It was the first everyday thing she'd said in over nineteen hours, and Reilley looked up at her from the chair. He was worn out over it himself, and the familiar sound of her voice was strange to him.

She stood in the doorway looking at him, biting her lower lip, clenching it in her teeth until it turned white, bulging out of the gap in the front

For a minute he looked at her. "I'm sorry," he said. Since they had gotten the news, it was the first time he had been able to get at her to let her know how he felt about it.

She looked at him and nodded. Then she went into the kitchen and began fixing supper.

He went into the bathroom and ran hot water in the tub to kill the spider.

"It's the weather makes them come into the house," he said when he came into the kitchen. "Squeezes them the same as us."

They hadn't finished eating when Donald knocked, then slammed open the front door into the living room. Although it was basic to his personality, being a fireman also had something to do with the way he always came into the house—like he was coming to put out a fire. Shoving in the door so that it would bounce off the wall on the backswing, shaking the house and making the dust rise out of the rugs. Just being a Lynch had a lot to do with it. Donald was the biggest of Kate's brothers, bigger than the father had been.

Reilley knew Donald needed the whole doorway to be able to get into the house. What he couldn't figure out was the violence of it.

They had talked it over a number of times, he and Kate. "I wonder what he'd do if we ever locked it on him?" she said. "Get an ax and chop it down?"

Sometimes they would just sit and think about why he did it.

"Was he like that at home?"

"He moved strong. We all did. Of course, we had more room there. It was an old house, and they put them together pretty solid in those days. Donald was the biggest."

Donald's visits not only made Reilley nervous, they also cost him money. But since Donald was the only one of the family who came around at all, he didn't feel he ought to say anything. Still, just the way Donald opened the front door set them back five or ten dollars right to begin with. And what he did to Kate's lamps and china and knickknacks and things once he got inside made Reilley's breathing go smothery and turned him red in the face. Also, Kate tended to forget herself and move around too much when he was there. Though she would complain and carry on about it very big after Donald had gone, when Reilley added it all up for her.

When they both got excited and started moving together, Reilley didn't like to stay in the living room with them at all, but would go stand in the kitchen door where he would be out of the way.

He didn't like to be that way about it, but inevitably Donald's visits took shape as a column of figures inside Reilley's head. Joyful spending was one thing, and he was blithe enough about shedding his hard-earned cash when he could think of it as bringing back heart's ease and gladness. But his work in the pay-roll department of the Central disposed him to a very dollary view of waste and destruction, and, since Reilley literally paid for them, Donald's visits had to be figured out in terms of profit and loss. Always considering that he was the only one of Kate's blood relations who would have anything to do with her.

The most expensive visit they ever had from Donald came after the St. Patrick's Day parade in 1949, when he blew in very excited from the green Irish whiskey and the brass band music of the Irish-American Friendly Society. He turned over the dining room table chasing Kate around it, and broke four place settings of her Wedgewood china. Then, before they could get him anchored into Reilley's chair, he stepped on the Atwater-Kent radio, and crushed the right lens of Reilley's reading glasses. It came to $83.36.

This time the splintery sound of the door coming open, and the way the house shook on the backswing, lit up the double-entry sheets inside Reilley's head, and he knew like it was a vision that a new record was going to be set. Nothing broke, because by now everything was either screwed down or broken already. But it jumped the radio off the station it was on, and dropped the top seat of the toilet in the bathroom.

"Kate!" Donald had a high blurry voice, with a sound in the middle of it like air escaping from a tire. "Have you heard, Kate? . . ." he said. "Jack's dead."

They knew what he was going to say, but they didn't know what to answer him. Kate kept on eating, but Reilley put down his fork and watched her.

"Yes," she said, not very loud.

"Jack's *dead*. . . . Kate?" he said. "Jack got killed last night. Where's *Kate*?" He stumbled into the kitchen, flinging the swinging door open and catching it when it bounced off the refrigerator. He had to crouch to get through the doorway with his fireman's bill cap on.

"Jack's dead, Kate . . ." he said, trailing off, looking down at them sitting at the table. He leaned against the open door and took off his bill cap slowly, holding it over his left breast and bowing his head slightly. "It is my duty to inform you . . ." he said, looking down at the floor.

"I said . . ." she held on to it, ". . . yes . . ." She looked at Reilley, then up at Donald.

He was still looking down at the floor. Up to now, he had been working along at getting out his message without paying any attention to them at all, the way they were taking it. The main thing was for him to lay down the burden he was carrying.

He was standing very erect, except for his head being bowed. For a long time he stood that way, then he rocked his head up slowly, pulling it back until he stood at attention, staring into the wall above their heads. "Jack's dead," he said, finishing it off, "Kate. . . ."

His face was a handsome face, but there was a gone-away look on it. Like the face of a half-wit—or of a man who is going to die soon, but not right away. His eyelids were droopy, folding down over eyes so black they seemed to be all pupil—or no pupil at all, just plain blank holes burned into his head. The skin had a painted-on white color—the color of an old woman's breast, with the same blue undertone from the veins just below the skin. Darker blue around the sockets of his eyes.

Across his left eyebrow and the bridge of his nose there was a scar, dead white against the blue-white of his face. The knife that had made it was in Donald's pocket—he kept it for a souvenir. The man it had belonged to was dead—which was something that still came up now and then around the firehouse barracks. Down there a real fair-fight killing was something that tended to have a very long conversational life.

"He was a good boy," Donald said, drawing himself up to attention to speak, and looking over their heads at the wall. "A . . . good . . . boy." The words came out one at a time, as if he had memorized them.

"Sit down and have some supper," said Reilley.

Donald looked at Kate, nodding his head downward. "How's she . . . taking it?" he said.

"I know about it already," she said. "I'm all right." She looked up at him standing by the refrigerator. "You want something to eat?"

"Sit down," said Reilley.

"You don't have something to drink?" he said, not sitting down. Kate looked up at him. "We're not holding a wake," she said. "Yes," he said. He ran his tongue over his lips slowly. "A little of the hair of the hound . . ." he said. "A *drop* of something . . ."

His lips were pale, but clearly defined—thin. "It certainly would . . ." he said.

Kate got up and started to clear away the supper dishes. "I'll do the dishes," said Reilley. She didn't answer him, but took his plate, then started to run the water in the sink."

"You can have something to *eat*," she said, speaking to Donald. "I'm not going to put any more whiskey in you.

Donald was sitting very erect in the straight-backed kitchen chair. He ran his tongue over his lips again. "A brew?" he said.

Kate turned to the sink and cut off the water. "I'll do the dishes," she said. "You two go in the living room."

Reilley looked up at her, then at Donald. Without getting up out of his chair, he reached over and opened the door of the refrigerator, taking out two cans of Miller's beer. "The church key's in the drawer," he said, pointing. "Give us a glass," he said to Kate.

She looked at Donald, then opened the cabinet. "One's all he gets," she said, putting the glasses on the table.

Donald tilted the can and the glass together, pouring the beer down the side to kill the head. He drank half the glass of beer, then he put it on the table in front of him and wiped his mouth with the back of his hand. Reilley was salting his, shaking the salt out into his left hand, then taking it up in pinches between his right index finger and thumb. The grains made diving trails of bubbles in the glass, foaming the beer on top.

"It ruins the taste," said Donald, looking across the table at him. Reilley looked up, then back at the glass. "I like to watch it," he said, taking another pinch and dropping it into the glass, fluttering his finger against his thumb. "It doesn't make that much difference in the taste."

"It makes it flat out."

Reilley looked up at him. "I never noticed that it made any difference," he said.

They both watched the salt grains making strings of bubbles in the glass.

Donald was sitting at the table with one hand on his glass of beer, the other in his lap. "There wasn't a priest," he said after a while. "He was dead when we dug him out. There wasn't time for a priest."

Kate stopped moving her hands in the sink. For a minute she stood there without saying anything. "They told me that," she said.

Donald twirled the glass in his hand, rotating it between his thumb and index finger. "Mother says he won't go to heaven," he said. He unfolded his eyelids, glancing up at her. "Jane says he's going to hell." He paused. "Mother didn't say that," he said. "Jane was the one said he was going to hell."

Kate didn't say anything. Reilley looked up at her, then back across the table at Donald.

"They said you were hateful to God for what you did," he said. "Leaving Johnny and going in with Reilly." He took a drink of the beer, emptying the glass. "Mother said that, too," he said.

Reilley looked across the table at him. Sitting down, they were more of a height. "Horseshit," he said. He said it as respectfully as he could, with the table between them. "They never even saw me."

"You know how they are," said Donald. "Just the two of them in that big house." He poured the rest of the beer into the glass. "When a priest says 'shit,' they both got to stoop and groan."

"It's nothing to do with you, Reilley," said Kate. "It's me."

"It's the priests," said Donald. "Mother's old and Jane's ugly. Just right for the bastards."

Reilley centered his glass on the place mat. "I wouldn't believe that Jack is going to hell," he said. He didn't look up at Kate. "I just wouldn't believe that."

"God does fearsome things . . ." she said. She had her back to them, looking out the window over the sink.

Donald drank down the rest of the beer. "They've got her by the short hairs, too," he said, talking to Reilley. "They know how to work the women all right. They kicked her soul out of the church, but they still got hold of her goddamn ass." He looked up at her, then back at the table. "God didn't put him in Hull Street Tuesday night," he said, holding the empty beer can upended over the glass. "He took himself in there." He put down the beer can and held the glass up to his mouth, holding it high to get the last drops out of the bottom. "It was too tight. When the wall came down, there wasn't any place to go." He held up the can between the thumb and index finger of his right hand, then he squeezed and the can folded in on itself with a snapping sound. He put the can on the table. "There wasn't any place to go," he said again. He looked at the can on the table. "Maybe *God* sent him in Hull Street," he said. "It wasn't no goddamn priest had anything to do with it."

Reilley shoved his can across to Donald, pulling the bent can over beside his glass.

"This weather's been getting me down," said Donald, pouring out of Reilley's can. "I feel like I've had my mouth full of a cat's tail, and my nose up his ass."

"It gets you down," said Reilly.

"We've been living in sin," she said. "I told you *I'm* the one. You weren't married before."

Donald looked at Reilley. "Makes you want to kick ass, don't it?" he said. He snapped the second can and dropped it on the table.

"Don't the love mean something to God?" said Reilley. "I would think he ought to notice something like that." He paused. "How is it *you* can be living in sin, and *I'm* okay?"

"I know it," she said. "It's just how I feel. I can't do anything about that." She looked down at him sitting at the table. "I'm not talking about *us*," she said. "I love you, too. I'm talking about God."

"You're talking about the goddamn priests," said Donald. "God wouldn't have nothing to do with it."

Kate didn't say anything.

Donald looked up at her. "Jack told Father Whelan to kiss his ass once," he said. "I heard him do it."

Kate turned back to the sink and began washing the dishes again. "All they know how to do is sit around jacking off and scaring the shit out of the women," he said. "I hate the bastards."

Kate didn't turn around. "You two go in the living room," she said. "I'm not going to argue about it."

Reilley and Donald sat down in the living room, and Reilley tried to talk to him, going on with the talk in the kitchen. But Donald started closing up, folding his drooping eyelids up and down in big, slow blinks—licking and sucking his lips, with both arms stretched out along the arms of the chair.

The sound of Kate sloshing the water in the sink came in from the kitchen.

Later they got him into the bedroom and onto the bed. Reilley wrestled him out of his clothes as well as he could, having to do it without Kate's help. She would have undressed Donald by herself and thought nothing of it, but the two of them doing it—being there together—she wouldn't do that. So she went back into the living room to straighten things up before they went to bed.

Donald lay stretched out on top of the spread, filling up the bed. Under his clothes he wore an old-fashioned union suit that buttoned down the front, with sleeves. It looked strange on him, childish. Reilley looked back from the door before he turned out the light. While he was watching, Donald raised his arm and crossed himself, making the moves with a quick, precise motion. He was moving his lips, but Reilley couldn't hear what he was saying.

After the lights were out and they had gotten into the bed together, Kate came over to Reilley and he put his arm around her. She was so solid that he had to prop up his pillow and almost squat on top of it to squeeze her in under his arm, but he liked holding her that way with the lights out in the room. Their bodies stretched out side by side under the covers, and he could feel her knee and the shank of her leg against his foot.

"Don't let go again," he said. "I couldn't stand it this morning."

"I'm all right now," she said.

He reached out to the table beside the bed and turned on the radio. "The Bells of St. Mary's" came up slowly as the tubes were getting warm.

She wasn't moving under his arm, and he couldn't see how she looked in the dark. "I thought a lot of Jack, too," he said.

"The Bells of St. Mary's" ended, and "An Irish Lullaby" came on.

"I was going to pieces."

"I know," he said. "I know you did. But I thought a lot of him, too."

For a while she didn't say anything. "There wasn't a priest," she said.

"It was too quick," he said. "It'll be all right."

"I can't help how I *feel* about it, Reilley," she said.

"I didn't know you still felt that way," he said. "I feel like we're good Catholics."

She didn't say anything. "I can't even open the casket," she said.

He moved away from her a little. "You're not going to open the casket, are you?" he said.

"I couldn't do it."

"You wouldn't want to do it," he said. "I'm sorry. You wouldn't *want* to do it. . . . It's not the Church that won't let you open it. . . ."

For a long time she didn't say anything.

"I can't even pray for him," she said.

"You can pray for him. What do you mean?"

"I can't *pray* for him."

For a while he didn't say anything.

"I'll pray for him for you," he said.

"An Irish Lullaby" ended, and there was a commercial for Pepsi-Cola. Then "Danny Boy" came on.

"Did you kill the spider?" she said.

"I ran some hot water in the tub," he said.

For a while they didn't say anything. "You'd better get some sleep," he said. "Tomorrow's going to be another bad day." He reached over and turned off the radio. In the dark they could hear Donald snoring in the other bedroom.

Suddenly Reilley sat up in bed. "He didn't break anything," he said.

"What . . . what? . . ." Kate didn't sound sleepy.

"He didn't break anything."

She lay back down. "Wait till tomorrow," she said.

After they had gotten quiet again, a big insect flew against the screen of the bedroom window. Until he went to sleep, Reilley could hear it beating its wings against the screen.

Kate was listening to it, too. It sounded as big as a bird.

Untitled song lyric

JOHNNY MERCER (1909–1976)

Johnny Mercer left his native Savannah at seventeen to pursue an acting career in New York. After a few minor roles, he published his first song, "Out of Breath and Scared to Death of You," written for the *Garrick Gaieties of 1930*. (Among Mercer's small stage roles was extra work in Eugene O'Neill's *Marco Millions* in 1930. With the success of that play and *Mourning Becomes Electra*, O'Neill purchased Casa Genotta, a beach cottage on Sea Island, Georgia.) After his first hit, "Lazybones," written with Hogy Carmichael, Mercer went on to work with Harold Arlen, Jerome Kern, Henry Mancini, Andre Previn, and Richard Whiting. Mercer earned eighteen Academy Award nominations for his songs, and won Oscars for "On the Atchison, Topeka, and the Santa Fe" (1946); "In the Cool, Cool, Cool, Cool of the Evening" (1951); "Moon River" (1961); and "Days of Wine and Roses" (1962). Mercer commented in his unpublished autobiography on the fact that he had never published a song about Savannah:

I guess the idea intimidates me so that I've been afraid to try. If it weren't a giant hit, I'd feel I let them down. And I don't know if that kind of song is in the cards anymore. They'll just have to be satisfied with a lot of songs that "sprang" from there . . . like "Blues in the Night," "Moon River," and . . . a State Song ["Georgia, Georgia"] that the Georgia legislature turned down after they had requested it be written, as being too "Savannah" for the whole state.

The following untitled lyric is previously unpublished.

> Hominy grits when you waken
> Peaches a breeze has just shaken
> Lyin' around for the takin'
> You're in Savannah

You're in Savannah
Where the Spanish moss hangs lazy on the trees
Where they say "Thank you, ma'am" almost as much as
     "If you please"

Even though folks are old-fashioned—
Bourbon and smiles are unrationed—
They can get pretty impassioned
About Savannah

So if you're walkin' through a tree-filled square
Where they say "Y'all come back, y'hear"

Traveler, you're in Savannah
My home town

from *Halloween*

BEN GREER (1948–)

> Ben Greer was born in upcountry South Carolina. He earned a
> bachelor's degree from the University of South Carolina where
> he studied with James Dickey and George Garrett. Greer went
> on to earn a master's degree from the Hollins College Creative
> Writing Program. During the 1970s Greer wandered—first to
> Maine where he was befriended by May Sarton, and later to
> work odd jobs in Cape Cod, Savannah, and South Carolina.
> Greer's novels include *Slammer* (1975), *Time Loves a Hero*
> (1986), and *The Loss of Heaven* (1988). Greer currently
> teaches at the University of South Carolina. *Halloween* (1978),
> excerpted here, is set in a dream vision of Savannah and is told
> through the Valium- and alcohol-soaked perceptions of the ail-
> ing Blake Pasque. The entire action of the novel takes place in
> a twelve-hour period on All Hallow's Eve.

Millis was musical. She had wanted to be a concert pianist. She
had tiny red hands which matched the color of her hair. Blake's
grandmother had told Millis that her hands were far too small,
her talent merely adequate. Nevertheless Millis graduated from
Converse Conservatory and went out on an up-country tour. She
played in three separate towns and quit. She became a grade-
school music teacher. She never married and became fat. She
developed a taste for her own misery, though she did not exclude
her sister's. She was a lover of bitter chocolates.

  Cross had never married either and had no use for music or
the stage. If anything, he loomed as the dark man in the wings
who knew well about absolute ends like the dropping of curtains
and blacking of lights. He had used Birddogs against Jess twice
before and had even threatened Blake's father with them. Blake
did not believe Cross to be an evil man, a man who deliberately
set traps and bound people because the suffering soothed him.

But Blake knew that his uncle understood entirely what he needed to survive and that he would pull from anyone in the family those strengths that assured him a safe portion of life. In this way his formal preoccupation with Jess frightened Blake, for if the pain of need was great enough, the method for relief could always be tallied as the expense of peace.

One cold night when Blake was seven years old his uncle slipped into his room, turned up the gaslight, and raked the bedded coals of the fire across the new log. The noise of the sputtering wood awakened Blake. Cross stood in the gold gaslight cradling a cup of coffee. He had been outside. The cold rolled off his greatcoat like a breathing. He pulled Blake from the bed and swooped him into the greatcoat, holding him fast between his knees. The new log tattled and spat, and his uncle smelled of cigarettes as he peeled a fat apple and told Blake how sick his mother had become and that he needed his help. He fed Blake slivers of white apple and pushed the cup of bitter coffee to his lips. He dressed him and carried him out into the dark.

After the Birddogs lifted him into the ambulance and the harsh doors slammed, Blake felt his knees crouch and his hands reach out into the dimness toward anything that might hold him close. The engine cranked. The ambulance lunged forward and he saw Jess lying beneath the tight leather straps, her face drawn and lonely. A tube led from her arm to a bottle hanging above her. She saw him and spoke easily. She said not to be afraid. Her voice felt silver to him and she smelled of her own flat, brown odor which somehow brought comfort, though too the whiskey rode her breath. For a while they looked out the glass window of the roof and played big dipper and man in the moon and he tried to be brave in his heart though his chest hurt like something broken and his hands held himself tightly so he would not wet. He tried to keep his eyes on the stars and the surprised old moon and away from her wet eyes. The sorrowing eyes running with black mascara. The cramped hands that despite her quiet voice tore their skin against the manacles. He turned his face from the tube, which was dripping something into her veins. Something dark and rolling into the heart of his mother.

"Buckles, Mama loves you," Jess said.

He settled his hand on hers and felt her cold fingers twisting.

"Mama loves her little boy blue."

"I love you, Mama."

"You have the ambergris now? You didn't forget?"

Blake took the silver compact from his pocket and held it for her to see. "I snuck it our of your sweater. Nobody saw me. I was like a jackrabbit."

"Just smooth it across my eyes now. Just easy rub it in."

The ambergris dissolved warmly between his fingers. He eased a palm onto her face. Delicately he traced the ambergris across her eyelids. The sweetness of the cream arose. He could feel the spheres, the beautiful lights moving warmly beneath his fingers.

"That's better, Buckles. That's a sweet baby." She opened her eyes and looked up at him from the mattress. "Pull the needle out, sonny."

"Cross said it makes your nerves not swell."

"They're going to do things to me now, aren't they?"

"They're helping, Mama."

"Don't let Mama go away down there and die."

"It's a hospital. It's got a swimming pool and big ole trees inside."

"What kind of trees?"

"Them sweetgum kind, I think. They got Coke machines, too."

"See Mama's arm? It hurts. They're shooting mud into the big blue vein."

"It's sleep, Mama."

"Pull it out, baby. It's some meanness in the night."

He could not look at her when she spoke to him now and her hands were jerking so hard. The mascara and ambergris melted down her cheeks. "Sleep now. I know. We'll play the night-night game. It'll make your nerves go away." He paused and then started off in the lilting, singsong voice she always used at night which brought him sleep. "E-v-e-r-y-b-o-d-y-'s g-o-n-e night-

night. The moo cow's gone night-night and the big ole barn's gone night-night and the pecans way up in the trees gone way on to night-night too."

"Dirty, bad needle. They stuck it in my elbow. They rammed my bones."

She was beginning to writhe. The blanket kept slipping form her body, and he was afraid to put it back because he might touch her with no clothes on. "And the ole hooty owl has gone night-night and the bobwhite has long ago gone night-night too."

"Oh, it hurts me.

"No, now. It's just the sandy man coming down in you."

"I can't see the moon."

"He's gone night-night. Why, the big ole moon's all rolled up in his covers, Mama."

The blanket fell away. He closed his face in his hands. He could hear her feet bucking against the manacles.

"It's a broken bottle stuck in my arm."

"Sleepytime," he said. The tears came down his face.

"Where am I going?"

"Rest now."

"Where is Mama going down to so fast, honey?"

"To rest is all."

"Nobody down here but me."

"The Lord's there, Mama. The Lord's with you in there."

"Hug me."

Blake felt his hands grinding together.

"Nighttime kiss," she said, the drug heavy in her voice. "Sweet snacktime now."

"You'll be alright now."

"Please hug Mama going far away so by herself."

He circled his arms around her neck and felt her breast against him. He shuddered.

"Take it out of me . . . so far down. The dark is . . . so lonesome."

She was becoming quiet. "He's in there. The Lord."

"Not for me, no."

"Now I lay me down to sleep—"

"He's not in here . . . in way down here."

"I pray the Lord my soul to keep."

"I can't see. No, no. I got no light . . . and they . . ." Her voice went away to mumbles.

"If I should die before I wake, I pray the Lord my soul to take."

He laid his face on her neck and repeated this many times until they passed into the gates of the asylum and the driver pulled him away. Another man came and they lifted Jess out of the ambulance. The October wind was mean and cold and blowing the black leaves. The two men peeped under the blanket and one let go a small whistle and they whispered together. Blake sat on the ground and felt the rage in him. The Birddogs climbed out of their car. They had followed all the way. He could hear the dimes ringing in their pockets. He watched the hospital men roll her into the elevator. They closed the screeching door and took her up into the strange-smelling building. He kept saying softly above the silver dimes of the Birddogs and the laughter of the men in the dark with his mother and the black wind: "I love you. I love you. I love you, Mama."

Alfbender let him off near the first of the downtown squares.

"Meet you at the Swan," Blake said.

Alfbender looked about the square. "You keep under the streetlights. Out of the dark."

Blake nodded. The car's gears grated into the night.

The Swan was only four blocks down. Blake had not been back for some time. On the stoops of the big houses around the square the first jack-o'-lanterns were glowing. Paper skeletons and monsters shimmered in the windows of the blue row houses. Two early trick-or-treaters rattled hug grocery bags.

"Hope you get lots of candy," Blake said.

"Screw you, mother," said a skeleton.

Kind words were hard to find.

He did not feel a lot of hope in seeing Jess again. Would she be high on pills or booze or acid? He smiled a bit when he felt the Valium working in his jaw.

Just before the Swan stood a gurgling iron fountain which rose almost thirty feet into the night. Two lights shone on it from the surrounding boxwoods and revealed scores of dark-eyed and prancing stallions, just by them larger and almost frightening swans, and toward the top of the fountain hollow-eyed cherubs blowing water from their trumpets. The top of the fountain was capped by a statue of Aphrodite. She was made of stone and exquisitely held the first moonlight along the length of her legs and the smoothness of her arms and neck. Two masks held in her right hand were glowing above the water. As a boy Blake often looked out of the Swan's windows and, seeing the statue, thought perhaps someone had built the entire fountain to honor Jess, for the figure looked so much like her. When he told Jess how the statue's beauty seemed so like her own, she hugged him and then explained the myth of Aphrodite. At the end of the story Jess said that his grandmother had possessed this same kind of spelling beauty. Blake had seen the old pictures of her. She was Black Irish from County Leitrim. Her hair was dark as a starless night, her eyes black as inkwells. Her neck and hands called her lady and graceful and beguiling. She had arrived in Port Sound to become a teacher. She had ambition and her mind was tough and surprising. Jess had told him that men cooed and plotted over her and that they were not men of the red-handed wharves or the sea but ample-bellied fellows in silk vests and chiming watches, the wearers of engraved cuff links and morning-star stickpins and whiskers blown out to the sides of their faces. Katherine Speer had been wary of her beauty, a beauty that was so successful, so full and wonderfully made, that she even sat in the lower part of the church to keep the men from creaking their starched collars as she passed by or dropping their change noisily upon the floor in order to swivel around and gamble a wink. Two years after her arrival she courted and married Whitney Pasque—a bantam man with one bad lung, two stricken legs, and four rosy-colored fishing sloops. She brewed his tea and they had their kids and Whitney Pasque died leaving money in the bank. Blake's grandmother turned her mind toward simple math then. She sold her old crew and bought another, this one of salesmen and bookkeepers—life insurance. She raised her company and her children. She instilled in both one prime maxim. "Acorns 'is' diamonds in your own back-yard."

Katherine Pasque had been a woman of mirrors and concern. She dreamed upon her image not in reckless vanity but rather as if she were storing the liveliness of her eyes and the radiance of her cheeks in dread of some coming and entire deprivation when none could find her beautiful and she on that account would lose the fascination with her existence. Her beauty did much more than sustain her, it sculpted an essential spirit of vivacity and resilience and pronounced her of value beyond any prestige that her success or her finely built house could acquire. Her beauty was her life.

Blake had feared his grandmother in the first of his life. She seemed to him severe and desolate. He remembered her as a woman at peace only when her family sat near. To Blake his aunt and uncle loitered about her, their hearts suppliantly ticking like small watches arranged about a great clock—all managing to record time but just faintly, their mechanisms barely touching against the metal of existence. Katherine Pasque tucked her children neatly into herself. She knew how to sort through every care and joy of her family, and if anyone was struggling in either too much joy or too much sorrow, she pulled them into herself and relived them of excess. By emptying out each child and sup-plying the necessary supports, she balanced out her household and embroidered each of her children more securely into her own life.

Laid out before her mirror, dressed in perfect lace, her silvery hair brushed down her shoulders, Katherine Pasque expired at eighty-five after a harsh year of desolation and dye.

"Madeira and Moonshine"

ALEXANDER A. LAWRENCE (1906–1979)

Alexander A. Lawrence was a lifelong resident of Savannah who distinguished himself as a writer, lawyer, jurist, and civic leader. He served as a United States District Court judge for over thirty years. His works of biography and history include *James Moore Wayne: Southern Unionist* (1943), *Storm Over Savannah* (1951), and *A Present For Mr. Lincoln: The Story of Savannah from Secession to Sherman* (1961). The following poem, from *Tongue in Cheek* (1979), was composed as a toast for the annual banquet of the Madeira Club, a Savannah salon which meets periodically for literary dinners. Metter, Georgia, was locally infamous for its stills. As early as 1832, Dr. William R. Waring, in a temperance paper prepared for the Georgia Medical Society, noted the affection of his fellow Savannahians for Madeira: "It is customary to invite guests who call on a Gentleman at any period of the day and especially at mid-day, to refresh themselves with brandy and water or with [Madeira] wine. It is a civility establish'd by Society."

Malmsey is great; Sercial is better
But give me the vintage brewed around Metter.
Distilled in the pinewood; aged in troughs,
Bottled in jars and stashed in hay lofts,
Oh what bouquet! One swig and a smell,
And a drinker has quaffed the water of hell.
The nectar of the gods came from the vine
But what can compare with Georgia moonshine?

"The Haunted Library"

MARGARET WAYT DEBOLT (1930–)

> Margaret Wayt DeBolt was educated at West Virginia
> University. Her journalism includes work as staff writer at the
> *Savannah News-Press* and the "Kitchen in the Hills" column in
> *Hillbilly Magazine*. Her writing draws on her interest in
> women's and Civil War history, regional folklore, and
> Appalachian life, particularly cooking. Her books, *Savannah: A
> Historical Portrait* (1976), *Savannah Sampler Cookbook*
> (1978), and *Georgia Sampler Cookbook* (1983) have won her
> a devoted local audience. The piece below is from *Savannah
> Spectres and Other Strange Tales* (1984).

The story has long been told in Savannah of a haunted house
which was located near Bonaventure Cemetery. Although the
tale first saw print in *Stories of Old Savannah*, by Margaret
Godley of the Savannah Public Library and Lillian C. Bragg in
1949 without the name of the estate involved, some believe that
it was Greenwich.

"The house stood about a quarter of a mile from one of the
avenues of oaks at Bonaventure," the story began. "It was large
and strongly built, much defaced by time in its last days. The
wild swallows made their nests in its chimneys; its court was
overgrown with weeds, and vines clambered over the windows.
It was finally removed, and a neat, small mansion erected not far
from its site."

The narrator states that her father "had always been one to
laugh at the idea of ghosts in haunted houses. Such things in
Savannah in the nineteenth century—impossible!" Then one
chilly February afternoon, as the early winter darkness came on,
he found himself weary after a day of hunting near Bonaventure,
in the time when it was still largely woods and marsh. The
young man suggested to his companions that they seek hospital-

ity for the night at the old house, whose owner was known to one of them, rather than ride back to Savannah in the dark.

The others objected, telling him that they had always heard the residence was haunted. He hooted in reply, and turned his tired horse toward its walled garden.

It was an area, added the writer, which had been "one of the old Colonial estates, rich in history, legend, romance, and beauty." Many years before the residence had been an elegant one, tastefully and expensively furnished and surrounded by fruit trees and flowers. Shortly after the War between the States, there had been a quarrel among the heirs. Those whom most of Savannah felt had the best claim to the property were unable to produce the necessary documents, and lost their home.

Heartbroken, they left the area. So, in time, did the next resident. Stories of unusual happenings in the old house under the oaks began to be told and embellished. As the young men were thinking of these things, the present owner appeared and graciously invited them all in for supper. Under the influence of some fine wine, they later admitted to him their misgivings about ringing his bell. He laughed easily, saying that he thought the idea of such things "exploded at the present day," and that he regretted he had no ghosts to show them. He did, however, suggest that the young man who had proposed the visit spend the night in the house library apartment, formerly the bedroom and study of the host's late father, where there were a number of rare volumes on the subject.

The others laughingly agreed, arranging to meet the next day and further discuss the matter over dinner in Savannah. Then they asked for their horses and rode on, leaving their friend alone with his host.

At first, the tale continues, the young man was comfortable in the combined library and bedroom. He examined its volumes, many now long out of print, and its excellent prints and paintings. These included several life-sized portraits of various members of the family, now long gone. There was a strong, virile-looking man in the regimental dress of the recent war; a beautiful young woman in a bridal veil; an older woman in brocade; a middle-aged man holding a roll of parchment in his hand, and several more. Finally, worn by the day's exertions, he fell asleep.

He awoke a few hours later to the sound of the great striking clock. A full moon shone in the windows, illuminating the room. As he glanced about his strange surroundings, he was startled to see a man—the man of the portrait, in uniform—now seated near him in a large leather armchair. The frame of the painting above him was empty.

Then he realized in terror that the other elaborate frames were vacant as well, for the persons who had occupied them were now moving about the room. There was the matron, whose brocade skirts rustled as she walked; the young woman more beautiful than ever under her bridal veil; a feminine relative who complained, "Are we to have no music or dancing anymore?"; and the man with the rolled parchment. It was between the latter and the officer that a conflict was ensuing, the watcher realized. Finally the veteran urged him, "Be just! Yield up what is not your own! Let not the innocent suffer!"

The man with the papers only shook his head. The handsome features of the other were now contorted with rage. Then, continues the story, the scene began to change. "The outlines of the figures first became tremulous and indistinct, and then they seemed to melt into one another. At length, all was dark, as the moon had gone behind the tall trees."

Exhausted by emotion, the young man managed to sleep again. He awoke to a servant entering the chambers, and a room full of sunlight. An uneasy glance told him that the ancestral pictures were solidly in their frames, although he felt as though they all were looking directly at him. At breakfast, and the later meeting with his friends, he found himself unable to speak of the night's events. He was, however, more interested than ever in what he could learn of the history of the house and family.

The old residence, the story continues, was eventually removed, "and a neat, small mansion was erected not far from its site." If this was indeed the last house to be built at Greenwich, it was, like the one at Bonaventure, destroyed by fire in 1923. Its occupants, the Torrey family, narrowly escaped with their lives.

Years later, after the older house was demolished, workmen excavating near where its foundations had been found a molding and nearly illegible piece of rolled parchment. Perhaps hidden in the confusion of the war years, it was one of the lost papers which might have helped the dispossessed heirs. But since the original estate had by then been divided and was decreased in value, nothing was done with the document.

It did, however, serve to convince the guest who had slept in the library during what songwriters Sir William Gilbert and Arthur Sullivan called the "the ghost's high noon," that such documents did exist. To the end of his days, the man who had scoffed at ghosts, was unable to look at a life-size portrait without a feeling of horror.

from *Sleeping with Soldiers*

ROSEMARY DANIELL (1935–)

> Rosemary Daniell attended poetry workshops at Emory
> University. Working variously as a journalist and poet-in-
> residence in Georgia, Wyoming, and South Carolina, Daniell
> has earned National Endowment for the Arts fellowships in
> creative writing in 1975–1976 and 1980–1981. She has con-
> tributed to *Mother Jones*, *New York Times Book Review*,
> *Philadelphia Inquirer*, and *Harper's Bazaar*. Daniell lives in
> Savannah where she conducts a women's writing group, Zona
> Rosa. Besides *Sleeping with Soldiers* (1985), excerpted here,
> Daniell's books include *Fatal Flowers: On Sin, Sex and Suicide
> in the Deep South* (1980) and *The Woman Who Spilled Words
> All over Herself* (1997); as well as two books of poetry, *A
> Sexual Tour of the Deep South* (1975) and *The Feathered Trees*
> (1976). "Ug-AH! ug-AH!," the final line in this excerpt, is the
> cheer associated with the University of Georgia Bulldogs' team
> mascot, Uga.

Following my divorce from Ben, I lived part of each year in my
home city, Atlanta, and the other part in the seaport town of
Savannah. Atlanta is serious business—a boomtown of narcis-
sistic neon, ever-expanding suburbs, and freeways to equal
Houston or L.A., a metropolis that can accurately be labeled
glossy. My second husband, an architect, had had his hand in
designing many of the glass phalluses, the sports arenas, the
broad shopping malls of a city that was rapidly losing its *Gone
with the Wind* mystique.

Savannah, by contrast, is a sleazily decaying, yet lovely, pastel
dream of tight cobbled streets, elegantly austere eighteenth-century and frilly Victorian nineteenth-century houses, overhanging
Spanish moss, masses of azaleas and oleander. It is said that the
first thing one is asked in Atlanta is "What do you do?"; in

Charleston, "Who were your ancestors?"; and in Savannah, "What would you like to drink?" When a New Yorker asked a Savannah society woman what she did, she looked at him, puzzled. "Why, ah *live*—ah *live* in Sa-vannah!" she replied with proper hauteur.

Indeed, it is a town in which everything—aristocracy, historic architecture, booze, drugs, even flowers—is excessive. My manicurist is a transsexual, my dentist wears a pistol in his boot, my internist mentions threesomes in Chicago over the examining table, and my plumber was, until recently, salvaging ships off Key West, when he was struck by the "Keys Disease"—a malaise in which one starts out in the morning to buy a loaf of bread and doesn't return home until after midnight. He was now in Savannah, he told me while disassembling the toilet tank, to help a local couple build a replica of Ernest Hemingway's house, and to save money for his coming trip down the Amazon in his 1930s yacht.

Then there are the legendary scenes of sex-and-violence, extreme enough to rival any dreamed up by Tennessee Williams: Poet Conrad Aiken heard his father shoot his mother, and then himself, in the bedroom of one of the beautiful town houses when the poet was eleven. During the twenties, a son of a wealthy Savannah family was said to be dating the singer-girlfriend of a local bootlegger; one night, someone rang the doorbell of the family mansion and, when the door was opened, threw the young man's severed testicles through the doorway—a story allegedly kept out of the local newspapers, yet passed down decade after decade. Savannah is the first place in which I had had among my everyday contacts—from repairmen to social acquaintances—a number of people actually involved in murder trials. ("Now don't say anything about that thing that happened in this building," a hostess whispered, referring to a particularly gruesome murder involving cocaine, solicitation, a blow to the head with a conch shell, a stabbing, a toothbrush shoved up the victim's anus, and an attempt to burn the body in a bathtub. "Her son was charged with it, you know.") Bars and cocktail parties—where women serve things with names like Jezebel (a spicy conserve poured over cream cheese, spread on crackers) and, of course, mint juleps—became frequent settings for psychodrama.

"Savannah's a seaport town—ships and sailors," a Savannah Police Department spokesman said on the front page of the *Savannah News-Press*, trying to explain a crime rate often among the highest in the nation; "It's no longer a question of how to control it—it's probably beyond control." If the unconscious is the seat of sex and aggression, Savannah is that part of the psyche made manifest.

Before long, the two cities—Savannah and Atlanta—had become metaphors for the two parts of myself. And for a woman in search of the macho man, Savannah was the natural habitat; even the mayor—a charismatic, four-times-elected, blue-eyed Greek-American patriarch—is macho; a black state representative was arrested for possession of cocaine with little loss of popularity; foreign sailors and drug smugglers walk the streets; and Army Rangers fill the waterfront bars.

It is the kind of town in which one might be walking down the street, hear the telephone in a nearby booth ring, and—as happened to my gay friend, Robert John—answer it to hear a stranger suggest meeting for sex; indeed, a place that might be symbolized by the black boy of about nine, walking on the sidewalk beneath my window one balmy morning, lustily singing at the top of his lungs:

> Why don't you jes'
> pull up yo' dress—
> All I wanna do is
> ug-AH! ug-AH!

from *The Distant Lands*

JULIEN GREEN (1900–1998)

> Julien Green was born to American parents living in Paris. He
> published over sixty books ranging from novels, essays, and
> plays, as well as fifteen volumes of his journals. Green lived
> nearly all his life in Paris and published almost exclusively in
> French. He was the first foreigner to be elected to the Académie
> Française. He resigned in 1996—citing his advanced age and
> distaste for honors—saying he felt "exclusively American."
> Green was a member of the American Academy of Arts and
> Sciences, and a winner of the Harper Prize, the Prix Marcel
> Proust, the Prix France-Amérique, and many other interna-
> tional awards. Green's collected works have been published in
> the Gallimard Pleiade series. His literary influences include his
> friends Jean Cocteau, Andre Gide, Jacques Maritain, and
> Francois Mauriac. Despite his long residency in Europe,
> because of his deep association with the American South—he
> attended and taught at the University of Virginia and his
> mother, Mary Hartridge Green, came from a Savannah family
> with colonial roots—many claim him as an American writer.
> Green once described himself as "a southerner lost in Europe,
> regardless of what I do." Green's novels show a distinct
> Southern Gothic influence. The following excerpt from his
> novel *The Distant Lands* (1987) draws on Savannah's long tra-
> dition of legal dueling, a tradition laid down in John Lyde
> Wilson's *The Code of Honor* (1838).

The colonial cemetery was a large park crisscrossed with
avenues where the finest trees in Savannah cast a constantly
moving shade over paths of pink brick. Sycamores, catalpas,
cork oaks, all bore in their foliage shreds of grey moss like long,
torn veils, stirred by the slightest breath of air. Originally from
Barbados and borne by the wind, this almost ethereal vegetation
added a melancholy element to even the most cheerful country-

side, and its strange attraction finally had its effect on the imagination. You could pull it out from the green depths, but it
would come back, like some obsession.

At four o'clock in the morning, it was daylight, but the town
was still sleeping and the cemetery empty. Rays of sunlight caught
the surface of the stone slabs scattered at random in the grass, and
those who were curious could read the names of soldiers from the
time of the Independence, but also of duellers that a saber blow or
pistol shot had laid beneath these romantic shadows.

Mr. Hudson arrived first, accompanied by his two seconds,
whom he had sought out straight away, just as they were preparing for sleep. In consequence, both of them wore an air of sullen
gravity. Arching his back in order to show off the slimness of his
waist, and with a smile on his lips, Hudson was wearing a look
of extreme satisfaction, his hat at a somewhat war-like angle
which seemed to suit him. His hand, in a pearl-gray glove, was
holding a whip with which he was striking himself lightly on the
calf. Coming almost immediately behind him, Major Burton
presented a quite different appearance. Ten years older than his
opponent, his features bore the marks of tiredness, and his quiet
face was that of a man attending a boring show. His seconds,
clearly soldiers in civilian dress, maintained a profound silence.
With the usual greetings exchanged, one of Hudson's seconds
recalled the conventions: a distance of twenty paces, single pistol shots to be discharged simultaneously.

It remained to measure out the distance when an incident
interrupted the operation. A galloping could be heard in the
avenue at the edge of the cemetery, and Charlie Jones appeared
on his bay mare.

Dressed in black from head to foot, he jumped to the ground
with the suppleness of a young man and cried:

"I offer my excuses, gentlemen! I request your attention for a
moment."

As soon as he saw him, Mr. Hudson changed color and in an
instinctive gesture, he put his hand to his hat and dropped his
whip, which fell at his heels.

Turning first of all to Major Burton, Charlie Jones said:

"Commandant, I have been informed of your difference of opinion with Mr. Hudson by Francis Brooks, who will be here very shortly. His very poor eyesight is the sole explanation for his slowness in getting here. What is more, I think I can see him, running and out of breath, adjusting his eye glasses."

"But I had told him that there was no point in his coming."

"It seemed indispensable to him, however. Francis Brooks is as much a man of honor as we are. Mr. Hudson," he said briskly, "if circumstances are no against it, I shall have a few words to say to you when you've settled matters with Major Burton."

Mr. Hudson nodded agreement.

At that moment, Francis Brooks appeared, wiping his forehead and trying, without success, to say something. His black hair was disheveled and he was holding a stovepipe hat that was visibly too big for a man of his size. He stuffed his handkerchief into his pocket, and in the same way that people remove their hats out of politeness, he took off his eyeglasses, then bowed. Everything in his appearance betrayed violent emotion, controlled with great difficulty.

"Pull yourself together," Charlie Jones said to him, "stand quite still next to me and watch. Watch carefully."

The young man drew as close as he could to Charlie Jones and did not move, but his face was running with sweat and his eyes were darting from one of the adversaries to the other.

Each of them, in shirt sleeves and gripping his weapon, was waiting for the signal to be given, the usual exclamation. In an almost unbearable silence, birds were calling from every corner of the cemetery and their songs collided in a kind of teasing and mocking chorus.

"Gentlemen, are you ready?"

A few seconds passed which seemed never-ending.

Without his eye glasses, Francis Brooks could see nothing, although he strained forward, and his heart raced in his chest.

"One . . . two . . . three. Fire"

A bullet whistled past the major's right ear, but he did not stumble, whereas a faint cry issued from Mr. Hudson's mouth.

They hurried round them.

"Mr. Hudson is so clumsy that he nearly killed me," said the major with a smile, "but either I am mistaken or he won't be waltzing any more this season."

Mr. Hudson had indeed had a bullet go through his arm, just below the shoulder.

When first aid had been administered to the wounded man, the two were asked if they wished to be reconciled. The major shrugged his shoulders.

"No objection," he said with indifference in his voice, "but the boy will not wish it. He's a firebrand. He aimed for the head, as was his right. If there's a war, he'll be good in a bayonet charge, he'll be a ferocious lover, but he'll never be a leader."

As if he had heard these words, Mr. Hudson cast a furious look in his direction that gave the lie to any hope of reconciliation.

Followed by Francis Brooks, who stuck to his side, Charlie Jones went up to him. They were dressing his wound. In a kindly voice, he asked him if he was in pain.

"It's bearable," said Mr. Hudson with a forced smile.

"The bullet passed through the arm and tore a muscle," said the doctor who was taking charge of the wounded man. "He'll have to wear a sling for at least three months."

"An arm in a sling, there's something to earn you the esteem of the whole of Savannah," said Charlie Jones gaily. "A record has been made of this meeting. Honor is saved. A reconciliation is proposed to bring an end to this affair. What do you think?"

The young man shook his head to say no. Then Charlie Jones did something that was peculiar to him and which amazed his friends. In some indefinable way, he began to change his appearance. His shoulders seemed suddenly broader, his whole height was drawn up in such a way that he gave the impression of having grown taller, and his face became more serious.

"Hudson," he said, "some day I shall have the chance to

speak to you at greater length. This morning, I ask you to think of the time when you used to work in my offices. You are free to act as you please, but in your place, I should not refuse the very honorable hand that is being extended towards you."

The two men looked at each other for a moment, each one seeking to guess at what the other was concealing in his eyes. Mr. Hudson finally said in a flat voice:

"I can only answer you when we are alone."

Charlie Jones turned immediately to the seconds:

"Gentlemen, may I ask you to withdraw for a few minutes? Is the first aid sufficient, doctor, for you to . . ."

"Yes, but I should be happier if Mr. Hudson could sit down. The pain can be very sharp."

"Oh, I can very well remain standing."

"Let them bring over that bench I can see in the path," ordered Charlie Jones. "You go off with the others, Brooks. But what are you hiding beneath the flap of your coat?"

"Later, if you please, Mr. Jones."

"All right. Off you go."

One of the benches used by strollers was installed beneath an oak from which fluttered the fringes of the eternal moss curtain.

They sat down.

"Hudson," said Charlie Jones, "a simple gesture can change a life. Shaking Burton's hand will earn you the esteem of the whole of Savannah society and will confirm your situation, which can only be helped by it. Do I have to spell things out?"

"You must understand me, sir. I had asked Miss Elizabeth to dance with me because I could see her on the arm of a man whom I judged to have no place amongst us."

"You can imagine that the people who were whirling around you did in fact overhear all that you were saying. After three minutes, the whole ball knew about it. Let's have it out, Hudson. Formerly you speculated wildly, and three times I saved you from complete ruin. Your furniture was seized, your house sold, you were in danger of prison for debt. Is that true?"

Hudson paled and did not answer.

"Right," said Charlie Jones, "when you'd come out of there, you would have got lost amongst the great and wretched hordes of Poor Whites. You had all the qualifications for it."

"I beg you, Mr. Jones."

"The subject is not pleasant, I agree, but we must come to the case of Francis Brooks. Son of a Poor White and taken up by me, he has done his studies, and now he is amongst the best of my architects. As shortsighted as a mole, he manages to get by with a whole series of magnifying glasses and succeeds brilliantly. Don't you admire him?"

"I'm no judge, and then . . ."

". . . and then you'd like to see me finish. Here you are. If you touch Francis Brooks, you'll have in me a tenacious opponent until the end of my days. I shall always be there to impede your progress. Do I need to remind you that, being related to none of the great Savannah families, it's better to set about things prudently if you want to—how shall I put it—climb?"

Mr. Hudson started rebelliously.

"Do you not think we have said enough on this subject, Mr. Jones? There comes a point when one cannot carry on being humiliated."

"And that is the time for wise decisions. In your case, for example, to shake Major Burton's hand. Your seconds are waiting for you, with the major's."

"With all the respect due to you, I beg you to note that you are exerting an unfair pressure on me. There is a name for it."

"Don't be a simpleton, Hudson. You are perfectly free to act however you please. I have simply warned you of the danger that is lurking."

In a voice trembling with annoyance, Mr. Hudson answered:

"How can I do other than obey you? I shall go then, fuming in my heart."

"Fuming in your heart," Charlie Jones repeated philosophically as he stood up. "Do you feel able to walk on your own? May I help you?"

Mr. Hudson gave him an indignant look.

"You're joking," he said.

With his left hand, he leaned on the bench and stood up. The doctor, who was standing some distance away with the group of seconds ran up to him.

"I'll accompany you, Mr. Hudson. It's vital. Are you in pain?"

Mr. Hudson turned a marble face towards him. All the vacuousness of his beauty emerged, lit up this time by the fires of anger.

"I am indeed in pain," he muttered through his teeth.

"That's only to be expected, it'll pass."

"Never. But leave me, I beg you. What should I look like if I had to be helped to take a few steps? They are coming over to me, what is more."

The formalities were gone through in accordance with custom, beside the unraised grave of a soldier, twenty-three, who had looked askance at an officer in the heyday of the revolution. The major held out his hand with a somewhat indulgent smile. It was touched, rather than shaken, by Mr. Hudson, whose furious look aimed more accurately than his right arm had done earlier.

During all this, Charlie Jones was waving to Francis Brooks to come over and speak to him. It was some time before the latter noticed him. They pointed him in the right direction and, with the help of his eye glasses, he came running up.

"Francis," Charlie Jones immediately said to him, "show me what you are hiding under your coat."

The young man unknotted a bag tied to his waist and pulled from it an imposing pistol of a bygone age. The brass butt was inlaid with ivory, and the barrel unusually long.

Charlie Jones took the object in his hands.

"Be careful, it's loaded!" cried Francis Brooks.

"And you're carrying it around in a bag tied to your waist? What are you thinking of? And where does this formidable life-preserver come from?"

"It was my grandfather's pistol, when he was fighting for Independence."

"It should be in a museum. We'll get the powder out first."

Francis Brooks stopped him with a gesture:

"But it's there to defend my honor."

Charlie Jones looked at him with an affectionate smile, but emptied the pistol all the same.

"Your honor has not been touched, dear Francis. You will never have to defend it by means of arms if I succeed in getting duels banned. Come with me."

He took him familiarly by the arm, and the two of them walked beneath the trees. The pistol shots had drawn a crowd, and Charlie Jones found himself being greeted at almost every step. His companion had taken back his venerable pistol, now empty, and replaced it in its bag, but he felt no less important for that alongside Mr. Jones—invulnerable too. For he had been afraid, and his nightmare was coming to an end in the soft light of morning filtering through the foliage and caressing the long, pensive gravestones, spread out here and there, in no particular order.

Charlie Jones stopped in front of one of them:

"Here lies a young man of twenty-three who died at the sword of a friend who loved him. Some insolence bandied in ill humor or in jest, no matter, it was an affront. An affront! That was the word that was always being heard. So swords were crossed. Over there, another grave. It is from 1820 or '22 and more tragic. It is the tragedy of a great medical man of the district, brought about by a young fool who was in love with his wife. It is not so long ago that all the young men in Savannah carried a pistol or a knife on them. Don't let yourself be provoked by anybody. Your infirmity makes it impossible for you to fight. But let's leave all that. See how good life is this morning. The park has never been more delicately lit. There is an invitation to happiness in the air. I'm going to go home on my bay mare. I'll see you later, Francis, come and find me on the building site."

He moved off immediately, walking at a good pace towards the mare that was waiting for him beside a servant.

Just as he was going to put his foot in the stirrup, Francis Brooks's voice, high-pitched and a little strangled, reached his ears:

"Do you think there will be a war, Mr. Jones?"

Charlie Jones seated himself comfortably in the saddle and said:

"Perhaps, if the politicians lose their heads, but not if we listen to Mr. Clay."

And, striking his mount with his cane, he took her away at a gallop.

Francis Brooks, with his hands stretched out in front of him, like a blind man, was trying to run after him shouting:

"Mr. Clay! Mr. Clay!"

That night Elizabeth barely slept. She had only just gone off, when she was wrenched from her sleep by the fear that pursued her into her dreams. She again saw herself leaning at the window, watching the back of Mr. Hargrove in his gig. The night remained silent, and the horse was at full gallop, but she could still see Mr. Hargrove's back, wrapped in his box coat, motionless. Seized with fear, she threw back her blanket and began walking around her room in bare feet.

On the table, the lamp had gone out, and the Bible, open at the eighth chapter of Isaiah, was waiting. The pages shone faintly in the moonlight. She touched them with her hand, irresolutely.

The memory of the ball came back to her with sudden violence, and she had to lean on the table for support. There were those three men around her, one silent, the other two exchanging words of anger that she did not understand. She felt her heart pounding in her chest.

What time could it be? When it was light, they were going to fight, and one of them would be wounded, perhaps killed. Was it possible? In times of trouble, she convinced herself that the only real world was what she could see and touch. The walls, the furniture around her, the whole room, all that reassured her, soothed her distress a little; but, without daring to admit it to herself, what troubled her the most was the fate of Francis Brooks. She trembled for him, because he looked like a lost child between those two angry men. At certain moments, the gaucheness of his movements and an element of clumsiness about his person made him seem comic, but this was in itself unbearable, because it was like an insult to a vulnerable and quite defenseless creature.

On the mantelpiece, a small Swiss clock decorated with forget-me-nots and edelweiss showed three o'clock. Elizabeth could only work out the time by feeling the hands with her fingers, for the sky was still dark. She did not want to go back to bed through fear of more nightmares. Again she wandered amongst the furniture to pass the time. Daybreak would bring news. She tried in vain to imagine the colonial cemetery which she visualized full of palm trees bending over the graves. To fight in a cemetery . . .

The thought came to her of pulling on the embroidered cord and asking for Nora, her black maid, who would fill the lamp. She did not dare nor did she want to. Nevertheless, she went over to the door beside which the cord hung and held it in her fingers, tempted in spite of everything, when her glance fell on a square of white paper, almost by her feet . . .

Another letter slid under the door . . . She seized it, turned it over. The envelope was stuck down. How could she read the name in the dark? Obviously the letter was intended for her. She remembered the old black servant who had hovered around her after dinner, saying strange things to her, and she spoke the name Hudson aloud. If it was from him, what a disappointment . . . She despised that man who had insulted little Francis Brooks. But despite everything, getting a letter was quite an event. She had only received four in her whole life: from her grandmother, from her old tutor, from her father while traveling, and from a mischievous friend who had written on behalf of an imaginary admirer. At the age of twelve, Elizabeth had wept with resentment, but this time, it was something different, she could feel it.

Suddenly, she turned the key and opened the door. How come she had not thought of that before? A night light burned on the staircase, shedding just enough light to enable the steps to be seen. It was a small bronze object, copied from Roman lamps, which consisted of a wick dipped in oil and was placed in a niche, at the feet of a marble statue of Hermes.

With the perfect eyesight of her sixteen years Elizabeth was able to make out the large, irregular hand and read this, standing on a step and leaning on the banister:

Elizabeth, if I may call you that, what is the point of writing this letter that a servant is going to slide under your door? When you read it in a few hours' time, I shall perhaps be dead. Tonight, at the ball, I did the most foolish thing I've ever done in my life, insulted a poor boy who could not fight with me, being my inferior, because it made me mad with anger to see you on his arm, you, whom I had been watching throughout the whole of the banquet, you whom I love to distraction, because you are the one I have been waiting for since my earliest youth. How beautiful you are, Elizabeth . . . Do you know it? You are Juliet's age. How beautiful you are, Elizabeth . . .

She lowered the letter. Under the shock of such a sentence, she felt something give way inside her. Never had a young man spoken to her in this way; in a kind of magical double image, she saw herself in Hudson's sentence as in a mirror, as beautiful, very beautiful, with her golden hair spread over the whiteness of her nightgown, and her pink cheeks that spoke of English fields, and she stopped hating that man.

After a few seconds, she resumed her reading:

My opponent is one of the best shots in the district. I have myself been put to the test with a pistol. I intend to shoot him in the head, for I can no longer live if I do not silence that mouth that spoke the outrage. So honor will be saved and it will no longer be in shame that I shall come and tell you again of my love . . .

This time, the letter dropped from her fingers, as she did not wish to believe what was yet so evident. Marry Mr. Hudson? She picked up the letter and put it back in its envelope, then returned to her room, locking the door in just as much haste as she had opened it.

Mr. Hudson's face appeared to her suddenly, as in a hallucination. Smooth and beardless, it made her feel ill at ease in a way that she did not understand. Could a man be too handsome? A certain perfection of feature produced boredom rather than love. And then, there was no question of love, even less of marriage. Living with a model from an art class!

She cast the letter into a drawer with the impatience of someone with too many admirers, but deep inside herself she realized that she was acting out her role very badly. They were going to fight over her. There was reason to feel important.

Dawn was breaking behind the roofs. A vague grey glimmer invaded the room. Leaning at the window, Elizabeth watched the shrubs emerge slowly from the shadows, then the borders of pink geraniums.

Suddenly she went and fetched the letter and waited for daylight to read the end of it. Perhaps at the very moment when she was casting her eyes over its final lines, he would fall dead, struck by a bullet in the forehead. In novels, there were gripping coincidences . . .

In the first rays of daylight, she was finally able to read these words:

> Forgive me for writing to you so extravagantly. I do not forget that you are still a very young lady and that you have perhaps never heard a man speak to you as I am doing now. Perhaps a man who is brushing with death has the right to press on. If I am to fall now, let it be in the intoxication of this avowal.
>
> Your unfortunate Philip

With her brow furrowed, she re-read the last lines without being sure of having properly understood them. In spite of the little attraction she felt towards Mr. Hudson, she was beginning to view him differently. His letter frightened her. She could not help pitying him, and, by the same token, herself also. So young and drama already in her life . . . very romantic, this situation . . .

Now she could bear to wait no longer. She wanted to know how it was all going to end, if the two men were now standing face to face. Somewhat confused, she was holding the letter in her hand, and, in a moment of good sense, thought she could see her mother casting her very British eyes over it, and at the same time saying: "Keep quiet, you little idiot, and don't make a fool of yourself."

This time without hesitation, she pulled on her bell cord. There was no answer for ten minutes. One could have thought that the shocked silence had closed its waves around this impetuous ringing, waking people up at the crack of dawn.

Finally, in a great shuffle of shoes along the ground, Nora came in, with her hair hastily tied up, her eyes drooping with sleep.

"Good-day, Miss Lizbeth. Is you feelin' poorly, Miss Lizbeth?"

"Yes, Nora. Good morning. What time is it?"

"I ain't rightly sure. The sun's comin' up. I reckon maybe four o'clock."

"Four o'clock! Oh, Nora, I'm worried. At four o'clock, two gentlemen are going to fight in the cemetery."

"The colonial cemetery? Seem like they's always always some two gentlemen there, every week. It's somethin' terrible."

"Nora, I hope they are not going to kill each other."

Nora then made that gesture that intrigued Elizabeth. She looked as if she were wrapping the top half of her body in some invisible cloak that was pinned to her shoulders.

Elizabeth watched her:

"What are you doing, Nora?"

"A prayer, Miss Lizbeth, for them two gentlemen."

"Very good," said Elizabeth, too embarrassed to enquire any further.

She took a few steps towards the window.

"I should like it to be over, Nora. Does a duel last very long?"

"I don't know. Never wanted to see. Miss Lizbeth, I's goin' to remake this bed. Go on back to sleep now."

"Certainly not. Lower the blind. The sun is beginning to shine."

Nora obeyed, and the orange canvas plunged the room into a golden half-light.

The large woman had not taken the time to put a white apron over her black dress, and she was moving to and fro in the room, trying to tidy up, picking up underwear that Elizabeth had dropped more or less anywhere. In reality, she was curious to find out why the young English lady was interested in this duel. She did not dare to say anything, but she hoped for a sigh of sadness that would allow of some attempt at consolation, and she moved her heavy frame about, making the floorboards creak relentlessly beneath her weight.

Elizabeth, however, remained silent, and walked about in the room avoiding Nora whose presence was annoying her somewhat now. She stepped in front of the portrait of Charlie Jones and raised towards him, once again, a long, tender look, full of reproach. Why had he not remained as he was then in the full flush of youth? Why did people change?

from *The Dangerous Lives of Altar Boys*

CHRIS FUHRMAN (1960–1991)

Chris Fuhrman grew up in Savannah. He attended Armstrong State College and Yale University before receiving a master's degree from Columbia University. Fuhrman died of cancer while working on the final revision of *The Dangerous Lives of Altar Boys* (1991). "Rebels of the Blessed Heart," from that book, is presented here. The teenaged narrator of the book is a reader of *Mad*. That magazine's best known and most frequent contributor is native Savannahian Al Jaffee (1921–), who introduced the comic's popular "Fold-in" feature in 1964.

Father Kavanagh had canceled his weekly hour of Religion with our class. I suspected it was because seeing "the artists" would bring to mind images from *Sodom vs. Gomorrah '74,* in much the same way as I was afflicted by watching Margie's brother Donny, sunken into the desk in front of mine, pulling at a scab on his neck. We'd been ordered to read silently. *The Return of Tarzan* was open on my desktop, but the pictures in my head were of Margie, Margie and me, Margie and Donny. I squirted a third layer of glue onto my left palm, spread it with my right finger, sucked the finger clean. It tasted vaguely plastic. I'd heard it was made from animal hooves. I blew on the hand, and Elmer the Cow glared from the Glue-All label.

Sister Rosaria, twirling a Kleenex-sheathed finger in her nostril, said, "All right, class. Take out your history texts." She inspected the tissue, then dropped it with the others in the wastebasket.

The classroom rustled and scraped, books slapped. Tim laid *1984* inside his history book and continued to frown into it.

The nun piped, "Who can tell me why there's a historical marker at St. John's Episcopal Church?"

Two hands floated. Eric Johnson, the doctor's boy, and Donny Flynn, his arm in a plaster cast decorated with swastikas and peace symbols. The answer to the question was undoubtedly a war. It was Donny's only topic of interest.

Eric knew everything. Rosaria called on Donny.

Donny dropped his arm pow! on the desk and said, "It was General Sherman's headquarters."

Rosaria bared coffee-stained teeth. "That's right. Yes. Good."

To compensate, Donny slouched back again in the juvenile delinquent mode, arms hanging.

Rosaria slipped on her harlequin glasses and then wrote WILLIAM TECUMSEH SHERMAN on the green chalkboard behind her. "During the Civil War, Sherman marched his troops here from Atlanta, setting fire to everything along the way until he came to the sea. He spared Savannah because of its beauty and gave it to President Lincoln for Christmas. That's why we have so many Victorian houses left." She clapped beige dust from her hands, sat.

We'd studied the Civil War already this year. I believe Rosaria was trying to nurse race relations, because of the purse-snatcher killing, and the duck.

Rosaria asked who'd read *Gone With the Wind*, or seen it, and a sudden crop of right hands sprang up. I'd sneaked into the movie a couple of years before with Tim and Rusty. I enjoyed Vivien Leigh's bosomy gowns, but the story wearied me like the soap operas. It was a tourist-shop picture of the South, unreal to me.

I ignored the nun's whiny praises of Margaret Mitchell. I stared around and imagined various girls out of their clothes. Angie Sipes chewed on her pen, licking at the cap between little bites. My stomach ached to think of the activities you might get a girl to agree to. I was scheduled to spend Friday night with Margie, but I found I couldn't imagine anything carnal between us, as if she was too pure to be thought about that way. Odd, especially since I couldn't help but picture her with Donny.

Rosaria droned. Beside me, Tim and Rusty exchanged pellets

of paper. Behind us, Wade had his head close to the desktop, sketching a wildcat with muscles so well-cut it looked skinned.

The windows were cranked open and from time to time bees wavered inside, hovered, then streaked down and across the street to where the azalea bushes were exploding lavender, pink, and white, and the bees became specks darting in and out of the blossoms.

"Let's open our texts to page 161," Rosaria said, and a general scrape and the faint crack of book spines resulted.

A generic watercolor adorned that page, soldiers in blue conquering soldiers in gray. But the figures on my copy dangled giant penises drawn in black ink, and several had painted lips and long lashes. They exhaled balloons filled with vile dialogue. I flipped the page so Rosaria wouldn't see. Across the next two pages, in bold Magic Marker, were the words ROSARIA SUX HIPPO DIX. I rested my arms across the words. Rusty and Tim snickered.

Slowly, I tore the pages out with my unglued hand, hoping to finish before Rosaria strolled the aisles. I wadded the pages into my pocket.

The nun said, "Francis Doyle," and my pulse stopped. I grimaced up at her and she said, "Please read aloud beginning on 161."

"I can't, Sister," I said. "My pages are missing."

She made me bring my book up. She soured her face over it, ran her finger along the serrations. "It looks as if someone deliberately tore this," she said. I was reflected mite-like in her glasses.

"I bought it secondhand."

"All right. Look on with someone else."

I scraped my desk over beside Tim's.

Rosaria said, "Not with Tim Sullivan."

I scraped back against Rusty's desk. Rosaria stared disgustedly, but allowed it.

The same pages were torn from Rusty's book, and the next two were psychedelic from squiggly lines he'd used to camouflage what Tim and Wade had drawn there.

"Chuck Spinnett," Rosaria said, "you have a nice reading voice. You begin."

Chuck commenced. He had a mild speech defect, due partly to the wires and rubber bands on his teeth. He slurred through *Manassas*, *Antietam*, and *Shiloh*. After, Rosaria said, "Class, this was the bloodiest war ever fought in the Western Hemisphere, ten times as bad as Vietnam. Now why was our country divided against itself in 1861?"

The air boiled with hands. None of them belonged to our gang. It was such a recycled subject that even Joey O'Connor abstained. I noted that the mood rings on the Kelly twins' fingers had turned different colors.

Rosaria called on Craig Dockery, Negro, breaker of duck wings.

"The Civil War was on account of the people didn't want to free the slaves like Lincoln say they had to."

"*Said*," corrected Lewis Epps, the darkest boy in the school.

"Very good, Craig," said the nun.

Donny Flynn stood up, unasked. "The South wanted to succeed from the unions but the Feds wanted to control everything." Craig cut his eyes at Donny.

"Yes, there was a matter of secession. But slavery is a stain on our past. The Confederacy was a lost cause even before it began."

Donny Flynn sneered. Craig Dockery elevated his chin at Donny.

Rosaria continued, "God inspired men like Abe Lincoln and U. S. Grant to look into their hearts and do what was best for mankind."

Tim said, "If God was on the Union side, why'd it take them four years to slaughter an army they outnumbered four to one?"

Rosaria blinked. "God doesn't interfere with free will."

"Oh. Maybe you should mention the part where Lincoln offers Robert E. Lee command of the Union Army, but Lee turns it down to defend the South, even though he doesn't own slaves, or that Grant was an alcoholic and a corrupt president—" Tim had folded his arms across his chest and was speaking rapidly in his Northern preemptive fashion, with Dockery and Flynn both muttering, then Tim raising his volume, "—and Sherman was insane, which made him good at setting fires and exterminating American Indians—"

"Well, I didn't want to bring all that in at an eighth-grade level," barked Rosaria, hoisting herself up and scowling like a beacon. "In fact, Lee and Grant were both gentlemen—"

"But weren't the slaves freed in the North mainly so they could fight?" All the heads swung to Tim, straining forward in his desk. "And Lincoln was willing to let Southerners keep their slaves if they'd give in to the Union—"

"That may be partly true!" All heads swung back to the screeching nun. She raised herself onto her toes and tilted forward, leaning on the desk. "But let's not stray into conjecture! Everyone's father isn't a history professor, Mr. Sullivan! The slaves were freed and—"

"Stayed on as dirt-poor sharecroppers—"

"They were free!" Rosaria shrilled, face purpling. I'd seen some spit fly at us. The students all whispered, mumbled.

Tim relaxed into his seat. "Right. They could starve or get lynched. And meanwhile the South gets turned into a backwards hog wallow."

Rosaria swung out from behind her desk and was lumbering down the aisle towards Tim. "If I were a little boy as small as you, I'd listen—"

"I do some outside reading so I'll know what's what."

Rosaria slapped the wood of Tim's desk. Craig cocked his chin as high as it would go, iced his eyes, and said, "Is he tryin to say slavery was supposed to be all right?"

Lewis Epps rolled his eyes. Tim flung his head as if dizzy and said, "Craig, don't leave your brain to Science." Donny turned to Craig and said, "I'd chain you up in a heartbeat," laughed. The whole class was chattering. Craig snarled, "Kiss my mother—"

"Class!" Rosaria screamed, smacking Tim's desk again, lines radiating from her eyes, her mouth. We got quiet.

She continued the lecture in a more detailed, qualifying way, but Tim was uninterested now. He was toiling over two scraps of paper with two different pens. He printed one in black, the other in sloppy green cursive. Both were a jumble of mis-spellings, abuses of grammar, and unnecessary quotation marks. A series of racial and sexual insults, in toilet-bowl language, challenged a fight on the softball diamond at lunch.

"Get this one onto Donny's desk," Tim whispered and gave it to Rusty. "I'll plant the other one with Craig."

I felt guilty about it, of course. Donny was Margie's brother, his arm was broken. And Craig was black. I stressed this in a half-sin-cere appeal to Tim, knowing he didn't want to seem prejudiced.

"Prejudiced against what? Sadistic assholes? Think about that duck screaming, think about Flynn delivering our comic book to Kavanagh. And Margie." He raised his eyebrows. "I'll bear full responsibility."

When we were dragging out our English books, Tim pelted Craig in the neck with the folded note. Rusty had just delivered Donny's.

They read them. Craig ripped his savagely and slung it across to the wastebasket and began massaging his arms. Donny waited for a quiet moment, then blew his nose into the note. Throughout the period they reminded me of tomcats yowling from opposite sidewalks, separated by a busy street, their backs humped and electrified.

I peeled the dried glue off finger by finger, and a cool relief filled my hand. I laid the translucent handskin on my desk. It was whorled and banded with the map of my identity, fingers spread. Stop, it seemed to be saying, or Help. With felt-tip pens, I colored it extravagantly, fingers like a peacock's tail, a strange face on each tip. I divided the palm into green earth and blue sky, drew clouds wearing smiles and sunglasses, trees bearing rain-bow fruit, skulls, crosses, dinosaurs, stars, and ringed planets.

It blazed from my desk, and people looked. A universe shed from my hand, the brightest spot in the room.

All the boys ate furious lunches.

I jogged to the park. The grass was lacquered with the week-end's rain, and the orange clay of the softball diamond had changed into soup. Donny and Craig were rolling, surrounded by shouting boys. Craig pinned Donny in the mud and sat on his chest. Both looked as if they'd been slopped with orange paint. Donny slugged Craig in the kidneys, his cast adding weight to the blows. Craig smacked him in the forehead. Black skin gaped out of Craig's torn shirt-sleeve.

Donny's face contorted like he was crying, but without tears. Craig, breathing hard, studied him cooly. "Awright," Craig said. "You give? I'll let you up, you promise to walk away. We're finished?" Craig poised his fist over Donny's nose.

"Okay!" Donny groaned, wincing. "Okay."

Craig got off of him. Donny sat up and wiped mud out of his eyes. Craig tried to scrape the slop from his knees, gave up, tucked his shirt in, and swaggered away towards the water fountain.

Donny snarled and charged at him, Craig spun around and began to slip, and Donny whacked him across the eyes with his plastered arm, and the cast cracked in two. Craig grabbed Donny's collar and the shirt ripped open as they both splattered down.

Their faces were horrible, rage and pain, the clumsy ugliness that makes you want to stop a fight. All the boys went "Oooh . . . "

Craig and Donny locked together on the ground, panting, and traded spasms of short, halfhearted punches. Then they lay there. Donny slowly worked his elbow around Craig's jaw, achieving a headlock. Craig pretzeled Donny's invalid arm up behind his back with the broken cast hanging on it. Their legs squeezed, relaxed, squeezed. Donny looked as if someone had mashed berries against his lips, and Craig's left eyebrow had a raw spot. They exchanged little punches, paused, hit.

Tim, on the other side of the ring, stepped forward and stooped beside them. "I just wanted you two pinheads to know that I'm the one who sent you those notes." He laughed, spit. Craig and Donny held each other.

Then Craig writhed free and scrambled, sliding, and Tim bolted and Craig ran after him. They ran figure eights around the field, Tim in quick bursts so that the larger boy reached out and snatched air as Tim ducked and doubled back, dodged behind the cyclone fence, laughed.

Craig stopped and bent over with his mouth wide, resting his hands on his knees. He looked at each of our gang, his yellowed eyes slit, first at Rusty, who waited with his head cocked and hands on his hips, then at Wade, as tall as Craig and flexing the cords in his forearms. Craig looked at me, straightened up, walked over. He knew I was the least dangerous.

My blood burned. My legs shook. I didn't know, at that age, that adrenaline always makes you shake if you don't spend it immediately. I had never fought a black kid, and never anyone that powerful. The shaking made me feel twice as cowardly.

Donny was hammering his cast against the metal fencepost, clang! Clang! Crunching the orange-smeared plaster into startling white pieces, then crumbling them from his arm.

"Why y'all think you're so bad?" Craig asked me.

"I don't," I said. "I have a hernia." I turned my back on him and started to walk away.

He grabbed my shirt at the shoulder and said, "I axed you a question!"

I whipped around and my shirt pulled out of his fist, the cotton smudged rusty, and Craig began to shuffle, throwing his fists loosely and swinging them in a circle, chanting "Rope-a-dope, rope-a-dope." It was a silly, affected display which nonetheless gave me time to consider the thinness of my arms and the new difficulty of filling my lungs. All faces were turned towards us. Rusty and Wade stood with fists balled, but etiquette required them to stay put until I was injured. Voices urged us to fight.

The secret baby inside me began bawling that this was unfair, ordering me to run, to beg Craig not to hurt me. I kept my mouth shut, though, and my face reasonably tough.

I gave him my back again. He shoved me, and my neck whiplashed.

I wheeled around and banged him in the mouth, felt his teeth nick my knuckles. He touched his lips, surprised. I was shocked and exhilarated. Then I wished I had hit harder, and again, because he'd already recovered. My classmates made noises of doom.

Curtis Simms, another black eighth-grader, stepped towards us. Rusty drifted nearer, and Wade. Blue-black Lewis Epps. Hurley, the white athlete. The black seventh-graders were coming.

Then I started stumbling, clouds and sky vivid and whirling, Craig's eyes crazy and his fist recoiling. The skin around my eye was swelling, kept swelling, and I feared it would burst. I pressed my hand to my cheek and felt liquid, looked at my fingers. Clear fluid, not blood. I had become biology, not me, just a body in animal peril.

Craig grew bigger fast. "Come on! I'll black your other eye!" I felt weaker, but dulled. Disgusted that this huge kid wanted to harm me. You can't hurt me, I thought, this isn't really me.

Wade and Rusty both jumped Craig, and they all fell into the mud together.

Black Curtis Simms launched at Tim, and they fell grappling, biting, and clawing. I couldn't stand the looks on their faces.

Everywhere, boys paired up and fell slithering through the mud, like salamanders. Wade's little brother, Steven, was grinding some boy's face into it. White boys were shoving white boys. I thought I saw two blacks fighting, the clay made it hard to tell. Beside me, Joey O'Connor was tussling with an anonymous orange kid who probably weighed half as much as him. Joey was a tongue-chewer. Three pink inches jutted out between his teeth. A hard uppercut from the other kid would cause him to bite off his tongue. Joey's eyeglasses were spattered blind. Through my confusion, I was afraid for him.

Then I saw that every blow being landed around me was to the body. The brawl had grown epic, spectacular, but beyond danger into wrestling. The faces had turned from ugly to comic. It was a herd of boys roughhousing in the mud.

Lewis Epps, minus his shirt, stumbled into me hard and I shoved him off and he sat in the slop. He got up, and I made automatic fists, and he charged and hugged my ribs and hoisted me off my feet and we toppled, splashing into it. Clay squished under my waistband, my collar. We rolled, churned, then stopped and looked at each other from an inch away. There was mud on the hairs in his nose. I couldn't recognize him.

"What the hell?" I said, tasting clay.

"I don't know." His breath was on my face. "I'm supposed to serve a funeral Mass after recess."

We untangled and started dragging people apart. Some allowed it, others made me feel like a hockey referee. They'd ignore you, roll over your feet, push you away. I found that if I shouted, though it hurt my hernia, they ceased. "The teachers are coming!" I yelled, cleaving apart boys I couldn't identify.

"Here come the teachers," bellowed Lewis Epps.

Boys rose, smirked, and searched for sucked-off shoes. They wiped their faces and flung clay from their fingers. My cheek was throbbing, my hand ached. Tim passed, slapping me on the splattery back.

"Young Henry Kissinger," he said. "Diplomat. Francis, man, you slay me."

Tim limped over to Craig, who was propped against the fence, straightening the tatters of his shirt.

"Look at my clothes," Craig said. "You're in for it, man."

"I don't give a damn what you think about me, Craig. You're a bully. You like to hurt anything that can't hurt you back. That's why you hit that duck, and that's why you went after Francis instead of the other guys. And that's the same attitude the slave traders had when they held a gun on your ancestors and forced them into a cage. Think about that for a while."

"You might know books, little man, but you don't know what's in my mind." Craig licked his lip where blood was hardening.

Tim cleared his throat and spit on the ground. "You've got a big blob of clay on your head, Dockery."

"You got some on your chin."

They wiped clay off. Tim shrugged and walked over to me and we plodded towards our oak tree.

A mud-covered tribe of boys was playing lazy soccer, easy softball. Rusty smiled down at his orthopedic shoes, which appeared to be finally ruined. Margie was sitting over on the bleachers. I waved. She waved.

Tim lay on the ground with his ankles crossed, fingers laced behind his head. "Don't worry, Francis," he said. "She knows Donny gets beat up all the time. You ever, ever seen him without stitches or a cast or crutches?"

"His one arm is all shriveled and small," I said. "Reminds me of a fiddler crab."

"Anyhow," said Rusty, "he got us into boocoos of trouble. I'm sorry I didn't get to fuck him up personally. Hell, he molested his own sister—" Rusty halted, looked past me, coughed, pulled at a seedling and studied it.

"Molested?" said Joey.

I was drained with anger. "You promised!"

"Well, Rusty is godfather of the gang." Tim met my eye. "I'm sorry, man, it preyed on my mind. I had to tell, just like you had to tell, and Margie too. That's why confession was invented." He sighed.

I hurried across the field, the street, into the school building, the lavatory. I got out of my shirt and soaked it in the sink. I anointed myself with water, dried with paper towels, wrung out the shirt. All the wrinkles were orange, in the shirt, my face, my elbows.

The teachers quizzed us about the clay, black eyes, bloody lips, and we blamed it on soccer and softball. They couldn't do anything.

For the rest of the day I didn't speak to anyone. After the bell, I ran home.

from *Midnight in the Garden of Good and Evil*

A Savannah Story

JOHN BERENDT (1939–)

John Berendt received his A.B. from Harvard University in
1961. He has served as an editor with both *Esquire* and *New
York* magazines. His *Midnight in the Garden of Good and Evil:
A Savannah Story*, excerpted here, was a Pulitzer Prize finalist
for general nonfiction in 1995. "The Book," as it is called in
Savannah, has been a *New York Times* bestseller for over four
years and was dramatized for the screen by director Clint
Eastwood.

There being no direct route to Savannah from Charleston, I
followed a zigzagging course that took me through the tidal
flatlands of the South Carolina low country. As I approached
Savannah, the road narrowed to a two-lane blacktop shaded by
tall trees. There was an occasional produce stand by the side of the
road and a few cottages set into the foliage, but nothing resem-
bling urban sprawl. The voice on the car radio informed me that I
had entered a zone called the Coastal Empire. "The weather outlook for the Coastal Empire," it said, "is for highs in the mid-
eighties, with moderate seas and a light chop on inland waters."

Abruptly, the trees gave way to an open panorama of marsh
grass the color of wheat. Straight ahead, a tall bridge rose steeply
out of the plain. From the top of the bridge, I looked down on the
Savannah River and, on the far side, a row of old brick buildings
fronted by a narrow esplanade. Behind the buildings a mass of
trees extended into the distance, punctuated by steeples, cornices,
rooftops, and cupolas. As I descended from the bridge, I found
myself plunging into a luxuriant green garden.

Walls of thick vegetation rose up on all sides and arched over-head in a lacy canopy that filtered the light to a soft shade. It had just rained; the air was hot and steamy. I felt enclosed in a semi-tropical terrarium, sealed off from a world that suddenly seemed a thousand miles away.

The streets were lined with townhouses of brick and stucco, handsome old buildings with high front stoops and shuttered windows. I entered a square that had flowering shrubs and a monument at the center. A few blocks farther on, there was another square. Up ahead, I could see a third on line with this one, and a fourth beyond that. To the left and right, there were two more squares. There were squares in every direction. I counted eight of them. Ten. Fourteen. Or was it twelve?

"There are exactly twenty-one squares," an elderly lady told me later in the afternoon. Her name was Mary Harty. Acquaintances in Charleston had put us in touch; she had been expecting me. She had white hair and arched eyebrows that gave her a look of permanent surprise. We stood in her kitchen while she mixed martinis in a silver shaker. When she was finished, she put the shaker into a wicker basket. She was going to take me on an excursion, she said. It was too nice a day, and I had too little time in Savannah for us to waste it indoors.

As far as Miss Harty was concerned, the squares were the jew-els of Savannah. No other city in the world had anything like them. There were five on Bull Street, five on Barnard, four on Abercorn, and so on. James Oglethorpe, the founder of Georgia, had been responsible for them, she said. He had decided Savannah was going to be laid out with squares, based on the design of a Roman military encampment, even before he set sail from England—before he even knew exactly where on the map he was going to put Savannah. When he arrived in February 1733, he chose a site for the city on top of a forty-foot bluff on the southern bank of the Savannah River, eighteen miles inland from the Atlantic. He had already sketched out the plans. The streets were to be laid out in a grid pattern, crossing at right angles, and there would be squares at regular intervals. In effect, the city would become a giant parterre garden. Oglethorpe built the first four squares himself. "The thing I like best about the squares," Miss Harty said, "is that cars can't cut through the middle; they must go *around* them. So traffic is obliged to flow at a very leisurely pace. The squares are our little oases of tranquillity."

As she spoke, I recognized in her voice the coastal accent described in *Gone with the Wind*—"soft and slurring, liquid of vowels, kind to consonants."

"But actually," she said, "the whole of Savannah is an oasis. We are isolated. Gloriously isolated! We're a little enclave on the coast—off by ourselves, surrounded by nothing but marshes and piney woods. We're not easy to get to at all, as you may have noticed. If you fly here, you usually have to change planes at least once. And trains are not much better. Somebody wrote a novel in the nineteen-fifties that captured it rather well, I thought. *The View from Pompey's Head*. It's by Hamilton Basso. Have you read it? The story opens with a young man taking the train from New York to Pompey's Head and having to get off at the ungodly hour of five in the morning. Pompey's Head is supposed to be Savannah, and I have no quibble with that. We're a terribly inconvenient destination!"

Miss Harty's laughter was as light as wind chimes. "There used to be a train that ran between here and Atlanta. The *Nancy Hanks*. It shut down altogether twenty years ago, and we don't miss it at all."

"Don't you feel cut off?" I asked.

"Cut off from what?" she replied. "No, on the whole I'd say we rather enjoy our separateness. Whether that's good or bad I haven't any idea. Manufacturers tell us they like to test-market their products in Savannah—toothpastes and detergents and the like—because Savannah is utterly impervious to outside influence. Not that people haven't *tried* to influence us! Good Lord, they try all the time. People come here from all over the country and fall in love with Savannah. Then they move here and pretty soon they're telling us how much more lively and prosperous

Savannah could be if we only knew what we had and how to take advantage of it. I call these people 'Gucci carpetbaggers.' They can be rather insistent, you know. Even rude. We smile pleasantly and we nod, but we don't budge an inch. Cities all around us are booming urban centers: Charleston, Atlanta, Jacksonville—but not Savannah. The Prudential Insurance people wanted to locate their regional headquarters here in the nineteen-fifties. It would have created thousands of jobs and made Savannah an important center of a nice, profitable, non-polluting industry. But we said no. Too big. They gave it to Jacksonville instead. In the nineteen-seventies, Gian Carlo Menotti considered making Savannah the permanent home for his Spoleto U.S.A. Festival. Again, we were not interested. So Charleston got it. It's not that we're trying to be difficult. We just happen to like things exactly the way they are!"

Miss Harty opened a cupboard and took out two silver goblets. She wrapped each of them in a linen napkin and placed them carefully in the wicker basket beside the martinis.

"We may be standoffish," she said, "but we're not hostile. We're famously hospitable, in fact, even by southern standards. Savannah's called the 'Hostess City of the South,' you know. That's because we've always been a party town. We love company. We always have. I suppose that comes from being a port city and having played host to people from faraway places for so long. Life in Savannah was always easier than it was out on the plantations. Savannah was a city of rich cotton traders, who lived in elegant houses within strolling distance of one another. Parties became a way of life, and it's made a difference. We're not at all like the rest of Georgia. We have a saying: If you go to Atlanta, the first question people ask you is, 'What's your business?' In Macon they ask, 'Where do you go to church?' In Augusta they ask your grandmother's maiden name. But in Savannah the first question people ask you is 'What would you like to drink?'"

She patted the basket of martinis. I could hear the echo of Captain Flint shouting for rum.

"Savannah's always been wet," she said, "even when the rest of Georgia was dry. During Prohibition, filling stations on Abercorn Street sold whiskey out of gas pumps! Oh, you could always get a drink in Savannah. That's never been any secret. I remember when I was a child, Billy Sunday brought his holy-revival crusade to town. He set himself up in Forsyth Park, and everybody went to hear him. There was great excitement! Mr. Sunday got up and declared at the top of his voice that Savannah was the wickedest city in the world! Well, of course, we all thought that was perfectly marvelous!"

Miss Harty handed me the basket and led the way through the hall and out the front door to my car. With the basket on the seat between us, she guided me as I drove through the streets.

"I'm going to take you to visit the dead," she said.

We had just turned onto Victory Drive, a long parkway completely covered by an arch of live oaks dripping with Spanish moss. In the center, a double colonnade of palms marched along the median strip as if lending architectural support to the canopy of oaks and moss.

I glanced at her, not sure I'd heard correctly. "The dead?"

"The dead are very much with us in Savannah," she said. "Everywhere you look there is a reminder of things that were, people who lived. We are keenly aware of our past. Those palms, for example. They were planted in honor of soldiers from Georgia who died in the First World War."

After driving three or four miles, we turned off Victory Drive onto a winding road that took us to the gates of Bonaventure Cemetery. A live-oak forest of a primeval dimension loomed before us. We parked the car just inside the gate and continued on foot, coming almost at once to a large white marble mausoleum.

"Now, if you should die during your stay in Savannah," Miss Harty said with a gentle smile, "this is where we'll put you. It's our Stranger's Tomb. It was built in honor of a man named William Gaston. He was one of Savannah's greatest hosts and party givers, and he died in the nineteenth century. This tomb is a memorial to his hospitality. It has an empty vault in it that's reserved for out-of-towners who die while visiting Savannah. It gives them a chance to rest awhile in one of the most beautiful cemeteries in the world, until their families can make arrangements to take them away."

I remarked that I hoped I would not tax Savannah's hospitality to that extent. We moved on past the tomb along an avenue bordered by magnificent oaks. On both sides, moss-covered statues stood in an overgrowth of shrubbery like the remnants of an abandoned temple.

"In Colonial times, this was a lovely plantation," Miss Harty said. "Its centerpiece was a mansion made of bricks brought over from England. There were terraced gardens extending all the way down to the river. The estate was built by Colonel John Mulryne. When Mulryne's daughter married Josiah Tatnall, the bride's father commemorated the happy union of the two families by planting great avenues of trees forming the initials M and T intertwined. I'm told enough of the original trees survive that you can still trace the monogram, if you put your mind to it." Miss Harty paused as we approached a vine-covered mound by the side of the path.

"This is all that's left of the plantation house," she said. "It's a piece of the foundation. The house burned sometime in the late seventeen-hundreds. It was a spectacular fire, by all accounts. A formal dinner party had been in progress, with liveried servants standing behind every chair. In the middle of dinner, the butler came up to the host and whispered that the roof had caught fire and that nothing could be done to stop it. The host rose calmly, clinked his glass, and invited his guests to pick up their dinner plates and follow him into the garden. The servants carried the table and chairs after them, and the dinner continued by the light of the raging fire. The host made the best of it. He regaled his guests with amusing stories and jests while the flames consumed his house. Then, in turn, each guest rose and offered a toast to the host, the house, and the delicious repast. When the toasts were finished, the host threw his crystal glass against the trunk of an old oak tree, and each of the guests followed suit. Tradition has it that if you listen closely on quiet nights you can still hear the laughter and the shattering of crystal glasses. I like to think of this place as the scene of the Eternal Party. What better place, in Savannah, to rest in peace for all time—where the party goes on and on."

We resumed our walk and in a few moments came to a small family plot shaded by a large oak tree. Five graves and two small date palms lay inside a low curbstone. One of the graves, a full-length white marble slab, was littered with dried leaves and sand. Miss Harty brushed the debris away, and an inscription emerged: JOHN HERNDON MERCER (JOHNNY).

"Did you know him?" I asked.

"We all knew him," she said, "and loved him. We always thought we recognized something of Johnny in each of his songs. They had a buoyancy and a freshness, and that's the way he was. It was as if he'd never really left Savannah." She brushed away more of the leaves and uncovered an epitaph: AND THE ANGELS SING.

"For me," she said, "Johnny was literally the boy next door. I lived at 222 East Gwinnett Street; he lived at 226. Johnny's great-grandfather built a huge house on Monterey Square, but Johnny never lived in it. The man who lives there now has restored it superbly and made it into quite a showplace. Jim Williams. My society friends are wild about him. I'm not."

Miss Harty squared her shoulders and said no more about the Mercers or Jim Williams. We continued along the path toward the river, which was just now visible up ahead under the trees. "And now I have one more thing to show you," she said.

We walked to the crest of a low bluff overlooking a broad, slow-moving expanse of water, clearly the choicest spot in this most tranquil of settings. Miss Harty led me into a small enclosure that had a gravestone and a granite bench. She sat down on the bench and gestured for me to sit next to her.

"At last," she said, "we can have our martinis." She opened the wicker basket and poured the drinks into the silver goblets.

"If you look at the gravestone," she said, "you'll see it's a bit unusual." It was a double gravestone bearing the names of Dr. William F. Aiken and his wife, Anna. "They were the parents of Conrad Aiken, the poet. Notice the dates."

Both Dr. and Mrs. Aiken had died on the same day: February 27, 1901.

"This is what happened," she said. "The Aikens were living on Oglethorpe Avenue in a big brick townhouse. Dr. Aiken had his offices on the ground floor, and the family lived on the two floors above. Conrad was eleven. One morning, Conrad awoke to the sounds of his parents quarreling in their bedroom down the hall. The quarreling subsided for a moment. Then Conrad heard his father counting, 'One! Two! Three!' There was a half-stifled scream and then a pistol shot. Then another count of three, another shot, and then a thud. Conrad ran barefoot across Oglethorpe Avenue to the police station where he announced, 'Papa has just shot Mama and then shot himself.' He led the officers to the house and up to his parents' bedroom on the top floor."

Miss Harty lifted her goblet in a silent toast to Dr. and Mrs. Aiken. Then she poured a few drops onto the ground.

"Believe it or not," she said, "one of the reasons he killed her was . . . parties. Aiken hinted at it in 'Strange Moonlight,' one of his short stories. In the story, the father complains to the mother that she's neglecting her family. He says, 'It's two parties every week, and sometimes three or four, that's excessive.' The story was autobiographical, of course. The Aikens were living well beyond their means at the time. Anna Aiken went out to parties practically every other night. She'd given six dinner parties in the month before her husband killed her.

"After the shooting, relatives up north took Conrad in and raised him. He went to Harvard and had a brilliant career. He won the Pulitzer Prize and was appointed to the poetry chair at the Library of Congress. When he retired, he came back to spend his last years in Savannah. He always knew he would. He'd written a novel called *Great Circle*; it was about ending up where one started. And that's the way it turned out for Aiken himself. He lived in Savannah his first eleven years and his last eleven years. In those last years, he lived next door to the house where he'd lived as a child, separated from his tragic childhood by a single brick wall.

"Of course, when he moved back to Savannah, the poetry society was all aflutter, as you can imagine. But Aiken kept pretty much to himself. He politely declined most invitations. He said he needed the time for his work. Quite often, though, he and his wife would come out here and sit for an hour or so. They'd bring a shaker of martinis and silver goblets and talk to his departed parents and pour libations to them."

Miss Harty raised her goblet and touched it to mine. A pair of mockingbirds conversed somewhere in the trees. A shrimp boat passed at slow speed.

"Aiken loved to come here and watch the ships go by," she said. "One afternoon, he saw one with the name Cosmos Mariner painted on the bow. That delighted him. The word 'cosmos' appears often in his poetry, you know. That evening he went home and looked for mention of the *Cosmos Mariner* in the shipping news. There it was, in tiny type on the list of ships in port. The name was followed by the comment 'Destination Unknown.' That pleased him even more."

"Where is Aiken buried?" I asked. There were no other gravestones in the enclosure.

"Oh, he's here," she said. "In fact, we are very much his personal guests at the moment. It was Aiken's wish that people should come to this beautiful place after he died and drink martinis and watch the ships just as he did. He left a gracious invitation to that effect. He had his gravestone built in the shape of a bench."

An involuntary reflex propelled me to my feet. Miss Harty laughed, and then she too stood up. Aiken's name was inscribed on the bench, along with the words COSMOS MARINER, DESTINATION UNKNOWN.

"Gambling, Liquor, and Vice"

TOM COFFEY (1923–)

> Tom Coffey worked in newspapers for fifty years. Starting as a newspaper delivery boy, Coffey eventually retired as editor of the *Savannah Morning News* and *Savannah Evening Press*. Two-time acting city manager of Savannah, Coffey continues as columnist and commentator in Savannah newspapers and on local television. *Only in Savannah: Stories and Insights on Georgia's Mother City*, from which the following piece was taken, appeared in 1994.

Willie Haar, who ran one of Chatham County's bootlegging operations from his seaside base on Tybee Island, once explained how easy it was to corrupt county policemen without really corrupting them very much. On nights when a liquor shipment was coming in from Canada or Cuba, he would give each Chatham County policeman assigned to patrol Tybee a cigar, around which would be wrapped a fifty-dollar bill.

"That was more money than the cop earned in two weeks," Haar explained. All he would ask them to do was to patrol a certain end of Tybee between the certain hours when he was expecting a boat shipment that would arrive on the other end of the island—and without telling them that a shipment was coming in. They'd understand without any detailed explanation, Haar said. Or, giving benefit of doubt, maybe they simply weren't all that curious.

Of course it was wrong for cops to take money, but one veteran officer explained to me that back in Depression days cops hardly earned enough to get by on, and most of them held second jobs, therefore "all of them would *take* to a certain extent." That "certain extent" phrase seemed to justify everything, like saying someone's a little bit pregnant. And, the cop elaborated, such deals with Willie Haar were merely I-won't-bother-you-

and-you-won't-bother-me gentlemen's agreements—in other words: see no evil, hear no evil, speak no evil.

There is an earlier reference to a raid on the Owls Club in downtown Savannah, and how it was obvious there had been a tipoff. Likely, some money-wrapped cigars were involved.

Leo Ryan, who started with the city force in 1940 and rose through the ranks to chief, recalled to me how one of his first assignments as a rookie was to drive over to a joint on West Broad Street, pick up a package, and bring it back to a superior.

"Hell, I didn't think anything of it until after I had picked up the package, a cigar box with a heavy rubber band around it," Ryan recalled. "I shook the box and could hear paper moving around, and then it dawned on me that there was money in the box. Sure as hell wasn't newspaper clippings."

Ryan said he was scared to death until he delivered the box to his superior and got it out of his hands. "I knew that was a gambling payoff," Ryan reminisced, "because the guy who gave me the box was a known numbers seller, as well as a collector from the street runners. But dammit, I was innocent, and somehow I dodged being sent ever again to that guy's place."

It was a rather smart method by Ryan's superior—use the cops who aren't in on the payoffs to make the pickups, then don't use them again lest suspicions arise.

Numbers-running was the principal form of gambling, lucratively complementing the slot machines and pinballs, and the card games and dice rolling that occurred in "secret" clubs like the Owls. The numbers game took several forms, ranging from the Cuban lottery's first-cousin bolita, to stocks-and-bonds and other versions and deviations, in which payoffs were based on stock market figures printed on the financial pages of the daily newspaper.

The numbers games were run by several kingpins, notably among them two white men named Snippy Garrity and Bubba Johnson. I use their names here because neither ever made any secret of the fact of their involvement. A black man named Sloppy Joe Bellinger also was a numbers kingpin, and his wife, Inez, succeeded him upon his death.

Sloppy Joe—so-called because of his obesity, rolls of fat forming several layers across his belt line—was an interesting character. He ran a nightclub on West Gwinnett Street and conducted his games from that base. It was there, in that huge metal building near the old city waterworks, that his funeral took place. At least two thousand overflowed the place to hear several tearful orations in tribute to Sloppy Joe's benevolence, which was no exaggeration—he gave to many charities and helped many black families individually.

Sloppy Joe also was a likable fellow; and he made the national news at one of his trials because he continually would doze off as the testimony against him was being recited from the witness stand. His lawyer explained that Bellinger suffered from something called Pickwickian syndrome, a malady peculiar to obese people. In fact, his lawyer cited the ailment in his plea for leniency.

Snippy Garrity and Bubba Johnson were the white bolita bosses who claimed certain territories of the community for themselves and took unkindly to anyone encroaching on the other's geographical turf. It was territorial encroachment that precipitated a fist fight between the two one night in the late 1940s in a men's room of the General Oglethorpe Hotel on Wilmington Island.

The General Oglethorpe, a resort hotel, is now the Sheraton, several times renovated and refurbished since that classic fight. But the men's room where the fight occurred looks much the same today—nicely appointed, clean-tiled, but not very large; two stand-up and three sit-down compartments, if memory serves. The night of the fight, the two were at the hotel as guests of the Quarterback Club's annual Bowl Party; which is the name assigned to the annual banquet of those football boosters.

I did not witness the fight, but heard about it quickly afterwards. Hardly anyone else at the banquet didn't lay claim to having actually witnessed it, and many gave contradicting and embellished accounts of how Snippy or Bubba, one or the other, ended the fight by shoving his adversary's head into a toilet bowl. And while I didn't see the fight, I will say this about it: If everyone at that banquet of about three hundred people who claimed to have seen the fight actually crowded into that small men's room and witnessed it, neither Snippy nor Bubba would have had room to throw a punch, much less maneuver the other into a stall for the coup de grace. Leave it at this: they did fight, and Lord knows who won or by what means the winner ended the fray. Anyway, Savannahians still hear varying accounts of that set-to, and this has been one of them.

Old-time Savannahians know what bolita is, but for the uninitiated I should describe the game, of Cuban origin and Savannah embellishment. Numbers were sold on the street by runners who worked for neighborhood bosses who in turn worked for territorial bosses. Most of the runners and players were black. A player could buy as many numbers as he chose, within the range of one to one hundred, and a ticket bearing the chosen number served as his receipt for whatever amount he had risked—a nickel, a dime, a quarter, and up into big money. Payoffs were made in proportion to the size of the bet, each daily take governing the amount to be paid out overall.

At the end of the day the winning number would be drawn— the location of the drawing changing daily—and divulged only to a few trusted players, who in turn were trusted by their peers among the bettors. At the time of the drawing, balls numbered one to one hundred were placed inside a cloth sack, and the operator would tie the sack shut with a stout cord.

Then the operator would shake the sack vigorously and toss it to one of the witnesses across the room. That witness, in turn, would shake the sack and toss it to another witness. And so on . . . the sack got tossed from one person to another about twenty times (even more if any of the invited in-players insisted), thus ensuring that the balls were well mixed. Finally the sack went back to the operator, who this time would catch the sack so that he held, through the fabric, one of the hundred balls.

Then, with another piece of twine, the operator would tie off that lone ball, after which he would use scissors to cut the trapped ball loose from the sack. Players who held tickets matching that ball's number would be winners.

The house kept all the money plunged on losing numbers. It was a profitable venture in which the game's bosses, their operators, and the politicians shared the largess. Considering that several games ran daily and many played bolita, it was big money.

Now, there was always the danger of too many players holding a winning number, thus siphoning off the profits. One of the dangers, I am told by a knowledgeable former operator, lay in the arrival in town of a new fortune teller in an era when itinerant seers and self-anointed prophets came and went to prey on the superstitions of Negroes. A new fortune teller in town would draw an outpouring of customers asking for a number, and the soothsayer would oblige—for a fee, of course.

The fear of the operation's moguls was that the seer would give each customer the same number, and if that number "hit" (the word for a number coming up), then it would be disastrous day for the house.

The operation's moguls, however, figured a way to overcome that danger—sew inside the cloth bag a pocket into which the person in charge of the drawing would, with sleight-of-hand, drop a ball with a number that wasn't heavily played that day. All the tossing and catching of the bag during the ceremony of the drawing could not dislodge that trapped ball, and the man operating the game knew; on the final toss, just where to catch the bag and grab the hidden ball.

Even compulsive gamblers who eternally harbor high hopes of a big payday concede that the house always wins. Maybe not always, but it did whenever the house ran a risk of losing big. Only in Savannah? Indeed, everywhere there is a gambling operation, even those that are legit.

Was gambling protected by the police? Anyone who was involved with it in those days says yes. Else, how could shoeshine boys at hotels and railroad stations sell numbers with impunity? Or waiters and bellhops? Or men and women with no visible means of support but who drove classy cars and moved from neighborhood to neighborhood, much the way drug dealers do today? How did Snippy Garrity's black chauffeur afford that sparkling multicarat diamond stickpin that he wore with impunity. No policeman ever stopped him to ask where he got it, the way some of the redneck cops would stop, frisk, and quiz any Negro who, to them, looked "suspicious" or overly prosperous.

Also, there is another version of why Snippy Garrity and Bubba Johnson came to blows, as earlier related. The fight happened shortly after political kingpin John Bouhan, whose party had been out of City Hall for two years, won back control of the city. As the story goes, Johnson had won favor with Bouhan and advised Garrity to take a hike—in other words, get out of the numbers business. The famed fight is said to have stemmed from that.

The story goes further. Bouhan's advisers, fearing that internecine warfare in the gambling community would cut into the profits enjoyed on the political periphery, advised Bouhan to try to reconcile Garrity and Johnson. Bouhan did, through an emissary. Garrity and Johnson reportedly lived happily ever after until federal agents, who long had been monitoring local gambling activities, heard that Garrity had a huge cache of cash buried underneath his home. The report proved true, and Garrity was arrested and convicted. After his release Garrity went straight, holding a job as a bridge toll-taker. Johnson's sway over gambling gradually came to an end in the mid-1950s after the election of the reform city administration headed by Mayor Lee Mingledorff.

Both Garrity and Johnson are deceased. So are most of the politicians and policemen who countenanced bolita and all other forms of gambling, and the ones still around are long retired and out of the swim.

Does bolita still flourish? I am told that it does, but that most of the games are small-time, operated independently, and that political protection no longer is needed because the games go virtually ignored on account of such other pressing crimes as drugs, murder, mayhem, and stealing. Only occasionally is there a gambling arrest, made when the principals become so careless as to be blatant. Also, there's the Florida lottery flourishing legally across the border, and Georgia has gone into the lottery business in the wake of a referendum in November 1992.

Vice is defined as an evil and immoral habit, which can embrace a multitude of sins. In Savannah officialdom the term has always meant one thing: prostitution—not only the oldest profession, but also the most long-running, because no community has ever stamped it out.

Two kinds now go on in Savannah, as in any community. There are the street-corner prostitutes who stand in the shadows and beckon to potential customers, and there are the B-girls who sit around bars waiting for "Johns" to pick them up. Police harass these whores, frequently arrest some, and sometimes arrest their Johns.

The classy prostitutes are the call girls, same as in other places. Now and then police will raid a house of prostitution, and some of those have turned up in ritzy neighborhoods; but I am told that call girls, obtainable through an intricate network known to hotel bellmen, and from escort services, command the highest prices.

There was a time, though, when whorehouses flourished, and nearly everyone knew where they were or could find out easily enough, and they operated with about 98 percent impunity, getting raided once in a while, just so the authorities couldn't be accused of completely ignoring them.

The best-known place—and its history remains a legend to this day—was Indian Lil's, situated on Indian Street just two blocks south of the Savannah River and a block west of West Broad, where the post office complex now stands.

Lillian Sims was the madame. She and her brother Joe ran a couple of other places along the cobblestoned West Broad ramp, across from the fire station. The three places, therefore, were within a block-and-a-half triangle.

There were also houses on Congress Street, the most famous being Ma's Place at the southwest corner of Montgomery Street;

and also on West Broad, Oglethorpe Avenue, Liberty Street, and in sundry other locations, including one as far south as beside the railroad crossing on Thirty-seventh Street, operated by Mamie Saxe. It's now my understanding that call girls operate out of residences in Ardsley Park, which remains Savannah's classiest residential section, even when pitted against the much newer subdivisions where mansion houses have been built.

As a kid, I delivered papers to several whorehouses, and in those Depression days the madames and girls were my best-paying customers because they always had money. Rumors among the *Evening Press* carriers were that those places would allow you to "take it out in trade," but either that was wrong or something was the matter with me because never did I, an adventuresome teenager who might have relished the experience, encounter such a tempting offer from those subscribers. In those days I was slight of build, about 125 pounds soaking wet, and I hadn't yet begun to shave.

The whorehouses were cleverly constructed, with false walls inside the closets, behind which patrons could hide in the event of a raid. After a raid a cop once told me that he couldn't understand why, with cars parked all around the house on Montgomery, he didn't find one gentleman inside the place.

Although I never met Mamie Saxe personally, she and I became telephone friends when I was managing editor of the *Morning News*. After several raids in succession, she called to ask that we stop writing her up because at the time she was under indictment for a felony crime and the publicity would prejudice a jury.

"Tell you what," I said to Mrs. Saxe, "you don't get raided anymore and we won't write you up." I recited the old news standard: If you don't want it in the paper, don't do it. She promised that she would be more circumspect, and believe it or not, we never printed her name again because the raids ceased. Form your own conclusion on whether it was circumspection or payoff to the cops.

Her name did appear once more, and that was as the owner of the house by the railroad, after the place caught fire and suffered heavy damage. A few days later a reporter came in with an intriguing observation—he swore that a note tacked on the front door of the burned-out house read: "Closed. Beat It." The double entendre evoked laughter in the newsroom.

Lillian Sims remained the queen of the madames, through all those days when whorehouses flourished. The word was that she had a heart of gold, extended credit to regular customers who were down on their luck, and sometimes carried on her books honest-faced seamen who promised to pay up next time they were in port.

She was said to be a generous contributor to charitable causes, a soft touch for a handout, and an otherwise nice and accommodating lady. From my days as paper carrier, I remember her that way; she'd always take a chance on the raffle tickets that I sold for good causes, and was a generous tipper at Christmas. But she never invited me inside, perhaps because I was a minor.

The best whores-at-the-lockup story I recall features Mike Davies, a handsome young reporter at the time, who was covering the police beat. Mike went on to become a Pulitzer Prize-winning executive editor in Kansas City, and now is publisher of the *Hartford Courant*.

Well, English-born Mike, who still cultivates his soft British accent, was about the handsomest reporter in town—well built and with facial features suggesting a blend of John F. Kennedy, Dan Quayle, and Peter Lawford. He was in the desk sergeant's office, getting the details of the just-finished raid, jotting down the names of the accused madame and her girls, all of whom were standing around, waiting patiently for their bondsman to show. Before he had finished taking his notes, Pretty Boy Mike had been propositioned by every one of those prostitutes, all of whom promised freebies. Mike vows that he never succumbed to the lurings, but admits that some of them looked mighty cute. They all thought he was cute and told him so.

Miss Sims and Mrs. Saxe have vanished from the local scene, but they're not forgotten. The last whorehouse raid of recollection occurred in 1989 in midtown. It was a well-run business, complete with records of drop-in customers as well as patrons who ordered call girls.

Police Chief David Gellatly announced at the time that the investigation wasn't complete and that soon he would be releasing information from the seized records, which he said contained the names of many prominent Savannahians. He never has, but you can bet there are still some husbands shuddering in anticipation of Gellatly's dropping the other shoe. Only in Savannah would one find so much fearful apprehension among the "prominent."

I have already related how Willie Haar, the bootlegging kingpin at Tybee Island, fixed it with the police so he could unload shipments of contraband booze from Cuba during Prohibition days. Haar was one of several bootleggers who, though liquor was illegal at the time, held the esteem of Savannahians.

For goodness' sake, Savannah-Chatham County historically has been a location where people like to drink, and anyone with a taste for bonded or otherwise good whiskey would rather have obtained liquor from someone capable of getting good brands than from moonshine distillers who flourished. Haar, Johnny Peters, and Jimmy Goethe, Peters's brother-in-law, were in Prohibition days the most prominently mentioned as being in the liquor trade; and in the same breath, were soft touches for anyone down on his luck.

Alas, the tales of Prohibition bootlegging all came to me secondhand, because my family brought me back to Savannah in 1935, after repeal of the Eighteenth Amendment that had banned liquor in America—the noble experiment that simply did not work. But from Willie Haar came a few first-person stories.

Haar recalled, also pleasantly and boastfully, his running game of cat-and-mouse with the federal agents. There was a time in his operation when Haar had to go to a city on the coast of central Florida to "make arrangements" (payment in advance) for a shipment of booze from Cuba. The designated place for the cash payment was a hotel.

By then, Haar knew by sight practically every federal agent who was on his case; and as he drove up in front of the hotel, he spotted one of them standing nonchalantly near the entrance. He knew that he couldn't walk into the hotel carrying a satchel filled of cash; the agent would tail him to the rendezvous and arrest both Haar and the shippers as soon as the cash traded hands.

Haar was prepared for such an eventuality. On such trips he always took with him various items for the making of disguises, and stashed in the trunk of his car were a fiery-red outlandish wig, horn-rimmed eyeglasses, and a hat unlike his customary style of headwear. So, after spotting the agent, Haar drove around the block and donned his disguise.

Again at the hotel's entrance, Haar parked his car and dismounted, carrying the satchel of money through the entrance right past the federal agent. So pleased was Haar with the success of his disguise, he turned around in the lobby, came back to the front door, and asked the agent for a light for his cigar. The agent obliged, and a smilingly grateful Haar gave the agent a cigar, then reentered the hotel.

So pleased by then was Haar that after completing his transaction inside the hotel, he came back through the front entrance, stopped, and engaged the agent in small-talk conversation, then sauntered to his parked car, tipping his hat to the unsuspecting agent as he left.

Talk about pushing one's luck! Only in Savannah . . . or, more precisely, only a Savannahian on a mission to Florida!

Another Haar story involved his softball team. His liquor operation employed a number of people, and for Sunday relaxation they played softball on a Tybee Island diamond. Haar recalled that while sitting on the team's bench he noticed suddenly that his three outfielders were leaving their positions and heading not toward the bench but, at a trot, toward the far end of the ball field. Then he saw his first baseman abandon his position and leave the field, followed by the other infielders and the pitcher, the catcher also hotfooting it away from home plate.

Haar looked behind him and saw the reason for the sudden departure of his softball team. Two cars of federal agents were approaching the parking area, and that was signal enough for Haar to beat a hasty retreat from the players' bench, all of his reserves following their boss in flight.

By the time the feds parked and dismounted, not a member of Willie Haar & Company was in sight. Players of the other team, the one at bat, simply shrugged when the revenue agents asked where their opponents were. Gee, they had been in the field only minutes ago.

The bootlegging that the newsmen of my vintage became privy to was performed by illegal distillers who plied their trade mostly in the black districts, and they were hounded by local, state, and federal officers.

The most notorious, I suppose, was a black man named Joe Delegal (pronounced "delly-gall"), who well may have been the most persistent moonshiner in any urban setting. They would catch Joe making 'shine in some abandoned ghetto house, confiscate and destroy his booze and still, haul him in, fine him, and turn him loose. In a week or two he'd have another still set up somewhere else, and the procedure would repeat.

I suspect that not all of Delegal's corn whiskey found its way into the sewers because, police avowed, it was high-quality stuff, tasty and of potent proof. I suspect that some of it found its way into policemen's liquor closets. I know that a half-gallon of it found its way to my house, a friendly cop having placed it in the back of my car one day, assuring that the crime laboratory had given it a passing grade. I sipped along on it for months.

At last report Mr. Delegal had retired from bootlegging, had taken up preaching, and was doing well at a small church in one of the neighborhoods where he once ran a still.

My chapter on Savannah politics recalls the integration of the city's police department during Mayor John Kennedy's administration in 1957. Among the early-ons was Fay "Jazzbo" Patterson, a former prizefighter who became the nemesis of

Savannah bootleggers and later moved into higher echelons of law enforcement in another state.

Officer Patterson had a sixth sense where illicit booze was concerned. All liquor stills were set up in well-concealed locations, and hard to find. Officer Patterson, however, could either sniff them out or find them with the help of informers. He also developed a knack of obtaining evidence—no easy task because whenever cops showed up, bootleggers had carefully preplanned methods for the hasty disposal of booze even while closed doors were being battered down.

At one location, while his fellow officers were gaining entry to a house where moonshine was stored for sale, Patterson crawled beneath the house with a washtub, and as the booze was being poured through the cracks in the floor, Patterson was filling the washtub for evidence, enough to gain a conviction. Such dedication—only in Savannah!

Savannah still has gambling. It still has vice and, no doubt, illegal liquor. The police remain alert to all three, sometimes make arrests through raids or stakeouts, but illegal drugs have come onto the scene as a better target for law enforcement. Not "only in Savannah" because that's the case in just about any city. And there's nothing glamorous or intriguing about the drug trade. It is a high-risk murderous trade for those who peddle drugs, and the customers are also victims, some of the world's most pitiful souls upon whom greedy criminals prey. There was a certain amount of romance in the older days of wholesale whoring, bolita-running, and liquor stills. Alas, the old order changeth. And society's besetting sin assumes different form, not to mention consequences.

"The Death of Tomochichi"

JA A. JAHANNES (1942–)

Ja A. Jahannes was educated at Lincoln University and
Hampton University and earned his doctorate at the University
of Delaware. His short fiction and poetry have appeared in *Black
Scholar, Catalyst, Ebony, Griot*, and *Snake Nation Review*, in
addition to several anthologies. He has written eight plays,
including two musicals, *Nealey's Playing Ground* (1988) and
Yes, Lord, One More Sunday (1997). Jahannes has received
numerous awards, including the Langston Hughes Cultural Arts
Award (1981), the Atlantic Center Arts Award (1986), and the
Joseph J. Malone Fellowship (1990), as well as grants from the
Rockefeller Foundation (1993), the Andy Warhol Foundation
(1993), and several from the National Endowment for the Arts.
In 1996, the Savannah Writers' Workshop depicted Jahannes's
life and literary influences as a part of its tribute to local literary
figures called *Native Voices*. The following poem appeared in
1993. He lives and works in Savannah.

The Yamacraw have no name
only
a footnote
because history said you were foolish
the lover of an intruder
who did not know your gods
but the rivers forgive you
the grasses forgive you
the mud under the cypress trees forgive you
the ghosts of the ancestors forgive you
you could not foresee the long line of insults
punctuated by oblique references to your soft skin
Dark chants echoed on the bluff near Savannah
they stole your honor
and you cannot rest

so I come to bury you
I too am child of trickery
your cousin of the African sun
I come to bury you
They will not let you be returned to the marshes
And the evergreens
They will keep covering their heads with tall tales
that you loved old Oglethorpe who made himself your
master
I am angry because
I have never believed you unworthy
Can I feel your spirit to know
If I am the knife of your justification
turning my blade
in the grotesque face of a fable
that dances on the place where they keep you alive
I have come to bury you
Die now like the old raccoon with lost teeth
Die peacefully and we will carry your spirit
to the top of city hall
and let it hover above the robbers of your memory

"Return to Savannah"

ABERJHANI (1957–)

Poet and writer Aberjhani's work has appeared in *The African-American Literary Review*; *Essence*; *Poets, Artists & Madmen*; and *The Savannah Literary Journal*. He is active in the Savannah Writers' Group and the Poetry Society of Georgia. (The society, based in Savannah, is one of the oldest such literary societies in the country.) *I Made My Boy Out of Poetry*, a collection of short fiction and poetry from which the following selection was taken, was published in 1997.

Memories: vicious
like a thicket made hot
with cobras. The wrong step
or an erroneous beat
of the heart
and I could turn
into a tower bursting with death.

Legends tell the tourists
that spectres roam this city
but I've no need of tales
to explain
the red-eyed shadows
hopping like squirrels
through the greenless branches
of my immediate apprehension.
I remember when they died.

Stand amazed, now,
watching them haunt
reflections of their former lives.

The tourists hear one story
but let me tell you another:
like the one about WillieMae
who had 14 children, 9 they say
still living, just like she is
a blackwoman working split shifts
at what used to be the old
Desoto Hilton Hotel.
14 children, 9 still living
spanking, feeding, loving her brood
in-between preparing pastries
for people who'd rather not know.

But her story contains no irony
the husband died a death that was actual
and non-literary, her southern blackwoman's
life failed to reflect
the bohemian aesthetics of drag queens,
singers, and polka-dotted eccentrics
that made John Berendt's garden party
glow so lusciously with decadence.

I could tell the story
of that scar, on WillieMae's right leg
where police dogs
attacked like Klansmen
because she insisted that her children
laugh like anybody's children
in the sun-caressed green of Forsyth Park.

But that history has not been preserved
like the architectural jewels
that adorn a shameless hypocrisy.
Nor has it been dramatized
at festivals or parades
stirring up the ghosts on River Street.
Nor immortalized
by a Ray Ellis watercolor
or a statue in the center of a square.

We could even flip this coin
of WillieMae's tale
and recite the parable of how
she fed an entire neighborhood
with one fried chicken
and Jesus came back just to tell her
"WillieMae you did my recipe proud.
Hear what I say girl?
You did my recipe proud."

Shall we speak of that woman's biography
like a hidden chapter of this city's life
or shall we simply point
at a stupid little Hitch Village boy
feet covered with red dirt
and blackberry stain,
snot flowing like panic and river water,
some curious doctor's fingers
lost between his thighs
his dream containing just enough genius
to save his mystified ass
from everything except
the slow knowledge of why
certain days stink putrid with agony.

Memories: vicious like a thicket
burning hot with cobras.
The wrong step
or an erroneous beat of the heart
and a man like me
could turn into a tower stinking with death.

Acknowledgments

Special thanks to the following individuals for their assistance in making *Literary Savannah* possible:

Mr. and Mrs. Leopold Adler II, Frederic Beil, John Berendt, Marion Boyars, Ken Boyd, Miriam Center, Faith Childs, Carol Christiansen, Mary Ellen Brooks, Sean Ferrell, Coleen Floyd, Patricia Flynn, Karen Gerwin, Tim Gillen, Suzanne Gluck, Anne Godoff, Richard Horwege, Hargrett Rare Book and Manuscript Library of the University of Georgia, Eileen Humphlett, Lila Karpf, Jane Kobres, Van Jones Martin, Amy Medders, Charles Modlin, Chris Paton, Patricia Powell, Paul Quick, Paula Scott, Ester Shaver, Welford Taylor, Christopher Tricarick, Martina Voight, Wendy Weil, Kay Young, and many others, as well as the authors themselves.

"The Haunted Library" from *Savannah Spectres* by Margaret DeBolt ©1984 by Margaret DeBolt. Reprinted by permission of Donning Company Publishers.

Selection from *Sleeping with Soldiers* by Rosemary Daniell ©1984 by Rosemary Daniel. Reprinted by permission of the Wendy Weil Agency.

"Rebels of the Blessed Heart" from *The Dangerous Lives of Altar Boys* by Mark Fuhrman ©1994 by the Estate of Mark Fuhrman. Reprinted by permission of the University of Georgia Press.

Selection from *The Distant Lands* by Julien Green ©1991 by the Estate of Julien Green. Reprinted by permission of Marion Boyars Publishers, Inc.

Selection from *Halloween* by Ben Greer ©1978 by Ben Greer. Reprinted by permission of the author.

"The Death of Tomochichi" by Ja A. Jahannes ©1993 by Ja A. Jahannes. Reprinted by permission of the author.

"Madeira and Moonshine" from *Tongue in Cheek* by Alexander Lawrence ©1979 by Alexander A. Lawrence. Reprinted by permission of Cherokee Publishing Company.

Selection from *Juliette Low and the Girl Scouts: The Story of an American Woman* by Anne Hyde Choate and Helen Ferris ©1928 and renewed by Girl Scouts, Inc. Reprinted by permission of Girl Scouts, Inc.

Selection from "A Matter of Vocabulary" by Alan McPherson ©1969 by Alan McPherson. Reprinted by permission of the Faith Childs Literary Agency.

Lyric poem and passage from the unpublished autobiography of Johnny Mercer (a: chapter I, pages 6 through 9, ca. 1973, from Johnny Mercer Papers, box 1, folder 3 and b: unpublished manuscript, n.d., from the Johnny Mercer Papers, box 15, folder 64) ©1998 by Special Collection Department, Pullen Library, Georgia State University. Reprinted by permission of Georgia State University.

Untitled poem by Ogden Nash ©1933 by the Estate of Ogden Nash.

"The King of the Birds" from *Mystery and Manners* by the Estate of Flannery O'Connor ©1969 by Flannery O'Connor. Reprinted by permission of Farrar, Straus, and Giroux, Inc.

"Kate" from *A Lion's Share* by Mark Steadman ©1974, 1975 by Mark Steadman. Reprinted by permission of the author.